Comparative Central European Culture

Comparative Cultural Studies
Steven Tötösy de Zepetnek, Series Editor

Comparative Cultural Studies is a contextual approach in the study of culture in all of its products and processes. The framework is built on tenets of the disciplines of comparative literature and cultural studies and on notions borrowed from a range of thought such as (radical) constructivism, communication theories, systems theories, and literary and culture theory. In comparative cultural studies focus is on theory and method as well as application and where attention is on the how rather than on the what. Colleagues interested in publishing in the series are invited to contact the editor, Steven Tötösy, at <totosy@lib.purdue.edu>.

Comparative Central European Culture

Edited by
Steven Tötösy de Zepetnek

Purdue University Press
West Lafayette, Indiana

Copyright 2002 by Purdue University. All rights reserved.

Library of Congress Cataloging-in-Publication Data
Comparative Central European culture / edited by Steven Tötösy de Zepetnek
   p.   cm.—(Comparative Cultural Studies)
   Rev. and expanded versions of papers originally presented at three different conferences held during 1999–2000: the 24th annual conference, American Hungarian Educators' Association (Cleveland, 1999); Central European Culture Today (University of Alberta, Edmonton, Sept. 1999); annual conference, Modern Language Association (Washington, D.C., 2000).
   "Selected bibliography for the study of Central European culture": p.
   Includes bibliographical references and index.
   Contents: Comparative cultural studies and the study of Central European culture / Steven Tötösy de Zepetnek—A comparative view of modernism in Central European literature / Andrea Fábry—Radnóti, Celan, and aesthetic shifts in Central European Holocaust poetry / Zsuzsanna Ozsváth—Comparative Central European culture: gender in literature and film / Anikó Imre—Austroslovakism in Anton Hykisch's novel about Maria Theresa / Peter Petro / Milan Kundera and the identity of Central Europe—Politics, history, and public intellectuals in Central Europe after 1989 / Katherine Arens—Comparative Central European culture: Austrian and Hungarian cinema today / Catherine Portuges—Comparative Central European culture: Displacements and peripheralities / Roumiana Deltcheva—Central Europe, Jewish family history, and Sunshine / Susan Rubin Suleiman.
   ISBN 1-55753-240-0
   1. Europe, Central—Literatures—History and criticism—Congresses. 2. Europe, Central—Intellectual life—20th century—Congresses. 3. Motion pictures—Europe, Central—Congresses.   I. Tötösy de Zepetnek, Steven, 1950– II. Series.
PN771.C577 2002
809'.8943—dc21

2001048284

Contents

Preface   vii

Steven Tötösy de Zepetnek
Comparative Cultural Studies and the Study of
   Central European Culture   1

Andrea Fábry
A Comparative View of Modernism in
   Central European Literature   33

Zsuzsanna Ozsváth
Radnóti, Celan, and Aesthetic Shifts in
   Central European Holocaust Poetry   51

Anikó Imre
Comparative Central European Culture: Gender in
   Literature and Film   71

Peter Petro
Austroslovakism in Anton Hykisch's Novel
   about Maria Theresa   91

Hana Pichova
Milan Kundera and the Identity of Central Europe 103

Katherine Arens
Politics, History, and Public Intellectuals in
  Central Europe after 1989 115

Catherine Portuges
Comparative Central European Culture:
  Austrian and Hungarian Cinema Today 133

Roumiana Deltcheva
Comparative Central European Culture:
  Displacements and Peripheralities 149

Susan Rubin Suleiman
Central Europe, Jewish Family History, and
  Sunshine 169

Steven Tötösy de Zepetnek
Selected Bibliography for the Study of
  Central European Culture 189

Contributors 207

Index 213

Preface

The volume *Comparative Central European Culture* is a collection of papers in comparative cultural studies applied in the study of Central European culture. First, it is proposed that a Central European culture, as controversial and debated the notion may be, exists. The concept of a Central European culture is constructed based on real or imagined and variable similarities emanating from historical, social, and cultural characteristics apparent in cultures ranging from Austria and the former East Germany to Romania and Bulgaria and Serbia to the Ukraine, etc., thus including the Habsburg lands and their spheres of influence at various times of history including now.

Second, it is proposed that precisely because of real or imagined and variable similarities and characteristics, it is advantageous to study Central European culture in a comparative manner, that is, in a wider context than the single-culture approach. The framework upon which the material of the volume rests, comparative cultural studies, is a new field of study where the notion of comparative is merged with the field of cultural studies from the basic premises of the discipline of comparative literature. The framework prescribes that the study of culture and culture products—including but not restricted to literature, communication, media, art, etc.—is performed in a contextual and relational construction and with a plurality of methods and approaches, inter- and multidisciplinarity, and, if and when required, including team work. In comparative cultural studies it is the processes of communicative action(s) in culture and the how of these processes that constitute the main objectives of research and study. However, comparative cultural studies does not exclude textual analysis proper or other established fields of study. In comparative cultural studies, ideally, the framework of and methodologies available in the systemic and empirical study of culture are favored.

Based on the two main premises, namely comparative cultural studies as a theoretical framework and the notion of the existence of Central European culture, the material of the volume represents shared meta-theoretical argumentation and intellectual and thematic coherence. In addition to the volume's intellectual cohesion, the material presented is based on a collective point of view with regard to the position of observation. The problematics of cultural criticism with regard to an "inside" as compared with an "outside" position of observation and perspective are well known. In the case of the scholarship in this book, the material has been written from the "outside." This means that the authors of the book reside intellectually (to various degrees) and physically outside Central Europe; in North America. At the same time, all except one contributor, the authors originate physically from Central Europe and most completed secondary schooling there while the majority completed graduate study in North America. It remains without saying that the locus of the observer is of high importance and thus the observation performed by the authors from the outside while originating from the inside offers an alternative view of the subject matter, so to scholarship produced in Central Europe proper. This delineation is not meant to set up an intellectual divide between the said "inside" and "outside," a differentiation of intellectual locus of observation or position of scholarship. Rather, it represents awareness of points of view and pluralism in scholarship.

The studies in the volume are revised and longer versions of papers presented at conferences held in 1999 and 2000, respectively. In a series of conferences conceived and organized by the editor of the volume, the first gathering consisted of a double panel, *Comparative Culture and Hungarian Studies*, organized for the 24th Annual Conference of the American Hungarian Educator's Association, held at John Carroll University, Cleveland in April 1999. The second conference was the result of an invitation by the Canadian Centre for Austrian and Central European Studies, University of Alberta. Invited as a member of the advisory board of the Centre, Steven Tötösy organized and convened *Central European Culture Today: An Invitational International Conference* in September 1999. Funded by the University of Alberta and the Ministry of Foreign Affairs, Austria, the conference was held over two days at the University of Alberta in Edmonton and in the Rocky Mountains in Banff, Alberta.

As the last task of a five-year service on the advisory board of the Hungarian Discussion Group of the Modern Language Association of America, the third gathering was organized as a panel, *Comparative Cultural Studies and Post-1989 Central European Culture*, held at the association's annual convention in Washington, D.C., December 2000 (see <http: // www.cultureonline.org/library/mla2000.html>). The selected papers offered to a number of university presses, the editor opted to publish the papers in the new series of books in Comparative Cultural Studies Purdue University Press now launches with the volume on Central European culture.

The process of the papers' peer review, the search for a suitable publisher, the editing of the papers, and all correspondence of the process of publishing are without financial assistance or payment of any kind. Residing in Massachusetts as an independent scholar at this time, the volume is a result of the editor's interest in culture scholarship in general and in Central European culture in particular. However, after electronic submission of the edited papers, further necessary tasks of the publishing process including copy-editing, typesetting, promotion and advertisement, etc., are with Purdue University Press.

The papers are presented in a sequence thematically arranged. The volume opens with Steven Tötösy's "Comparative Cultural Studies and the Study of Central European Culture," a paper intended to establish the intellectual raison d'être of the volume. Following an introduction of comparative cultural studies and the notion of in-between peripherality as a postcolonial space describing Central Europe and Central European culture, Tötösy applies the proposed theoretical and methodological postulates to selected texts. The examples discussed are memoirs published by second-generation North Americans with ethno-cultural backgrounds in the region and their constructions of Central European culture.

Based on the notion to study Central European culture comparatively, the papers are grouped in thematic and periodic sequence. Andrea Fábry, in her "A Comparative View of Modernism in Central European Literature" explores Central European modernism in a European context. Fábry explores texts by Jaroslav Hašek and Franz Kafka on the one hand, and Kafka and James Joyce on the other, thus arguing for the study of modernism in a widely conceived European cultural and literary landscape. She proposes the re-assessment of the critical canon, one that marginalizes Central European modernists against their West European contemporaries and she argues that knowledge about and an understanding of Central European culture and literature enriches our knowledge about the varieties of literary, critical, political, and intellectual stances in and of the modernist movement.

Zsuzsanna Ozsváth's paper, "Radnóti, Celan, and Aesthetic Shifts in Central European Holocaust Poetry," is a study of two great Central European poets of the Holocaust, Paul Celan and Miklós Radnóti. Ozsváth argues that the texts of these two poets reveal essential commonalities that point toward a shared cultural experience, that of Central Europe. Striking among them is the poets' belief in the power of poetry, which they viewed as capable of controlling, perhaps even transcending, the peril that threatened the world. Such beliefs were, of course, not uncommon in the Western literary tradition. Important, however, is that despite both poets' encounters with violent anti-Semitism, and despite their labor camp experiences, they still regarded these beliefs as integral part of their own foundational Central European cultural and intellectual ethos.

Anikó Imre, in "Comparative Central European Culture: Gender in Literature and Film," discusses her topic in the context of Central European national cultures of the 1980s and 1990s. Imre analyzes the analogous gender structures that underlie both nation and literature in these transitional cultures. She challenges both social science studies of postcommunist transitions and studies of Central European literatures and cultures for their traditional neglect of gendered desire as a political factor. Thereby, Imre adopts a deconstructionist, feminist, and post-colonial approach to Hungarian postmodernist literature and film, which, similar to other cultures of the region, combine an intense interest in the female and the feminine with the refusal of political commitment conveyed in poetic forms. Imre investigates the interrelationships among these features in order to point to a male intellectual culture emasculated by colonization whose use of "poetic pornography" disguises an effort to defend patriarchal privileges threatened by the effects of the transition from communist ideology and Soviet colonialism to post-communist democracy.

Peter Petro's "Austroslovakism in Anton Hykisch's Novel about Maria Theresa," is an analysis of Hykisch's novel, *Milujte kráľovnú* (*Long Live the Queen*, 1984) considered a representative text of Central European culture. In Petro's view, the novel is a literary phenomenon, prescient of post-1989 nostalgia for the multicultural Habsburg empire. Hykisch's historical novel depicts events and an atmosphere before the appearance of nationalism in the Habsburg lands while it is also a literary work that presents a twentieth-century version of a phenomenon of nineteenth-century Slovak history and culture called "Austroslovakism." Petro argues that Hykisch's novel is a particular blend of Central European cultural belonging and against political control over the arts at the time of the novel's publication.

Hana Pichova's "Milan Kundera and the Identity of Central Europe" is a discussion of Kundera's difficult relationship with his homeland and with his identity as a Central European writer, as manifested in his writing. Pichova examines the relevance of Kundera's theme of identity in the context of Central Europe and its cultural direction at the turn of the twentieth century. Kundera, once a communist poet, then a censored novelist, and finally a successful émigré writer in France, has struggles to place himself outside of politics and inside the great adventure of the novel. Yet, even after the collapse of the Soviet empire and communism in Czechoslovakia, Kundera and his works remain subject to politics. He has been accused of abandoning Czech culture, his Central European roots, and of writing solely for the West. Consequently, he is marginalized, shrouded in anonymity, and to this day only partially published in the Czech Republic. In many ways Kundera's otherness and in-between state can be seen as mirroring the fate of Central Europe itself.

Katherine Arens's "Politics, History, and Public Intellectuals in Central Europe after 1989" is a presentation of the politico-cultural map of contemporary Central Europe. Arens reflects on the writings of three authors and their function as public intellectuals, Otto von Habsburg, Peter Handke, and Milo Dor. When studying Central European culture, a discussion of thinkers and writers and their works is of relevance because they often make a great impact as public intellectuals and their actions influence politics and everyday life. Arens's analysis points to a map of Central Europe shared by the said three, nominally Austrian intellectuals, who are in fact of widely varying political stripes but sharing cultural backgrounds. Based on her analysis, Arens argues that Habsburg, Dor, and Handke do not accept the Cold War's map of the region, but instead set it firmly within the traditional boundaries of Europe, culturally, historically, and politically.

Catherine Portuges, in her paper, "Comparative Central European Culture: Austrian and Hungarian Cinema Today," builds on the premise that after more than a decade since the fall of the Berlin Wall, Central European culture ought to allow for a significant moment for reflection on the changes wrought by the post-communist transition in Central European cinema. Alongside radical transformations arising from the privatization of film studios and funding structures for co-productions taking place in the European market are thematic concerns in films that revisit aspects of Habsburg history, such as the inscription of nation and generation in films produced in Austria and in Hungary today. Portuges argues that the upheavals of the past decade have fostered a reconsideration of minority, ethnic, and gender identities within broader cultural and social contexts represented in contemporary film and video, including fiction, experimental, documentary, and avant-garde forms. Portuges's paper offers a comparative perspective on selected works from the region that highlight these transitional phenomena, situated both within a framework of Austro-Hungarian history and the contemporary landscape of a globalized film economy.

Roumiana Deltcheva traces in her "Comparative Central European Culture: Displacements and Peripheralities" manifestations of cultural similarities in post-Soviet Central European film. Deltcheva applies the notion of in-between peripherality and post-coloniality developed for the study of Central and East European cultures and combines it with the thematic metaphor of travel and the road. While the metaphor of travel and the road is apparent in films of the 1990s from the region as well as from the West about the region, the notion has undergone transformations and these transformations challenge the validity of East-to-West unidirectionality in films of earlier decades. Deltcheva also analyzes a number of films with regard to a specific notion of the metaphor of travel in Central and East European culture, namely the "long journey home," Europe.

Susan Rubin Suleiman's "Central Europe, Jewish Family History, and *Sunshine*" is a discussion of István Szabó's film, *Sunshine* (1999). The film, as a historical narrative of a century and a half of Hungarian history in the context of the Austro-Hungarian empire through the lives of four generations is the story of a quintessentially Central European family. *Sunshine* is understood in Suleiman's analysis in the context of Szabó's earlier films, notably the Hungarian films he made in the 1960s and the German trilogy *(Mephisto, Colonel Redl, Hanussen)* he made in the 1980s. In particular, *Sunshine* can be seen as a reworking and "rereading" of Szabó's best-known Hungarian film, *Apa (Father* 1966). Finally, Suleiman discusses some Hungarian reactions to the film. The film provoked passionate and lengthy debates in the Hungarian press, concerning Jewish identity in contemporary Hungary as well as Szabó's aesthetic and ideological choices.

The volume is completed by Steven Tötösy's "Selected Bibliography for the Study of Central European Culture." The selection of items for the bibliography is predicated on providing a tool for a multi-disciplinary and contextual study of the region's culture, with focus on the period after the fall of communism and the demise of Soviet hegemony.

The intellectual and thematic cohesion of the papers in the volume rests on several concepts. First, all authors underwrite, to various degrees, the notion of the existence of a Central European culture. And this basic premise applies to the proposition both historically and with regard to contemporary times including the period since the demise of the Soviet empire and communism. In the papers, shifts in taxonomy between "Central Europe" and "Central and East Europe" indicate differentiations with regard to historical and cultural demarcations within Europe. In scholarship as well as in social and everyday discourse, taxonomical shifts—based on as well as resulting in—of cultural and historical demarcations with regard to the region show continuous evolvements of inclusion and exclusion. In many ways, there is a core—from a historical perspective the Habsburg "imagined community" and/or from a contemporary perspective the German investments, economic and political—and from there each culture as a layer represents cultural and geographical proximity or distance from the core. And there are also forty years of Soviet colonialism and communism. The point is that while no one has described successfully as of yet the culture of Central Europe, most agree that it somehow exists. Granted, the agreement that it exists comes most easily when proposed by or viewed from the outside, for example from the point of view of North American scholarship. But even those in the inside—Central Europeans *in loco*—often argue for the notion at least rhetorically (although also, often, ironically). The authors of the papers in this volume suggest in their work that the cultures of the region confirm rather than deny variable similarities, whether of an imagined or a real "Central Europe," or both as I suggest.

An important plane of cohesion of the work presented in the volume is the comparative mode, that is, the implicit or explicit agreement of the authors to the proposed theoretical framework of comparative cultural studies. Application of the comparative mode ranges from the analysis of one text whose content points to a Central European historical theme as in Petro's paper or as in Pichova's paper on Central European identity to Arens's paper on the function of public intellectuals whose activities represent Central Europe-ism or to Suleiman's paper about a Central European Jewish family's history in film and as in Ozsváth's paper on similarities in ideology and poetry of poets of the Holocaust. The papers presented in this volume succeed in an exemplary fashion by showing scholarship in the comparative and contextual mode about Central European culture. Obviously, the material of the volume cannot cover Central European culture sufficiently. On the other hand, it presents selected topics about the culture of the region in both in-depth and broad horizons. The papers speak for themselves and their merit is subject to the opinions of their audience.

Steven Tötösy de Zepetnek
Winchester at Boston, April 2001

Comparative Cultural Studies and the Study of Central European Culture

Steven Tötösy de Zepetnek

In this paper, I first present principles of comparative cultural studies followed by a brief description of the framework's methodology, the systemic and empirical approach. This introduction of theory and method is then followed by a brief description of the notion of Central European culture—real or imagined—defined as an in-between peripheral and (post)colonial space. Next, with the objective to exemplify Central European culture as represented in literature, the framework and method are applied to samples of second-generation North American Jewish memoirs about Central Europe and to samples of contemporary Eastern German and Hungarian prose.

Comparative cultural studies is a field of study in the humanities and social sciences where tenets of the discipline of comparative literature are merged with the field of cultural studies. In comparative cultural studies the objects of study are culture and culture products including literature and other expressions of art. Work in comparative cultural studies is performed in a contextual and relational manner and with a plurality of methods and approaches, in inter-disciplinarity, and, if and when required, in team work. In comparative cultural studies it is the processes of communicative action(s) in culture and the how of these processes that constitute the objectives of research and study. However, comparative cultural studies does not exclude textual analysis proper or other established fields of study.

The framework of comparative cultural studies is constructed from several fields and disciplines in the humanities and social sciences. Epistemologically, it is rooted in radical constructivism, in the discipline of comparative literature, and in cultural studies. Comparative cultural studies is not to be understood as a "master theory"; rather, it is one framework among several, to be tested and applied, thus to be used as a tool in order to understand and to produce new knowledge. From the disciplinary, epistemological, ideological, and intellectual bases of the framework, I extrapolate an incipient set of principles as follows below. For now, the principles represent a basis for discussion and a clear statement without lengthy descriptive argumentation but which are in need of further theoretical work and development as well as exemplification by application. I also contend that the principles of a comparative cultural studies presented here are innovative precisely because curiously enough, notions of cultural studies in most cases lack a comparative, that is, a contextual, pluralist, and supra-national range and depth of thought and application (see, in detail, Tötösy, "The Empirical," *Comparative Literature* 13–41, "Systemic and Empirical," "From Comparative"). The ten basic and general principles of comparative cultural studies are as follows.

The first principle of comparative cultural studies is the postulate that in and of the study, pedagogy, and research of culture—culture is defined as all human activity resulting in artistic production—it is not the "what" but rather the "how" that is of importance. This principle follows the constructivist tenet of attention to the "how" and process. To "compare" does not—and must not—imply a hierarchy: in the comparative mode of investigation and analysis a matter studied is not "better" than another. This means—among other things as listed below—that it is method that is of crucial importance in comparative cultural studies in particular and, consequently, in the study of literature and culture as a whole.

The second principle of comparative cultural studies is the theoretical as well as methodological postulate to move and to dialogue between cultures, languages, literatures, and disciplines. This is a crucial aspect of the framework, the approach as a whole, and its methodology. In other words, attention to other cultures—that is, the comparative perspective—is a basic and founding element and factor of the framework. The claim of emotional and intellectual primacy and subsequent institutional power of national cultures is untenable in this perspective. In turn, the built-in notions of exclusion and self-referentiality of single culture study and their result of rigidly defined disciplinary boundaries are notions against which comparative cultural studies offers an alternative as well as a parallel field of study. This inclusion extends to all Other, all marginal, minority, border, and peripheral, and it encompasses both form and substance. However, attention must be paid of the "how" of any inclusionary approach, attestation, methodology, and ideology so as not to repeat the mistakes of Eurocentrism and "universalization" from a "superior" Eurocentric point of view. Dialogue is the only solution.

The third principle of comparative cultural studies is the necessity for the scholar working in this field to acquire in-depth grounding in more than one language and culture as well as other disciplines before further in-depth study of theory and methodology. However, this principle creates structural and administrative problems on the institutional and pedagogical levels. For instance, how does one allow for development—intellectually as well as institutionally—from a focus on one national culture (exclusionary) towards the inclusionary and interdisciplinary principles of comparative cultural studies? The solution of designating comparative cultural studies as a postgraduate discipline only is problematic and counter-productive. Instead, the solution is the allowance for a parallelism in intellectual approach, institutional structure, and administrative practice.

The fourth principle of comparative cultural studies is its given focus to study culture in its parts (literature, arts, film, popular culture, theater, the publishing industry, the history of the book as a cultural product, etc.) and as a whole in relation to other forms of human expression and activity and in relation to other disciplines in the humanities and social sciences (history, sociology, psychology, etc.). The obstacle here is that the attention to other fields of expression and other disciplines of study results in the lack of a clearly definable, recognizable, single-focused, and major theoretical and methodological framework of comparative cultural studies. There is a problem of naming and designation exactly because of the multiple approach and parallelism. In turn, this lack of recognized and recognizable products results in the discipline's difficulties of marketing itself within the inter-mechanisms of intellectual recognition and institutional power.

The fifth principle of comparative cultural studies is its built-in special focus on English, based on its impact emanating from North American cultural studies which is, in turn, rooted in British cultural studies along with influences from French and German thought. This is a composite principle of approach and methodology. The focus on English as a means of communication and access to information should not be taken as Euro-American-centricity. In the Western hemisphere and in Europe but also in many other cultural (hemi)spheres, English has become the lingua franca of communication, scholarship, technology, business, industry, etc. This new global situation prescribes and inscribes that English gains increasing importance in scholarship and pedagogy, including the study of literature. The composite and parallel method here is that because comparative cultural studies is not self-referential and exclusionary; rather, the parallel use of English is effectively converted into a tool for and of communication in the study, pedagogy, and scholarship of literature. Thus, in comparative cultural studies the use of English should not represent any form of colonialism—and if it does, one disregards it or fights it with English rather than by opposing English—as follows from principles one to three. And it should also be obvious that is the English-language speaker who is, in particular, in need of other languages.

The sixth principle of comparative cultural studies is its theoretical and methodological focus on evidence-based research and analysis. This principle is with reference to methodological requirements in the description of theoretical framework building and the selection of methodological approaches. From among the several evidence-based theoretical and methodological approaches available in the study of culture, literary and culture theory, cultural anthropology, sociology of culture and knowledge, etc., the systemic and empirical approach is perhaps the most advantageous and precise methodology for use in comparative cultural studies. This does not mean that comparative cultural studies and/or its methodology comprise a meta theory; rather, comparative cultural studies and its methodologies are implicitly and explicitly pluralistic.

The seventh principle of comparative cultural studies is its attention and insistence on methodology in interdisciplinary study (an umbrella concept), with three main types of methodological precision: intra-disciplinarity (analysis and research within the disciplines of the humanities), multi-disciplinarity (analysis and research by one scholar employing any other discipline), and pluri-disciplinarity (analysis and research by teamwork with participants from several disciplines). In the latter case, an obstacle is the general reluctance of humanities scholars to employ teamwork in the study of culture including literature. It should be noted that this principle is built-in in the framework and methodology of the systemic and empirical approach to culture (see below; for an outline of inter-disciplinary work in the humanities, see Tötösy, *Comparative Literature* 79–82).

The eighth principle of comparative cultural studies is its content against the contemporary paradox of globalization versus localization. There is a paradoxical development in place with regard to both global movements and intellectual approaches and their institutional representation. On the one hand, the globalization of technology, industry, and communication is actively pursued and implemented. But, on the other hand, the forces of exclusion as represented by local, racial, national, gender, disciplinary, etc., interests prevail in (too) many aspects. For a change toward comparative cultural studies, as proposed here, a paradigm shift in the humanities and social sciences will be necessary. Thus, the eighth principle represents the notion of working against the stream by promoting comparative cultural studies as a global, inclusive, and multi-disciplinary framework in an inter- and supra-national humanities.

The ninth principle of comparative cultural studies is its claim on the vocational commitment of its practitioners. In other words, why study and work in comparative cultural studies? The reasons are the intellectual as well as pedagogical values this approach and discipline offers in order to implement the recognition and inclusion of the Other with and by commitment to the in-depth knowledge of several cultures (i.e., languages, literatures, etc.) as basic parameters. In consequence, the discipline of comparative cultural studies as proposed advances our knowledge by a multi-facetted approach based on scholarly rigor and multi-layered knowledge with precise methodology.

The tenth principle of comparative cultural studies is with regard to the troubled intellectual and institutional situation of the humanities in general. That is, the tenth principle is with reference to the politics of scholarship and the academe. We know that the humanities in general experience serious and debilitating institutional—and, depending on one's stand, also intellectual—difficulties and because of this the humanities in the general social and public discourse are becoming more and more marginalized (not the least by their own doing). It is in this context that the principles of a comparative cultural studies is proposed to at least to attempt to adjust the further marginalization and social irrelevance of the humanities.

For method in comparative cultural studies the systemic and empirical approach is favored while other methodologies may be just as appropriate and useful. Briefly, in the systemic and empirical approach the main question is what happens to products of culture and how: It is produced, published, distributed, read/listened to/seen (etc.), imitated, assessed, discussed, studied, censored, etc. The approach originates as a reaction to, and an attempt at, solving inconsistencies and problem of hermeneutical studies and it is a contextual approach. It is also a inter- and multi-disciplinary approach borrowing from a number of areas in the humanities and social sciences including (radical) constructivism (e.g., Glasersfeld; Foerster; Schmidt; for an overview of constructivism, see Riegler), systems theories (e.g., Even-Zohar, Luhmann; Schmidt; Wallerstein), the empirical (e.g., Schmidt), cultural anthropology, ethnology, reception theory, the sociology of knowledge, cognitive science, etc. As seen in the work of scholars in Germany, Holland, Belgium, Hungary, Italy, Israel, Canada, the United States and elsewhere in several fields and areas of study, there are several types of systemic and/or empirical approaches which can be grouped into a general and umbrella approach termed the "systemic and empirical approach" (see Tötösy, "Systemic Approaches," "Bibliography of Studies").

The principal intent of scholars working with the approach can be characterized as an attempt at reducing metaphorical interpretation as the dominant approach in the humanities and to focus on process and context. That is, it is proposed that the study of culture and literature should be with focus on the study of processes and contexts and that this type of study be based in systems theories and the notion of the empirical defined as observation and knowledge-based argumentation. The system(s) of culture and actions within are observed and described as depending on two conventions (hypotheses) and that are tested continually. These conventions are the aesthetic convention (as opposed to the convention of facts in the daily language of reference) and the polyvalence convention (as opposed to the monovalency in the daily empirical world). Thus, the systemic and empirical approach as method concentrates to study not only the "text" in itself—"text" is defined here as any cultural product—but roles of action within the system(s) of culture, namely, the production, distribution, reception, and the processing of culture products. The steps to be taken in the systemic and empirical approach are the formation of a hypothesis, practice, testing, and evaluation (for detail, see Tötösy, "Systemic Approaches," "The Empirical," *Comparative Literature* 13–41, "Systemic and Empirical," "From Comparative," "Comparative Cultural").

The designations of "Central Europe" and "Central European culture" are matter of considerable controversy and debate (see, for example, Ash; Hanley, Stastna, and Stroehlein; for a bibliography on the concept, see Tötösy, "Selected Bibliography for the Study"). However, in my view there is a geo-political space called Central Europe that, consequently, contains a landscape of culture(s) comprising of real or imagined (i.e., Anderson's concept) and variable similarities of shared histories, cultural practices, institutions, social and behavioral similarities, etc. As a combination of geography, history, economics, cultures, politics, etc., Central European culture is a landscape of cultures of spaces ranging from Austria, the Czech and Slovak Republics, Hungary, Poland, Romania, Bulgaria, Western Ukraine, the former East Germany, and the countries of the former Yugoslavia, etc., thus including the Habsburg lands and spheres of influence, historically, of Austrian and German centers. While the region existed as a cultural space with specific characteristics before, with its some forty years of Soviet-Russian and communist history it has acquired additional and further characteristics of (post)coloniality. In the context of (post)colonial studies the postulates are that Central and East European cultures are peripheries of dominant European cultures such as the German and French. However, because of their indigenous cultural self-referentiality, Central European cultures are not only peripheral but also in-between, that is, in-between their own national and cultural self-referentiality and the cultural influence and primacy of the major Western cultures and economic and political centers they have been and continue to be influenced by. In addition, they are in a post-colonial situation following their historical experiences of Soviet and communist colonialism; the residues of these experiences remain significant elements of the region's cultural and artistic as well as social expressions (for more detail, see Tötösy "Post-Colonialities," "Cultures," "Configurations;" see also Moore).

Europe is not homogeneous and the North American designation of Eurocentrism as a negative construction is at times questionable because the designation does not account for the differences and hierarchies within Europe. In reality, there are several centers, France, Germany, and England, and there are "near centers" such as Italy, the Benelux, the Nordic countries, etc., and these centers reflect economic and political power. And then there are several peripheries such as Southern and East Europe, Portugal, the Baltic countries, etc. In this differentiated view of Europe, Central and East Europe comprises the successor states of the Austrian empire and beyond, with their

Austro-German and German economic, cultural, political, etc., spheres of influence. In general social discourse as well as in scholarship, Central and East European cultures, owing to their situation of peripherality, need proclaim within Europe that they are Europeans and that they belong to Europe while the sliding scale of cultural hierarchies based on economic realities from West to Central and to East Europe remains an established practice although more implicit than explicit, yet practiced rather than admitted and discussed.

After the Second World War, the primary colonization of Central and East European countries occurred by the ideological, political, economic, institutional, etc., leadership-by-force of the Soviet center, the communist politburo, directly and/or indirectly from Moscow, in politics, the economy, in and via the structures of social, educational, cultural, etc., institutions including military occupation in most countries of the region. There was also the everyday and ideological oppression performed, in all walks of life, by the local communist nomenclatura of the country. However, Soviet colonialism of Central and East Europe is to be understood not only within the traditional definition of colonialism but also in terms of what I define as "filtered colonialism," a type of colonialism that manifested itself in a secondary colonialization through ideological, political, social, cultural, and other means during and after the forty-year period of Soviet colonialism. Filtered colonialism is to be understood as a result of and following primary colonization, as penetration and imprint of cultural processes and behavior. For example, filtered colonialism is relevant when contemporary literatures of the region are discussed in the context of postmodernism: Halina Janaszek-Ivaničková draws the conclusion that innovation in the literatures of the region occurred before 1989 when under primary colonialism of the Soviet center and then suggests that postmodern tendencies "which are characteristic of postindustrial and postmodern societies, and which made themselves felt with such vigor in post-communist—in some ways, owing to the economic and political influence of the USSR, 'post-colonial'—countries after 1989, do not, upon closer inspection, constitute recent phenomena in these countries" (806; see also Pilař). In other words, the existence of postmodernity in Central and East Europe involves Soviet colonialism both before and after 1989–90 and it is thus that after 1989–90 the impact of Soviet colonialism remains and element in and of the region's culture(s).

The paradigms of center/periphery and center/margin are established concepts in postcolonial studies and the concept of peripherality with regard to culture exists in a number of varieties such as border writing (see, for example, Jay), in Amin Malak's ambivalent affiliations and in-betweenness, Homi K. Bhabha's third space and notion of hybridity, François Paré's locations of exiguity and the margins, etc. With specific reference to Central and East European literature as border and margin, Tomislav Longinović's designation of the region's culture as borderline is relevant, similarly to Marcel Cornis-Pope's view, who writes, in a Central European context, about the Romanian avant-garde that "living in a provisional state, on a *margin* that, considering the more general position of Romanian literature in Europe, was in fact a *margin of the margin*" (119; author's italics). A framework similar to my own is Anna Klobucka's notion of semi-periphery. Klobucka develops her framework for the study of "semi-peripheral" cultures and literatures such as Poland, Hungary, Portugal, etc. Klobucka's framework is based on the notions of world system and semi-periphery initially proposed by Christopher Chase-Dunn and Immanuel Wallerstein.

As postulated in the proposed framework of comparative cultural studies and in the method of the systemic and empirical approach, it is the processes of cultural mediation, filtering, assimilation, and creative alterations of cultural knowledge that contain provide data for the understanding of the center and periphery and periphery and in-betweenness configuration and specific situation of the region. Concepts of center/margin and center/periphery can also be understood that in some instances, while the center holds leverage, the margin/periphery responds by "other affirmations and negations" owing to the margin's/periphery's relative sovereignty (Minh-Ha 216). And this is precisely the case of Central and East Europe culture. They are located in in-between peripherality where strategies of polyvalence conventions mediate the center's impact into cultural self-referentiality. While the notions of center/periphery or center/margin—for example in Itamar Even-Zohar's polysystem framework or Trinh Minh-ha's concept of oppositions—focus on aspects of the margin, in the case of Central and East Europe these concepts are not entirely applicable because of national self-referentiality and relative sovereignty of these cultures—and where they are ever present factors in the cultural and social discourse of the region and beyond. The reference to national cultural sovereignty in the countries of the region is important for the reason that the idea and possibility of cultural colonialism by the former Soviet center is strenuously objected to by Central and East European intellectuals, while the influence of a Western center such as that of Germany is accepted as a given. This opposition is based on the perception and insistence that Soviet colonialism exerted no direct cultural influence while the notion that the region's culture(s) and literature(s) have been influenced via the center's primary colonialism and thus a secondary and filtered impact occurred in the processes of culture is also and consequently rejected. The implicit and explicit denial of the impact of the Soviet center and communism on the cultures of Central and East Europe is a blind spot on the intellectual and scholarly landscape although it may well be that it is rhetorical in nature and in time it will be acknowledged and understood.

While postcolonial paradigms of center/periphery and center/margin are useful and partially applicable in the study of Central and East European culture(s), what they lack is methodology and precise taxonomy and are often political or rhetorical in nature. The notion of in-between peripherality and the framework of comparative cultural studies serve as an alternative, with built-in elements such as the systemic and empirical approach as method, precisely defined taxonomy, attention to empirical evidence, and with attention to both textual and extra-textual (that is, systemic)—properties and relationships in/of culture. For this line of thought, I borrow aspects of polysystem's concept of center/periphery. For example, Even-Zohar postulates that a dominant culture or a base source "imposes its language [culture] and texts on a subjugated community" (68) and this can be applied to Central and East Europe, albeit with an extension: When the indigenous culture is in content and form self-centered and self-referential—as in the case of Central and East European cultures and literatures—the leverage and power of a superseding colonialist center, that is, a dominant culture, is not immediately obvious or clear. This is especially the case from the perspective of the subjugated community. Rather, the influence on various and specific aspects of culture, resulting from the colonialist center, can be observed and analyzed as the in-between position of the peripheral subject. Thus, in the post-colonial cultures of Central and East Europe, there are three principal centers and sources of influence: the indigenous center, that is, the self-referential national culture but that in reality is never as homogeneous as proclaimed and propagated and that includes many kinds and types influences such as the German influence in Austria and Hungary or the French in Romania, etc., the Western centers with varied German, French, etc., influences; and finally the Soviet communist/socialist center, its impact filtered over forty years of colonialism.

The existence of a Central European culture has been and still is contested. For example, Milan Kundera—here from the platform as public intellectual—argues that

> the geographic boundaries of Central Europe are vague, changeable, and debatable . . . Central Europe is polycentral and looks different from different vantage points: Warsaw or Vienna, Budapest or Ljubljana . . . Central Europe never was an intentional, desired unit. With the exception of the Hapsburg emperor, his court, and few isolated intellectuals, no Central European desired a Central Europe. The cultures of the individual peoples had centrifugal, separatist tendencies; they far preferred to look to England, France, or Russia than one another; and if in spite of that (or perhaps because of that) they resembled each other, it was without their will or against their will. . . . ("Three Contexts" 12; see also Kundera, "The Tragedy;" on Kundera and Central Europe, see Pichova)

If the existence of a Central Europe and thus of a Central European culture is questionable as Kundera suggests, he admits that they "resemble" each other and this is where the "outside," the locus of observation and perception plays a crucial role: looking at the region from the outside allows, at the very least for the notion of variable similarities and thus the designation of a Central European culture. But I argue that in social discourse, it appears, the existence of a specific space called Central Europe is generally accepted, although it must be admitted that the acceptance of the notion is more often than not exercised from the "outside." That is, while Central Europeans themselves, as Kundera suggests, take a differentiated, disinterested, and/or ironic view of the notion of a real or imagined Central Europe and Central European culture, when the notion is used from the outside of Central Europe it is more readily accepted and applied. For example, when Milan Kundera lives in Paris, or Josef Škvorecký or George (György) Faludy live in Toronto, that is when they become of a hybrid, Hungarian or Czech *and* Central European. Individual members and groups of nationalities—ethnic groups in North America and other locations of emigration and/or exile—interact in many aspects when before they would not. Thus, Czechs and Hungarians, for example, discover kinship and the Central European dimension when they live in Toronto or Berlin. This perspective of the locus of observation (a constructivist postulate) is, then, obviously an important aspect of the construction of the landscape of Central European culture and this is also the case when it comes to scholars who study the cultures of the region.

In scholarship, the difficulty arises when Central European culture is to be explained with examples. As introduced above, I propose that the exemplification of the notion of Central European culture ought to be executed with and within the framework of comparative cultural studies (with the framework's built-in methodology, the systemic and empirical approach), followed by the notion of Central European culture as (post)colonial in-between peripherality (see also Deltcheva; Imre). The next step, then, is the application of the proposed theoretical underpinnings. For this, I present a brief study of memoirs by second-generation

Canadian and American Jews of Central European parentage and whose texts contain much material supporting the notion of an imagined Central European culture. In turn, this exemplification supports the primary proposal, namely that there exists a Central European culture—real and/or imagined—and in this case, most interestingly, twice removed: in time (second generation) and in space (North America).

There is also a third component in this equation and that is the particular combination of the Jewish and the Central European. In my view, Jews living in the region—orthodox or assimilated or anywhere in between—represented the quintessential of Central European culture, so until the Holocaust when the Nazis and Germany together with Central Europeans amputated their cultures by anti-Semitism ending in genocide. What I mean is that neither German culture nor any of the national cultures of Central Europe could be lived and can be understood without the history and the presence of Jewries and their contributions in any area or walks of life, be that literature, the visual and plastic arts, music, or engineering, medicine, business and economics, etc.

Before I present samples of Jewish memoirs about Central Europe, a brief excursion into the question of the image of matters Central European in English-language culture may be useful. From classics such as Matthew Lewis' *The Monk* to nineteenth-century bestsellers in North America such as Ralph Connor's *The Foreigner,* etc., the image of cultures from the region have not been presented, generally speaking, in a positive context. Particularly in the period of high immigration in the nineteenth and early twentieth centuries, American and Canadian representations in literature and social discourse and, consequently, perceptions were in negative and racist contexts often arguing that the "sheepskin-clad peasant" from Poland, the Ukraine, or Hungary—all listed at various points of entry in the United States and Canada as Austrians from the Austro-Hungarian empire—will not be able to adapt to the superior culture of America or Canada (see, e.g., Papp de Carrington; for a bibliography with items on image studies, see Tötösy "Canadian Ethnic"). Similarly, since the Second World War in particular in films such as about the Transylvanian/Hungarian/Romanian (e.g., *Dracula*), the

Hungarian (e.g., *My Fair Lady*), the Austrian (e.g., *Sissy, Sound of Music*) have shaped much of the public perception. Although it is difficult to gauge the frequency of themes and the content of the themes as such, it is perhaps safe to say that in English-language culture(s) Central European themes have become more frequent of late as well as less negatively presented. In the last few years, examples include such texts of prose fiction as Tibor Fischer's *Under the Frog* (1992), Jill Tweedle's *Eating Children* (1993), Kazuo Ishiguro's *The Unconsoled* (1995), Milan Kundera's novels (see, e.g., Petro; Pichova), Tamas Dobozy's *Doggone: A Novel* (1998), Josef Škvorecký's *Two Murders in My Double Life* (1999), Jill Paton Walsh's *A Desert in Bohemia* (2000), Simone Zelitch's *Louisa* (2000), Alan Furst's *Kingdom of Shadows: A Novel* (2000), Jody Shields' *The Fig Eater: A Novel* (2000), John Wray's *The Right Hand of Sleep* (2001), or narratives by public intellectuals such as Michael Ignatieff's *Scar Tissue* (1993) or personal narratives such as Eva Hoffmann's *Exit into History: A Journey through the New Eastern Europe* (1993) and Modris Eksteins' *Walking Since Daybreak: A Story of Eastern Europe, World War II and the Heart of Our Century* (1999), or in film such as *The English Patient* (see Tötösy, "Michael Ondaatje's"), etc.

Criticism published in mainstream media such as *The New York Times* accords high literary and cultural value to some of these texts, for example to Furst's novel (see Smith) and Shields' novel as a first novel or that of Tweedle received excellent reviews and endorsements, and Fischer's novel received several awards such as the Betty Trask Award (1992). A brief note about Shields' *The Frog Eater*: the author describes in her novel Central European culture truly "imagined" and with much of the stereotypes attributed to this culture. What is "imagined" is, for example, that in Shield's Austria of 1900 one would be able to order Hungarian dishes *in Hungarian* in restaurants in Vienna, the daughter of a Hungarian landowner would be married to a police inspector in Vienna and that the Hungarian gentry would know intimately the culture and customs of Gypsies, etc., situations possible only in a Central Europe imagined this way today. Such fictionalizations are acceptable (I guess) owing to poetic license and because the author describes a Central European culture, "imagined," indeed. Nevertheless, the author's (and the publisher's editors') oversight of spelling is, while of little or no importance to the readership at large, irritating: Hungarian terms and names are misspelled throughout, "Erszébet" instead of Erzsébet, "Rosza" instead of Rózsa, "Jószef" instead of József, etc.

In contemporary American and Canadian English-language literature, memoir writing is a genre with a significant and growing corpus. In Central Europe proper, too, after 1989 and since there has been a large output of memoirs. In Hungary, for example—although of course memoirs have been published under the socialist/communist period—after 1989 memoirs of all possible persuasions appeared in large numbers. I am especially partial to Imre Kertész' *Sorstalanság* (1975; for my purposes the text—translated by Christopher C. Wilson and Katharina M. Wilson and published in 1992 with the title *Fateless*—in fact belongs to "contemporary" Jewish memoirs in English about Central Europe). Within the genre of memoirs about the Holocaust, *Fateless* is of particular significance because it predates representations of the Shoah with "laughter," as in Lina Wertmüller's film *Seven Beauties* (1975) or Nicola Paviani's film *Life is Beautiful* (1997). Kertész's bittersweet, at times biting, irony laced with intelligent humor is a masterpiece, although among scholars of Holocaust literature it would have detractors precisely because of the "laughter" the author describes in the concentration camp and the humor he attributes to life under the most horrific circumstances. Another text I find of particular poignancy is André Stein's *Hidden Children: Forgotten Survivors of the Holocaust* (1993), a collection of oral histories as told by child survivors from Central and East Europe. Among recent Holocaust (auto)biographical histories with a Central European background similar to those I discuss below, of note is Eugene L. Pogany's *In My Brother's Image: Twin Brothers Separated by Faith after the Holocaust* (2000), the story of a Hungarian Jewish family and their conversion to Catholicism, their conscious assimilation into Hungarian culture and urban Central European society, and the Holocaust and Anca

Vlasopolos' *No Return Address: A Memoir of Displacement* (2000), a fictional autobiography of a family of Hungarian, Jewish Romanian, and Romanian Greek intellectuals, their lives, and the lives of their relatives and friends in communist Romania.

On the other end of the spectrum, there are memoirs by the former upper class whose members were, in the rule, patriotic and nationalist, anti-Semitic, and conservative while at the same time very much Central European in their outlook towards Austro-German culture and with family, friends, and contacts over the whole region. A good example of this category of memoirs is Jenő Koltai's *Egy honvédtiszt visszaemlékezései. Korkép a XX. Századból* (*Memoirs of an Officer: A Portrait of the Twentieth Century*) (1989; not translated into English). While resonating with much nostalgia, Koltai's writing is void of emotion and suggests an emotionally dry, truncated life. On the other hand, he represents most aspects of the patriotic Hungarian aware of his Central Europeanness, with commitment to honoring the codes of the upper-class bourgeois officer serving in the country's professional army. What is fascinating in the text is the author's description of a Central European landscape of culture and social life in the interwar period of Czechoslovakia, Hungary, Austria, and Germany.

John Willett writes in his paper "Is There a Central European Culture?" that

> the elements of a new Central European culture must come from even farther a field than they did before Hitler and Stalin. We certainly cannot expect them to depend on the spontaneous German-Jewish-Yiddish tradition that once seemed to link the comedian Peischacke Burstein in Vilnius with the writer Ettore Schmitz in Trieste: however unforgettable, the source is barred, buried under the masonry of the great concentration camp memorials. But the essence of mid-Europe surely is that its cultural inspiration must come from both East and West, and its role be to test ideas against one another and use the result in its own creativity. (15)

Willett touches on several issues pertinent to my line of thought. The importance of Jewish culture in its varied forms on and in Central Europe is a given (see above; see also Braham; Johnston). However, while I understand the history of Central European Jewries tragic as Willet does, I do not find it "barred" and "buried" (on this, see also Ozsváth). Instead, I understand Central European Jewries as a quintessential synthesis and expression of Central European culture very much present and with a future.

As proposed in the perspective of a Central European culture and as seen from a locus removed in time and space, I discuss briefly Desider Furst and Lilian R. Furst's *Home Is Somewhere Else: Autobiography in Two Voices* (1994), Julie Salamon's *The Net of Dreams: A Family's Search for a Rightful Place* (1996), Elaine Kalman Naves's *Journey to Vaja: Reconstructing the World of a Hungarian-Jewish Family* (1996), Susan Rubin Suleiman's *Budapest Diary: In Search of the Motherbook* (1996), Magda Denes's *Castles Burning: A Child's Life in War* (1997), and Judith Kalman's *The County of Birches* (1998).

In a geo-cultural context, Salamon's *The Net of Dreams* is perhaps the most "Central European." Her idea and research of the book began by the impetus of reading, in 1993, about Steven Spielberg's plans to film his *Schindler's List* (6) after which she traveled to Poland and other areas of Central East Europe such as Huszt, now in the Ukraine, and formerly a Hungarian town. Salamon's description leading into the history of the mixture of nations is intriguing itself: "This was the land of the *shtetl*— and of Gypsies, Slovaks, Hungarians, and Ukrainians—an ignorant backwater that had been annexed by the USSR after World War II. Now Communism was finished and the place where my parents were from had been reshuffled again. Their birthplace had lost the status of affiliation with Czechoslovakia or the former Austro-Hungarian Empire" (13).

What is significant in this brief excerpt is the reference to Czechoslovakia (the interwar period) and the Austro-Hungarian Empire (the period prior to the 1919) and thus the setting of the notion of Central Europe, geographically and culturally. The Salamon family history, like that of Susan Rubin Suleiman or that of the Sonnenscheins' in István

Szabó's film *Sunshine* (see Portuges; Suleiman) stretches across Central and East Europe in time, in space, and in cultural parameters. It includes the particularities of their education (the Austro-German *Gymnasium* and university), their knowledge of languages and cultures, and the necessities of maneuvering from one cultural context to another but altogether being in a Central European space. Salamon's interpretations and explanations of matters and things Central European—be those in the particular Slovak, Hungarian, Ruthenian, Jewish, or Czech—extend over much detail. For instance, at one point she explains a specific instance of the usage in Hungarian of the familiar (*te*) and polite (*maga*) forms of address and other forms of address they used such as the Ukrainian-Czech mixture of *zolotik* ("little golden one") in their social and individual contexts (205). Salamon's narrative of memory is concentrated on family and family history and the memory of the horror of the Holocaust runs through it. Yet, the Central European cultural space as well as spaces the family's history and the histories of individual members occupy the book's narrative and they involve us as readers not only as historical evidence but also as evidence for a culture and literature of the region.

Elaine Kalman Naves's *Journey to Vaja: Reconstructing the World of a Hungarian-Jewish Family* is the most historical among the texts introduced here (it also has the least mistakes with diacritics and the translation of phrases and terms). The Jewish-Hungarian families whose history is told in the book, the Schwarz-Székács, the Weinbergers, the Rochlitz, etc., belonged to that stratum of Jews in Hungary who assimilated and became members of the educated upper-bourgeoisie of the country (see Braham; Ozsváth). In the case of the author's family, they produced members who were members of the Austro-Hungarian officer corps (the crème de la crème of pre–First World War and interwar society) and upper-government officialdom, landowners, industrialists, and the urban intelligentsia such as one Aggie Békés, who earned a doctorate in comparative literature from the University of Debrecen in the 1930s (section of photographs, n.p.). Jews in Hungary underwent perhaps the most widespread and deepest possible process of assimilation, for the reason that Kalman Naves describes as "during the forging of Magyar nationalism, they cast their lot wholeheartedly with that of the emerging Magyar nation—only one of the many ethnic groups in the polyglot Austro-Hungarian Empire which included Slovaks, Ukrainians, Slovenes, and many other nationalities. Even the orthodox among Hungarian Jews described themselves with self-conscious pride as *Magyars of the Israelite faith*" (15; on this, see also Ozsváth; Suleiman). In many instances, assimilation and magyarization resulted in access of numerous Jewish-Hungarian families to both non-titled nobility and to the ranks of the aristocracy and the large numbers of the urban strata of Hungarian Jews created much of the country's industrialization. Although assimilation and "voluntary" magyarization occurred to all of Hungary's national minorities such as Germans, Slovaks, Romanians, etc., in the case of Hungarian Jews the results of cultural and emotional assimilation explain much of the proposed character of Central Europeanness of the region's Jewries (for the Jewish nobility of Hungary, see McCagg; Lukacs 91–93; see also Molnár and Reszler; the above mentioned autobiography by Koltai contains descriptions with regard to the assimilation of Hungary's ethnic German population).

Magda Denes's *Castles Burning: A Child's Life in War* is a doubly sad book in view of its author's recent death in 1996 (all other authors of the memoirs under discussion here are alive today). The story of Denes's family is particularly poignant because of her father's abandon of his wife and daughter in 1939. The story of this Jewish-Hungarian family, again in the context of its position as educated upper bourgeoisie, is of particular interest for my argument of Central Europeanness because the story unfolds in "travel." What I mean is the telling of the tale when Magda Denes—after surviving the Holocaust in hiding—flees Hungary in 1946 with her mother and grandmother and how she perceives and experiences life as a refugee with and among all the other nationalities in the refugee camps. The narrative contains much reference and description of the self-confidence of the educated and cultured Central European (a theme in itself). Here is an excerpt: "I always suspected Ervin of having a bit of the prole [proletarian] in him. Anyway, now he wants to emigrate to Palestine with her, and he wants to fight for a Jewish state. I don't even know what that means. Jews are intellectuals, not farmers or soldiers" (147). Denes eventually ends up in New York where she becomes professor of psychoanalysis and psychotherapy at Adelphi University.

Susan Rubin Suleiman's *Budapest Diary: In Search of the Motherbook* is bitter-sweet in many instances of her narrative of recollection of Budapest life and death during the war and the Holocaust. The book's title itself is intriguing: *Budapest Diary: In Search of the Motherbook* and it is similar to Tibor Fischer's (another second-generation Hungarian) *Under the Frog* (1992), in that it contains a translation from the Hungarian. Fischer's un-English *Under the Frog* is a translation of the Hungarian phrase describing when one is in bad circumstances (as in quality of life): *a béka segge alatt* ("under the arse of a frog"). Suleiman's *Motherbook* is a translation of *anyakönyv*, the official name of one's birth certificate in Hungary and a term of nostalgia and patriotism in Hungarian literature and even in general discourse. Thus, the title of the book sets the scene, the author's search and re-discovery of her Hungarian background and history. In the first chapter, "Prologue: Forgetting Budapest," Suleiman describes her escape from Hungary as a ten-year-old, in the last months when the border was still open to Czechoslovakia. After stops in Košice and Bratislava—Kassa and Pozsony/Pressburg (the Hungarian and German names of the cities, respectively)—the Rubin family of three arrives in Vienna, free. After immigrating to the United States, Susan Rubin becomes an academic with a Ph.D. in French literature and her life is with clear distance to her cultural background in the American melting pot. Although with a brief interest in Hungary during the 1956 Revolution and its aftermath of Hungarian refugees arriving in the United States, it is only in the early 1980s—upon the illness of her mother, her own divorce, and the stress of raising two sons as a single mother—that "Zsuzsa" (the Hungarian version of Suleiman's first name) takes new interest in Hungary, Poland (her mother's background), and her unresolved past. After the dissolution of communism in 1989, she is invited to Budapest as a guest professor and she spends an extended period there in 1993. In Budapest—and it is in these chapters where the cultural reading I am interested in is written—Suleiman immerses herself in the intellectual life of scholars, writers, and artists and makes many interesting observations. While her descriptions of life and letters in Budapest may be uninteresting and at times contrite to a reader familiar with matters Central European and Hungarian, they are valuable for the North American reader because in North America these matters are of little or no importance or interest. Suleiman's writing is such that among the many interesting aspects of Central European and, within that, specifically Hungarian scenes, situations, and cultural varieties of matter, some may be of particular interest to the English-speaking and North American reader. Interestingly, there is one instance where Suleiman falls prey to that most Hungarian characteristic, cultural nationalism. In Suleiman's case this could perhaps be better described in terms of enthusiasm and over-valuation of things Hungarian: "I felt elated by the beauty of the city. 'It really is a great capital; it really can be compared to Paris.' I told myself as the cable car rose above the river." Well, yes, Budapest is a beautiful city, indeed, but in my opinion and despite the often repeated comparison to Paris it was never like Paris or Vienna and it is not comparable to them today either. . . .

Desider Furst and Lilian R. Furst's *Home Is Somewhere Else: Autobiography in Two Voices* is a dual autobiography. For her book, Lilian Furst edited autobiographical writings her father left her and added her own recollections in some chapters. Desider Fürst was born in Hungary, studied dental surgery from 1919 to 1926 at the University of Vienna, became a naturalized Austrian citizen in 1928, and practiced dentistry in Vienna until 1938. He fled Austria with his wife, also a dentist, Dr. Sári Fürst-Neufeld and daughter, Lilian, after the German annexation of Austria in 1938, to settle in England. The Fursts, similar to the Salamons and the family of Susan Rubin (Suleiman), had relations all over Central and East Europe, including Poland, Hungary, and Austria. They were educated with active interest in literature, theater, and the arts. Lilian's father and mother both had an M.D. and specialization in dental surgery from the University of Vienna. And their families and relatives suffered the Holocaust everywhere. Yet, Lilian and Desider Furst's memoirs of their lives and the lives of their families are imbued with nostalgia for the lost world that before the Shoah was theirs, a world that their memories recover and dress in sunshine.

In addition to their value in the corpus of the genre of memoir literature, the above texts are seminal descriptions of culture, history, and everyday life of pre-Holocaust Central Europe. These memories of real events are formations of an (imagined) Central Europe, a landscape with a culture of its own. Cumulatively, the texts reclaim a world destroyed and, by preserving and transporting its images to today, they locate a Central European culture of today. While these memoirs suggest and demonstrate variably similar perspectives of a Central European culture, they are also inseparable from the Holocaust and the history of the genocide of Jews remains part of Central European culture and its postcolonial situation.

From the sizable corpus of post-1989 cultural production, Thomas Brussig's *Helden wie wir* (1995; translated by John Brownjohn as *Heroes Like Us* and published in 1997) and Péter Esterházy's *Kis Magyar pornográfia. Bevezetés a szépirodalomba* (1984; translated by Judith Sollosy as *A Little Hungarian Pornography* and published in 1995) serve my second set of examples of Central European culture. In Brussig's case, the inclusion of the former East Germany in the designation of Central European culture needs to be explained, however. The in-between situation of the former East Germany obtained immediate relevance after the changes of 1989 and the collapse of the Soviet center, as follows. The historical as well as current cultural, political, economic, and other arguments for closer ties among all Central and East European countries are largely related to German and French economic and cultural influences as I suggested previously. There are, however, further differentiations. While Germany is the main center in its economic, political, linguistic, and cultural influence on the region, France exerts only limited economic or political influence in some countries such as Romania and Poland and France exerts significant cultural influence in these countries, including their literature (recently, Bulgaria even joined the Group of Francophone Nations). A further influence is of increasing importance: in many ways the United States, in culture as well as in its language, has begun to exert significant techno- and popular-cultural influence after the fall of Soviet colonialism in 1989, as well as limited economic and industrial impact on the region. The designation of the former East Germany (I refer to it as "Eastern Germany") as both a Central European cultural space and in-between peripheral rests on two observations. One, culturally and historically, Eastern Germany retained many characteristics similar to those to be found in Poland or Hungary, for example, such as the persistence of features of certain feudal characteristics associated with the *Junkerstaat*. Second, Eastern Germany was, similarly to the other countries of the region under Soviet colonialism, a communist and totalitarian state. And third, there is a growing sense that *die Wende* brought more than an acceptable level of economic as well as cultural colonialism over Eastern Germany exerted by Western Germany. An internal peripheralization is occurring within the new Germany, represented, for example, by the "Wessies" and the "Ossies" perspective including an economic as well as cultural colonization from the former West Germany towards the former East Germany (see, e.g., Grant; Mayer-Iswandy; Pape; Spieker). Thus, owing to the recent feudal past of the area (*Junkerstaat*), its some forty-years-long Soviet colonization and communist history, and its current colonial situation *vis-à-vis* the former West Germany suggest that Eastern Germany is an integral and functional part of the Central European cultural landscape.

I argue that contemporary Central and East European culture(s) show(s) postcolonial characteristics in that it feeds on and is influenced by the cultures of Western centers of power (economic and political as well as cultural) while it also manifests the effects and residues of filtered colonialism from the period of Soviet colonialism; thus the location of peripheral in-between. In particular, the literatures of the region show all elements of the postcolonial situation and they can be read as "narratives of change" with characteristics as follows. The emergence of the erotic and the sexual in literary texts albeit from a strong patriarchal perspective; the shift in the social status of the male author and its repercussions apparent in literature, and the observation that the themes of urbanity, memory, and sexuality/eroticism are manifested prominently in the texts as "subjective sensibility" (see Tötösy "Urbanity," *Comparative Literature* 121–72, "Configurations").

Brussig's novel belongs to the genre of post-1989 *Wende-Literatur* along with such novels as Günter Grass's *Ein weites Feld* (1995), Ingo Schramm's *Fitcher's Blau* (1996), Detlef Opitz' *Klio, ein Wirbel um L.* (1996), Monika Maron's *Animal triste* (1996), or Christa Wolf's *Medea* (1996). Brussig's *Heroes Like Us* is an irreverent novel (see, e.g., Upchurch). The author was born in 1965, he lives in the former East Berlin, and he is counter-establishment whether this concerns the former East Germany or the new, post-1989 Germany. The novel contains all the features I term as "narratives of change" above: urbanity, memoir textuality, and sexual narrative. The narrative of urbanity in the novel is in the tradition of the Berlin novel (e.g., Döblin's *Berlin Alexanderplatz*). The significance of the sexual narrative is not foremost in specific passages. Rather, the author uses sexual imagery and language for his historicization of urbanity and the politics of both before and after *die Wende* in an ironic and often satirical context and mood. Memoir textuality is a main feature of the novel but this is somewhat dissimilar from what I observed in the case of Hungary and Romania because in its structure and content it is not far in its genre properties from the *Bildungsroman* flowing over into the specifically German concept of *Vergangenheitsbewältigung* (dealing with the country's Nazi past), here applied to the history of the East German state. A most interesting feature of the text is the authors ironic and again, more often satirical treatment of Christa Wolf, a prominent author of the former East Germany. Here, the author is, theoretically speaking, in a systemic mode because he reflects on Wolf's stature and literary significance as well as her performance during and shortly after the fall of the Berlin Wall. Whether the novel also manifests the characteristics of the patriarchal male voice is subject to further analysis but preliminarily I would suggest that this is not the case, or at least not as strongly as in the case of other Central European literatures such Hungarians Endre Kukorelly's and Péter Esterházy's or Romanian Mircea Cărtărescu's texts (see Tötösy, *Comparative Literature* 121–72; see also Imre).

Along with Péter Nádas, whose *Emlékiratok könyve* (*A Book of Memories*, 1997, trans. Ivan Sanders and Imre Goldstein) may earn him one day the Nobel Prize in literature, Esterházy is recognized as one of Central Europe's and Hungary's prominent postmodern writers. Nádas's *Book of Memories* and Esterházy's *A Little Hungarian Pornography* or his *She Loves Me* (1995), similar to Brussig's novel, contain all features of the categories of a "narrative of change" in Central European literature. Esterházy's texts are prominently and explicitly sexual and with an unabashedly patriarchal point of view (see Imre) and Brussig's text is similar both thematically and in descriptions of relationships and women. Irony, often in conjunction with history and sexuality and women, is a foremost characteristic of the texts of both authors. For instance, when Esterházy uses irony and satire about Hungarian historical sanctities such as Prince Ferenc Rákóczi, he writes: "The tempo: take it slow, take it slow, good Master Rákóczi and she does her pleasure as if her gullet were her clitoris" (1; my translation) or "Then, flinging caution to the wind, Klára began to sob. My Husband is himself undecided. He says he loves me, and he's telling the truth, I know he is! The other day, too, he comes bolting out of the john and without prior notice says how while he was pissing, holding his dick, it hit him, he loves me" (6; my translation; further on Esterházy see also Tötösy, *Comparative Literature* 140–41). The novel is an accumulation of memoir material in loosely fitted sequential portions. Interesting is how the author connects his personal memories growing up in communist Hungary to the overall history of the country, more often than not through relating both aspects of memory to a sense and historical perception of the history of the Habsburg loyalist Esterházy family. The author is concerned with several issues characteristic of narratives of change such as the focus on the male voice. For instance, the book's first section's first sentence reads as follows: "Today's prose writer is a dour, endearing figure of a man" (156) and all sections portray maleness imbued with sexuality: "and while he watches the red-haired monkey taking possession of the frightfully beautiful princess who puts up almost no resistance at all he grabs his own member" (156) or "They stopped, whereupon he noticed how the woman had inadvertently spread her legs so her thighs would not rub together in the sweltering heat" (158). At the same time, the sections describe a sense of the social relevance of authorship of fiction: "I have no love for this intoxicating, loathsome and maddening world and I am bent on changing it" (157). The writer's life *is* text: "Today's prose writer is the kind of man whose life is the kind of life that doesn't progress from one place to the next. Consequently, the novel does not progress from here to there either" (157).

Brussig's novel about life in East Berlin is especially poignant to readers who lived under communism. References and descriptions such as the Berlin adolescent's yearning for objects and things western like glossy magazines, unavailable in the countries under Soviet and communist hegemony at the time, stand out and the flavors of everyday life in East Berlin are no different from those in Budapest or Prague. Finally, one aspect of the "narratives of change" ought to be briefly referred to: although dissimilar to Hungarian or Romanian literature where sexual language has not existed until recently while in German-language literature this is no novelty, Brussig's use of sexual language and imagery confirms this category of the proposed characteristics of Central and East European narrative.

The above brief applications of the proposed framework of comparative cultural studies in the study of Central and East European literature serve as examples for the argument that there exists a Central European culture based on variable similarities. In the first application the notion is evident in memoirs of second-generation North Americans of Central European background while in the second example the notion is found in textual characteristics and thematic similarities found in texts from the corpus of Eastern German and Hungarian literature.

WORKS CITED

Anderson, Benedict. *Imagined Communities: Reflection on the Origin and Spread of Nationalism.* London: Verso, 1991.

Ash, Timothy Garton. "Does Central Europe Exist?" (1986). *The Uses of Adversity: Essays on the Fate of Central Europe.* By Timothy Garton Ash. Cambridge: Granta, 1991. 161–91.
Bhabha, Homi K. *The Location of Culture.* London: Routledge, 1994.
Brussig, Thomas. *Helden wie wir.* Berlin: Volk und Welt, 1995.
Chase-Dunn, Christopher. "Resistance to Imperialism: Semiperipheral Actors." *Review* (Fernand Braudel Centre) 13.1 (1990): 1–31.
Deltcheva, Roumiana. "Comparative Central European Culture: Displacements and Peripheralities." *Comparative Central European Culture.* Ed. Steven Tötösy de Zepetnek. West Lafayette: Purdue UP, 2002. 149–68.
Deltcheva, Roumiana. "East Central Europe as a Politically Correct Scapegoat: The Case of Bulgaria." *CLCWeb: Comparative Literature and Culture: A WWWeb Journal* 1.2 (1999): <http://clcwebjournal.lib.purdue.edu/clcweb99-2/deltcheva99.html>.
Denes, Magda. *Castles Burning: A Child's Life in War.* New York: Simon and Schuster, 1997.
Esterházy, Péter. *Kis Magyar Pornográfia. Bevezetés a szépirodalomba.* Budapest: Magvető, 1984.
Even-Zohar, Itamar. *Polysystem Studies* Special Issue *Poetics Today* 11.1 (1990): 1–268.
Foerster, Heinz von. *Wissen und Gewissen. Versuch einer Brücke.* Frankfurt: Suhrkamp, 1993.
Furst, Desider, and Lilian R. Furst. *Home is Somewhere Else: Autobiography in Two Voices.* New York: State U of New York P, 1994.
Glasersfeld, Ernst von. *Radical Constructivism: A Way of Knowing and Learning.* New York: Falmer, 1995.
Grant, Colin B. *Literary Communication from Consensus to Rupture: Practice and Theory in Honecker's GDR.* Amsterdam: Rodopi, 1995.
Hanley, Sean, Kazi Stastna, and Andrew Stroehlein. "Central Europe Review: Re-Viewing Central Europe." *Central Europe Review* 1.1 (28 June 1999): <http://www.ce-review.org/99/ 1/hanley1.html>.
Imre, Anikó. "Comparative Central European Culture: Gender in Literature and Film." *Comparative Central European Culture.* Ed. Steven Tötösy de Zepetnek. West Lafayette: Purdue UP, 2002. 73-94.
Janaszek-Ivaničková, Halina. "Postmodern Literature and the Cultural Identity of Central and Eastern Europe." *Postcolonial Literatures: Theory and Practice/Les Littératures post-coloniales. Théories et réalisations.* Ed. Steven Tötösy de Zepetnek and Sneja Gunew. Thematic Issue *Canadian Review of Comparative Literature/Revue Canadienne de Littérature Comparée* 22.3–4 (1995): 805–11.
Jay, Paul. *Contingency Blues: The Search for Foundations in American Criticism.* Madison: The U of Wisconsin P, 1997.

Johnston, William M. *The Austrian Mind*. Los Angeles: U of California P, 1972.
Kalman Naves, Elaine. *Journey to Vaja: Reconstructing the World of a Hungarian-Jewish Family*. Montréal: McGill-Queen's UP, 1996.
Kalman, Judith. *The County of Birches*. Vancouver: Douglas and McIntyre, 1998.
Klobucka, Anna. "Theorizing European Periphery." *symplokē: a journal for the intermingling of literary, cultural and theoretical scholarship* 5.1–2 (1997): 119–35.
Kundera, Milan. "Three Contexts of Art: From Nation to World." *Cross Currents: A Yearbook of Central European Culture* 12 (1993): 5–14.
Kundera, Milan. "The Tragedy of Central Europe." *The New York Review of Books* (April 1984).
Longinović, Tomislav Z. *Borderline Culture: The Politics of Identity in Four Twentieth-Century Slavic Novels*. Fayetteville: U of Arkansas P, 1993.
Malak, Amin. "Ambivalent Affiliations and the Postcolonial Condition: The Fiction of M.G. Vassanji." *World Literature Today* 67.2 (1993): 277–82.
Mayer-Iswandy, Claudia. "Between Resistance and Affirmation: Christa Wolf and German Unification." *Postcolonial Literatures: Theory and Practice/Les Littératures post-coloniales. Théories et réalisations*. Ed. Steven Tötösy de Zepetnek and Sneja Gunew. Thematic Issue of *Canadian Review of Comparative Literature/Revue Canadienne de Littérature Comparée* 22.3–4 (1995): 813–35.
McCagg, William O., Jr. *Jewish Nobles and Geniuses in Modern Hungary*. Boulder East European Monographs, 1972.
Minh-ha, Trinh T. "No Master Territories." *The Post-Colonial Studies Reader*. Ed. Bill Ashcroft, Gareth Griffiths, and Helen Tiffin. London: Routledge, 1995. 215–18.
Molnár, Miklós, and André Reszler, eds. *La Génie de l'Autriche-Hongrie. Etat, société, culture*. Paris: PU de France, 1989.
Moore, David Chioni. "Is the Post- in Postcolonial the Post- in Post-Soviet? Toward a Global Postcolonial Critique. *PMLA: Publications of the Modern Language Association of America* 116.1 (2001): 111–28.
Ozsváth, Zsuzsanna. "Radnóti, Celan, and Aesthetic Shifts in Central European Holocaust Poetry." *Comparative Central European Culture*. Ed. Steven Tötösy de Zepetnek. West Lafayette: Purdue UP, 2002. 53-72.
Pape, Walter, ed. *1870/71–1989/90 German Unifications and the Change of Literary Discourse*. Berlin: de Gruyter, 1993.
Papp de Carrington, Ildikó. "From 'Hunky' to Don Juan: The Changing Hungarian Identity in Canadian Fiction." *Canadian Literature* 89 (1981): 33–44.

Paré, François. *Exiguity: Reflections on the Margins of Literature*. Trans. Lin Burman. Waterloo: Wilfrid Laurier UP, 1997.
Pichova, Hana. "Milan Kundera and the Identity of Central Europe." *Comparative Central European Culture*. Ed. Steven Tötösy de Zepetnek. West Lafayette: Purdue UP, 2002. 103-14.
Pilař, Martin. "Making Both Ends Meet, or, Czech Literature after November 1989." *Postcolonial Literatures: Theory and Practice/Les Littératures post-coloniales. Théories et réalisations*. Ed. Steven Tötösy de Zepetnek and Sneja Gunew. Thematic Issue of *Canadian Review of Comparative Literature/Revue Canadienne de Littérature Comparée* 22.3-4 (1995): 845-51.
Riegler, Alex, ed. *Radical Constructivism* (1996-): <http://www.univie.ac.at/constructivism>.
Salamon, Julie. *The Net of Dreams: A Family's Search for a Rightful Place*. New York: Random House, 1996.
Schmidt, Siegfried J. "The Empirical Study of Literature: Reasons, Plans, Goals." *The Systemic and Empirical Approach to Literature and Culture as Theory and Application*. Ed. Tötösy de Zepetnek and Irene Sywenky. Edmonton: Research Institute for Comparative Literature, U of Alberta and Siegen: Institute for Empirical Literature and Media Research, Siegen U, 1997. 137-53.
Schmidt, Siegfried J. *Kognitive Autonomie und soziale Orientierung. Konstruktivistische Bemerkungen zum Zusammenhang von Kognition, Kommunikation, Medien und Kultur*. Frankfurt: Suhrkamp, 1994.
Smith, Dinitia. "A Spinner of Spy Novels Whose Heroes Still Fight the Nazis." *The New York Times* (26 February 2001): B1, B6.
Spieker, Sven. "The Postutopian Subject in Soviet and East German Postmodernism: Andrei Bitov and Christa Wolf." *Comparative Literature Studies* 32.4 (1995): 479-96.
Suleiman, Susan Rubin. "Central Europe, Jewish Family History, and *Sunshine*." *Comparative Central European Culture*. Ed. Steven Tötösy de Zepetnek. West Lafayette: Purdue UP, 2002. 169-88.
Suleiman, Susan Rubin. *Budapest Diary: In Search of the Motherbook*. Lincoln: U of Nebraska P, 1996.
Tötösy de Zepetnek, Steven. "Selected Bibliography for the Study of Central European Culture." *Comparative Central European Culture*. Ed. Steven Tötösy de Zepetnek. West Lafayette: Purdue UP, 2002. 189-206.
Tötösy de Zepetnek, Steven. "Comparative Cultural Studies and Constructivism." *Frame: Tijdschrift voor Literatuurwetenschap* 15.1 (2001): 38-60. Online version at <http://clcwebjournal.lib.purdue.edu/library/totosy(constructivism).html>.
Tötösy de Zepetnek, Steven. "Systemic and Empirical Approach." *Online Dictionary of the Social Sciences*. Comp. Robert Drislane and Gary Parkin-

son. Edmonton: Athabasca U and ICAAP: International Consortium of Advancement of Academic Publication, 2001. <http://datadump.icaap.org/cgibin/glossary/SocialDict/SocialDict>.

Tötösy de Zepetnek, Steven. "Selected Bibliography of Work on Canadian Ethnic Minority Writing (to 1999)." *CLCWeb: Comparative Literature and Culture: A WWWeb Journal (Library)* (2001): <http://clcwebjournal.lib.purdue.edu/library/caneth.html>.

Tötösy de Zepetnek, Steven. "From Comparative Literature Today Toward Comparative Cultural Studies." *CLCWeb: Comparative Literature and Culture: A WWWeb Journal* 1.3 (1999): <http://clcwebjournal.lib.purdue.edu/clcweb99-3/totosy99.html>.

Tötösy de Zepetnek, Steven. "Bibliography of Studies in the Systemic and Empirical Approach to Literature and Culture." *CLCWeb: Comparative Literature and Culture: A WWWeb Journal (Library)* (1999): <http://clcwebjournal.lib.purdue.edu/library.html>.

Tötösy de Zepetnek, Steven. "Michael Ondaatje's *The English Patient*, 'History,' and the Other." *CLCWeb: Comparative Literature and Culture: A WWWeb Journal* 1.4 (1999): <http://clcwebjournal.lib.purdue.edu/clcweb99-4/totosy99-2.html>.

Tötösy de Zepetnek, Steven. "Configurations of Postcoloniality and National Identity: Inbetween Peripherality and Narratives of Change." *The Comparatist: Journal of the Southern Comparative Literature Association* 23 (1999): 89–110.

Tötösy de Zepetnek, Steven. *Comparative Literature: Theory, Method, Application*. Amsterdam and Atlanta, GA: Rodopi, 1998.

Tötösy de Zepetnek, Steven. "Selected Bibliography of Theoretical and Critical Texts on Canadian Ethnic Minority Writing." *Ethnic Minority Writing and Literary Theory*. Ed. Joseph Pivato. Special Issue *Canadian Ethnic Studies/Etudes ethniques au Canada* 28.3 (1996): 210–23. Online version at <http://clcwebjournal.lib. purdue.edu/library/caneth.html>.

Tötösy de Zepetnek, Steven. "Ethnicity and Center/Periphery: Cultural Identity in Germany and (East) Central Europe." *Culture, Identity, Europe/Kultur, Identität, Europa*. Ed. Rien T. Segers. Special issue of *SPIEL: Siegener Periodicum zur Internationalen Empirischen Literaturwissenschaft* 14.1 (1995): 38–49.

Tötösy de Zepetnek, Steven. "The Empirical Science of Literature/Constructivist Theory of Literature." *Encyclopedia of Contemporary Literary Theory: Approaches, Scholars, Terms*. Ed. Irene R. Makaryk. Toronto: U of Toronto P, 1993. 36–39.

Tötösy de Zepetnek, Steven. "Systemic Approaches to Literature—An Introduction with Selected Bibliographies." *Canadian Review of Comparative Literature/Revue Canadienne de Littérature Comparée* 19.1–2 (1992): 21–93.

Upchurch, Michael. "Nazi and Stasi: The Soundtrack." *The New York Times Book Review* (21 December 1997): 11–12.
Wallerstein, Immanuel. *After Liberalism.* New York: The New Press, 1995.
Wallerstein, Immanuel. "The Relevance of the Concept of Semiperiphery to Southern Europe." *Semiperipheral Development: The Politics of Southern Europe in the Twentieth Century.* Ed. Giovanni Arrighi. Beverly Hills: Sage, 1985. 31–39.
Willett, John. "Is There a Central European Culture?" *Daedalus: Journal of the American Academy of Arts and Sciences.* Thematic Issue *Eastern Europe . . . Central Europe . . . Europe* 119.1 (1990): 1–15.

A Comparative View of Modernism in Central European Literature

Andrea Fábry

According to Marshall Berman, "It is easy to imagine how a society committed to the free development of each and all might develop its own distinctive varieties of nihilism. Indeed, a communist nihilism might turn out to be far more explosive and disintegrative than its bourgeois precursor—though also more daring and original—because, while capitalism cuts the infinite possibilities of modern life with the limits of the bottom line, Marx's communism might launch the liberated self into immense unknown human spaces with no limits at all" (114). Indeed, this particular brand of nihilism emerged during socialism in Central and East Europe and created a special genre as an avenue for its biting and scathing satire, a genre Charles Eidsvik termed the "comedy of futility" (91). This comedy of futility may be one of the most popular (as well as most lingering) artistic achievements of the socialist period in Central and East Europe, as many recent "post-socialist" (post-1989) films still rely on the genre's self-reflexive and ironic outlook on life for their portrayal of how ordinary heroes can sabotage capitalism (using the very methods their ancestors used to counter socialism). Despite its popularity and prevalence in Central and East European culture, the comedy of futility remains an undertheorized and unexplored genre, one that still baffles scholars and critics with its suspicion of all ideologies and its questionable taste.

But how could we even start to explore the intricate lineages of family relations among texts as varied in terms of period and culture of origin as Bohumil Hrabal's fiction, the filmic adaptations of his works by leading directors of the Czech New Wave as well as central works of the Czech cinema such as Miloš Forman's *Firemen's Ball,* Jiři Menzel's *Crime at the Nightclub,* and Jaroslav Papoušek's *Homolka* trilogy, or Hungarian classics of at least three decades of socialism such as Péter Bacsó's *The Witness,* Péter Gothár's *A Priceless Day,* Péter Tímár's *Sound Eroticism,* and recent (post-1989) films such as Jan Sverak's *Kolya,* Viatcheslav Kryshtofovich's *Friend of the Deceased,* Emir Kusturica's *Underground,* Róbert Koltai's *We Shall Never Die,* and Péter Tímár's *Zimmer frei.* One way to approach the notion is through looking for common themes. Many characters in the above-mentioned works—for example, Hrabal's Uncle Pepin and Miloš's Hruma, Forman's firemen, Menzel's inapt lawyer, the indifferent Homolka family, the dam guard who bears witness to the 1950s, the factory manager and the fire marshal who foster healthy eroticism in the factory they supervise, etc.—go back to the figure of Švejk, the unruly hero of Jaroslav Hašek's 1923 classic of anarchist satire, *The Good Soldier Švejk.*

In order to formulate my proposal of a Central European modernity in literature, I re-evaluate Hašek's place in a revised canon of Central European modernity in the light of the assumption that Hašek created an entire tradition of "communist nihilism." The question is this: if Hašek is responsible for the model of socialist sabotage in which the "little man" "unwittingly" opposes oppressive state apparatuses, negating not only the legitimacy of these apparatuses but also the viability of any opposition to this illegitimate state, why was he celebrated as a forerunner of socialist humanist consciousness and action during socialism?

In the past, Hašek and his contemporary, Kafka, were idolized as classics of modernist literature, based on their differing treatments of political agency in an absurd modern world (for a comparison of Kafka and Hašek, see Kosik; Goetz-Stankiewicz). In addition, the two authors were also contrasted as authors of elitist versus popular inclinations, as men of tragic versus satirical visions, as well as writers of enigmatic and complex works versus transparent and commonsensical literature. For my purposes here, I concentrate on the first distinction that depicts Kafka and Hašek as authors favoring passivity and action, as captured in the following quote from Karel Kosik "What is the Kafkaesque world? It is the world of the absurdity of human thought and action, of human dreams, a world of a monstrous and unintelligible labyrinth, a world of human powerlessness in the network of bureaucratic machines, mechanisms, reified creations. Švejkism is a way of reacting to this world of absurd omnipotence of the machine and of reified relations" (88). As this passage suggests, the Kafkaesque (an adjective) connotes a state of the world, an overbearing human condition, while Švejkism (a noun) is a method of opposing that world. The two authors in this schema come to complement each other—while Kafka's heroes are "walled in a labyrinth of petrified possibilities" (88), Hašek's heroes come to the rescue to prove that "man is still a man, both a product and the producer of reification" (88). In other words, the noun of Švejkism points beyond itself to a verb of action whereby the Kafkaesque can be reversed through conscious human intervention. In this vein of interpretation, Švejk becomes a hero who wittingly pits a particular branch of idiocy against the powers that be to sabotage the war effort of the monarchy under the guise of vehement participation. By overdoing his tasks, he also deconstructs his mission in order to expose the frail logic of the military and imperial establishment of the Habsburg empire.

This reading of the Kafka-Hašek difference lends itself naturally to a Lukácsian interpretation whereby the two novelists can be seen as eminent representatives of modernism and realism as defined in Lukács's dual schema—Kafka shows a static and allegorical landscape in his works, where human beings are out of touch with their own destinies as well as are unshaped by history (modernism), while Hašek leads his actively defiant hero through a dynamic minefield of history (realism). Lukács's schema points to an important breach between modernism and historicity, namely that any impulse toward being modern entails the eradication of historical consciousness, yet modernness can only be achieved through a conscious contrast with the historical. As opposed to traditional accounts of modernism that concentrate solely on technique, Lukács attempts to reunite modernist form with its content to reveal underneath the façade of modernist style a stern refusal of history. For Lukács, as for Fredric Jameson today, the elaborate modernist style hides something (more precisely, the lack of something)—and that missing thing for Lukács is a dialectic between the individual modernist heroes' subjectivities and the realities they move in. Modernist protagonists do not move in or are moved by historical realities; they are without personal histories, as well as without actual historical surroundings that would impact their potentialities. In addition, the world itself depicted in modernist works is without history and change, only the narrator is in motion, the reality of the novels itself is static.

Since modernism severs the tie between individual subjectivity and the static world, its view of historical agency is demolishing—Lukács quotes Kafka's fly metaphor from *The Trial* to illustrate the paralysis of the modernist hero's lack of agency and how much of the modernist view of the world is presented "from the perspective of a trapped and struggling fly" (Lukács 607). Milan Kundera argues for a similar perspective in the modernist novel where "the monster comes from the outside and is called History; it no longer has anything to do with the train the adventurers used to ride; it is impersonal, uncontrollable, incalculable, incomprehensible—and it is inescapable" (Kundera 1986, 11). Kafka seems to be depicting the inhuman thrusts and unpredictable twists of such a train from the perspective of a hapless passenger, while Hašek present us with a hilarious view of a man fully enjoying himself on the same ride, throwing sandbags out the window to fasten the pace, disconnecting as well as sidetracking trains, and committing other acts of mischief to influence his ride according to his taste. The question rarely contemplated, however, seems to be whether any continuity exists between the writings of Kafka and Hašek besides the common locale—the impersonal centralized and alienated bureaucracy of the Habsburg empire, the historical locus of Central Europe and its culture—and whether the Kafkaesque and Švejkism are as incompatible as the abstract potentiality of modernism and the concrete potentiality of realism. In order to wrench away Kafka and Hašek from the neat periodical categories of Lukács, I intend to point out some of the shared themes and continuities between the two authors' oeuvre.

First of all, Kafka himself is markedly different from the kind of modernisms represented by Proust, Woolf, or Joyce. Consider the following passages, both about church towers, one taken from Proust's first volume, *Swann's Way,* and the other from *The Castle.* In the following scenes, we see two church towers and two strollers away from their childhood homes who pause to compare the towers, the ones present and the ones left behind in the past. Both strollers are forced to a halt by their contemplations, and resume their narrative only after the temporarily distraction caused by their observations.

The reflection of Proust's narrator upon the church steeple comes at the very end of a long section on the steeple of Saint-Hilaire in Combray. This section is representative of the modernist technique that Erich Auerbach called "multipersonal representation of consciousness" (536) or what Joseph Frank called "the spatial form" (68). The comparison of the two steeples is not part of a linear narrative development—Proust's narrator did not arrive in Paris after he duly related to the reader of all the consequential events of his childhood at Combray (as a narrator of a realist novel would have done) and now, pausing in front of the church steeple, he looks back to those dear times just once more. Instead, the overall design of Proust's narrator is rather one of conveying his entire narrative in a flashback—we are hearing about the childhood, teenage, grown-up memories of a man who "for a long time went to bed early" but of whose present surroundings and lifestyle we know very little of. The overwhelming part of the novel is, therefore, made up of past reminiscences, but even the past is not related to the reader in a temporal order, but is strung together through an associative logic.

The section of the book which collects all of the narrator's thoughts on the steeple of Saint-Hilaire cuts back and forth between various moments and scenes such as the narrator getting up and getting ready for mass at nine o'clock in the morning, him and his mother going to the store on their way to or from mass, him going to call for letters at the postoffice at five o'clock, or coming in from his walk in the evening. Some of these bursts of memory are connected to other church steeples, one in a quaint Norman town not far from Balbec, or one that can be seen from a particular window in Paris. At the very end of this wide array of associations upon steeples, we reach the present:

> And so even today, if, in a large provincial town, or in a quarter of Paris which I do not know very well, a passer-by who is "putting me on the right road" shows me in the distance, as a point to aim at, some hospital belfry or convent steeple lifting the peak of its ecclesiastical cap at the corner of the street which I am to take, my memory need only find in it some dim resemblance to that dear and vanished outline, and the passer-by, should he turn round to make sure that I have not gone astray, may be amazed to see me still standing there, oblivious of the walk that I had planned to take or the place where I was obliged to call, gazing at the steeple for hours on end, motionless, trying to remember, feeling deep within myself a tract of soil reclaimed from the waters of Lethe slowly drying until the buildings rise on it again; and then no doubt, and then more anxiously than when, just now, I asked him to direct me, I seek my way again, I turn a corner . . . but . . . the goal is in my heart. (72)

The presence of this moment is disappointing—whatever walk or social obligation Proust's narrator has been heading towards, it obviously cannot compare to the act of remembering, to the past moments materializing over the drying bit of soil reclaimed from Lethe. The present of this novel is self-effacing, it is a void characterized by the lack of colorful past observations and experiences. It is only by refusing to live the presence that the narrator can fully capture time and restore the past—the careful and precise rebuilding of past impressions demands his annihilation and denial of the present. As a result, after this passage on the present, Proust's narrator quickly returns to the immaterial past. Kafka's protagonist, by contrast, lives in the present. When he stops to contemplate the church tower, he is on one of his futile yet self-confident missions to reach the castle. On one of his first, brazen walks towards the castle, he looks up to observe his goal, which seems now more like a bunch of village buildings patched together, including a church building:

> And in thought he compared the church tower in his homeland with the tower up there. The church tower, tapering decisively, without hesitation, straightaway toward the top, capped by a wide roof with red tiles, was an earthly building—what else can we build?—but with a higher goal than the low jumble of houses and with a clearer expression than that of the dull workday. The tower up here—it was the only one in sight—the tower of a residence, as now became evident, possibly of the main Castle, was a monotonous round building, in part mercifully hidden by ivy, with little windows that glinted in the sun—there was something crazy about this—and ending in a kind of terrace, whose battlements, uncertain, irregular, brittle, as if drawn by the anxious or careless hand of a child, zigzagged into the blue sky. It was as if some melancholy resident, who by rights ought to have kept himself locked up in the most out-of-the-way room in the house, had broken through the roof and stood up in order to show himself to the world. Again K. stood still, as if he had greater powers of judgment at a standstill. But he was distracted. Behind the village church, beside which he had stopped—it was actually only a chapel with a barnlike annex to accommodate the congregation—was the school. (8–9)

K.'s reminiscences of the childhood church tower do not bring summary conclusions about the uselessness of the present—even though the present tower compares just as unfavorably to the past church tower as the steeples do in Proust (as a matter of fact, the present tower turns out to be a presidential tower belonging to the Castle). The past tower in Kafka does not achieve symbolic dimensions—while Proust's narrator arrives at the conclusion that "it was always to the steeple that one must return, always the steeple that dominated everything else, summoning the houses from an unexpected pinnacle, raised before me like the finger of God" (71), for Kafka's narrator, the church tower retains its material, earthly qualities. The narrator here for a minute either intervenes in K.'s recollection of the details of his childhood church to articulate his opinion that man can never create anything immaterial ("what else can we build?") or it is K. himself who arrives at this conclusion (K., the protagonist and Kafka's narrator are very close, albeit not enmeshed like Proust's narrator and the man whom in a later volume is called Marcel). For Proust's narrator, that steeple can become a guiding finger of his existence (search out all past steeple associations, nevermind the present), but for Kafka's narrator, whatever one ought to imagine that tower to be (house of god, finger of god) it will always remain a material, "earthly building." As the metaphor of the residential tower as a melancholy resident suggests, whatever is locked up inside (us) will always protrude into the outside world, there are no parts of our interior that we could seal off from the materiality of outside existence.

In addition to a certain continuity of narrative technique, we can observe a measure of continuity in characters between *The Castle* and *The Good Soldier Švejk:* Švejk is just as much of an opportunist as K.—they are both calculating and self-serving men who immediately become abusive when they rarely get the opportunity to wield power over others. It is surprisingly quick how K., a man awoken in the middle of his sleep at the beginning of the novel by a castle functionary insisting that he needs permission to spend the night at the inn, can start off his relationship with his assistants by stating that they are not to speak to anyone without his permission. K. recuperates his authority by putting his own assistants into a dependent position—if he needs permission to do things, other people will have to depend on his authority to go about their businesses. K. thereby imitates and perpetrates the absurd power structure of the castle and renounces his right to pitch an idealist alternative against that system. Whenever we would be ready to ask how can an innocent victim of the circumstances, a land surveyor summoned by accident, become a school janitor without an immediate remedy and apology from the castle, we see K. becoming complicit in his own fate, illustrating how people rationalize and make space for themselves within oppressive state apparatuses. K. shows himself collaborating on his own destiny, and implicitly, in the destiny of other characters as well.

We can find twin moments in both novels (these similarities can be somewhat explained by the common milieu of the two works, the lost world of the Austro-Hungarian Monarchy). One of such twin moments worthy of comparison is Švejk's visit at Judge Advocate Bernis (91–95) and K.'s visit at the chairman (57–74). Both Švejk and K. encounter authorities in these scenes: K. meets the chairman employed by the Count and Švejk is led in to see an army judge. K. sought to meet the chairman out of his confident assumption that he can sort out his status while Švejk is summoned and has no illusions concerning his lack of control over the events (in this sense a Lukácsian distinction is correct as Švejk is more of a "realist" than K. and refuses to believe in the abstract potentiality K. clings to.)

Both characters' fates depend on lost files—in *The Castle* the chairman's wife and K's assistants search jointly for the file that would explain whether K. is really needed as a surveyor in the village or not, while in Švejk's case, the judge himself looks for Švejk's file personally to be able to extract a confession out of him. In each situation there are tremendous piles of cases, a large portion of which never gets done. "Colleagues" within the same authority double-cross each other, the apparent miscommunications between departments delay the cases and cause even more paperwork, while, for example, the chairman explains to K. that such a miscommunication was an unfortunate accident that resulted in K. being summoned to the village for no reason and Švejk's judge relates bitterly to his visitor the exact details of how he changed the case number for a file to cover up for his mistake. In neither case is the file found.

In Kafka's text, the authority figure tells K. the story of the file in order to support his own viewpoint, namely, that the land surveyor is not needed but K. never gets to see the files; in Hašek's novel the outsider narrator informs us of the true story of the file in a bracketed paragraph (how it was found after the war, where it was misfiled, and what it contained). But even though we learn the contents of the file, it still doesn't explain anything or support any logical explanation as to why Švejk is in prison—it is entirely a narrative and authoritative decoy and is revealed by the narrator as such. The missing file of K. sides Kafka, the author with the authorities—just like the judges and bureaucrats use the files as canvases to their fabrications (the files provide an empty form into which plausible offenses can be deposited to match the pre-imagined punishments), Kafka uses the files to move his protagonist toward a pre-set destiny uncontrolled by his deeds and past. But the "real" file related to us by the narrator in *The Good Soldier* is just as mythological as K.'s file in *The Castle*, which functions as a Platonic idea (see Kundera). Here, the file is also an empty sign whose meaning is momentarily deposited by the characters involved: whether K. imagines the truth to be contained in it or various judges fill it with punishable offenses does not alter the sign-like function of the file.

Next, I briefly discuss aspects of text and context in Hašek and in Joyce with reference to the ongoing debate about whether there is a Central European literature as such (the corpus of works on this is large; for a bibliography, see Tötösy; see also Konstantinović; Tötösy; Willett). Both *The Good Soldier Švejk* and *A Portrait of the Artist as a Young Man* feature lengthy passages describing a sermon and I believe that the differing treatments of these scenes by the two authors reveal a great deal about the divergence between their world views. There are several meeting points between these passages: both sermons are at first collective, but are soon followed by a one-on-one conversation with a priest (in the case of Joyce, this priest is not the priest of the sermon, but a priest to whom Stephen confesses in a city chapel. In *Švejk*, the priest is the same chaplain who holds the sermon in the garrison jail). Both protagonists have front-row seats to the sermon (Švejk and his fellow prisoners from cell 16 are in their underpants right under the pulpit, Joyce's Stephen sits on the front bench of the chapel, as we are informed whenever the narrator cares to let us know). Both protagonists are touched by the sermon personally—and the sermon brings about a change of fortune in their lives (in *Švejk,* this is a direct change of fortune: since Švejk proved himself to be so cooperative with authority, he is chosen as batman to the chaplain. In *Portrait*, the sermon brings about a purification of the protagonist's interior, which presumably leads the exterior events of him being considered for the vocation). The difference, at first sight between the two passages, is purely stylistic—Joyce relies on the characteristic modernist technique of a multiple reflection of consciousness and of multiple time strata as described by Auerbach. The following passage, taken from Stephen's conversation with the director of his college in chapter four, illustrates the essence of this technique:

> Of course it is, of course. Just imagine when I was in Belgium I used to see them out cycling in all kinds of weather with this thing up about their knees! It was really ridiculous. *Les jupes,* they call them in Belgium. The vowel was so modified as to be indistinct. What do they call them? *Les jupes.* O! Stephen smiled again in answer to the smile which he could not see on the priest's shadowed face, its image or spectre only passing rapidly across his mind as the low discreet accent fell upon his ear. He gazed calmly before him at the waning sky, glad of the cool of the evening and the faint yellow glow which hid the tiny flame kindling upon his cheek. The names of articles of dress worn by women or of certain soft and delicate stuffs used in their making brought always to his mind a delicate and sinful perfume. As a boy he had imagined the reins by which horses are driven as slender silken bands and it shocked him to feel at Stradbrooke the greasy leather of harness. It had shocked him, too, when he had felt for the first time beneath his tremulous fingers the brittle texture of a woman's stocking for, retaining nothing of all he read save that which seemed

to him an echo or a prophecy of his own state, it was only
amid softworded phrases or within rosesoft stuffs that he
dared to conceive of the soul or body of a woman moving with
tender life. But the phrase on the priest's lips was disingenuous for he knew that a priest should not speak lightly on that
theme. The phrase had been spoken lightly with design and
he felt that his face was being searched by the eyes in the
shadow. (110)

Within the exterior event of the conversation, on the word *les jupes*, uttered in that very conversation, Joyce strings a series of time capsules: we get present glimpses of the priest's facial expression (lack of a smile) and Stephen's reaction to the word (calm gazing and a "faint yellow glow"), as well as past glimpses of Stephen's memories, conjuring up a smell ("a delicate and sinful perfume"), a touch ("the brittle texture of a woman's stocking"), and a sound ("softworded phrases"). Even further back in time, the disappointment women's articles of clothing caused for Stephen are likened to his childhood disappointment in the texture of reins, which, further back in time, had been imagined by him as silk. After Stephen's string of associations with the word *les jupes* are elaborated, the narrator returns to the present situation, where a word like *les jupes* can only be uttered with a specific design, as a tool of Jesuit craft (a thought which will open up new sets of associations and memories in Stephen's mind in the continuation of the scene).

In the sermon section, the interior event itself upon which the temporal and spatial excurses are grafted extends over a five-day period of time (a period of time which is described in the priest's speech as "one brief moment"). Over the five days of the spiritual retreat, we hear the sermon itself (sometimes directly, sometimes filtered through Stephen's consciousness), we are told of some of Stephen's actions (his going home, his eating of his dinner, his conversation with his schoolmates, his school lessons, his fit and prayers, as well as his trip to the Church street chapel and his confession there). In addition to these exterior occurrences, we hear Stephen's introspection over the sermon ("Every word of it was for him"), remember both his past sins ("the sordid details of his orgies"), and childhood memories (his life at Clongowes) with him as well as see his visions (of him and Emma joined by God, for example).

At times the exterior happenings are at first indistinguishable from interior events: after one of Stephen's hallucinations during which "flames burst forth from his skull like a corolla, shrieking like voices: Hell! Hell! Hell! Hell! Hell!" the narrator remarks, "Voices spoke near him: On hell" (89). At first reading, the voices speaking in this sentence (uttering "on hell") seem to be identical with the imaginary voices of the flames which shriek "hell," but upon further, more careful reading, the sources of the second voices turn out to be located in Stephen's schoolmates who are discussing the sermon at school next day.

In another passage, where Stephen is listening to the second day's sermon of the retreat on death and judgment, it is quite impossible to say at first whether we are reading the sermon as it is filtered through Stephen's consciousness (i.e., Stephen imagining the day when he would die and be judged as a sinner) or whether the priest uses a third person singular narrative to convey an emotionally powerful message about one exemplary sinner and his sermon is related to us by the narrator (without direct quotation of the full text of the sermon which is usually signaled in the text with dashes marking the beginnings of spoken paragraphs). In the entire text of the retreat, the imaginary and real happenings mingle just as much as the utterances and thoughts of various characters and the narrator mingle, making it problematic to pinpoint the sources of consciousness in which certain sentences and observations are centered.

In contrast, Hašek's narration of the sermon starts with a lengthy biography of the chaplain (83–85). Joyce's narrator only gives us one sentence about Father Arnall prior to his sermon ("He wore about his shoulders a heavy cloak; his pale face was drawn and his voice broken with rheum" 77), compared to the narrator of *The Good Soldier,* who still has confidence that he knows everything of his character and by conveying his knowledge to us readers, he can help us understand that character. Joyce's narrator is not particularly interested in the Father's appearance, life story, character, or even perhaps in his sermon, as much as he is interested in the interior effects of the Father's presence in Stephen's life. The narrator of *Portrait* discards the life story of the Father as irrelevant to the transformation and reversal his speech brings about in the protagonist's life. On the contrary, Hašek wants us to understand fully where the character who is going to change the course of events in his protagonist's life is coming from and aims at presenting the plot as a text created out of interlacing interests of crisscrossing character-bobbins. At the same time, Hašek refuses to concern himself with the interior of his protagonist—whether Švejk is a "prize royal oaf" (95) who indeed does not understand the ways of the world or a sophisticated trickster who pretends to be an idiot can never be inferred satisfyingly from the text which is nearly completely devoid of passages relating Švejk's thoughts or feelings to the reader.

After the chaplain's life story, we hear the sermon about the "thorny path of sin" (85), but this sermon is radically different from Father Arnall's four-part retreat. Father Arnall's sermon was constructed and structured pedantically, relating the events in the afterlife of a sinner, starting from death moving through judgment and reaching hell. His speeches on hell were carefully divided into a description of hell's physical characteristics (explaining in more detail the properties of hell pertaining to the four senses of sight, smell, touch and hearing) and his second-day description of the spiritual qualities of hell (the pain of loss, the threefold pain of conscience, and the pain of extension). In contrast, Hašek's chaplain is profoundly unprepared, loses his own track of thought, relapses into German several times (86), mixes registers ("What the hell does the Lord's Prayer mean to you?" 85), and, being unaware of the whole ritual, technique and text of the mass, proceeds without a single reference to the Bible. It is indeed as if the extreme structural pedantry of Father Arnall's speech was designed to contrast and set off the meandering logic of Stephen's interior thoughts, to distinguish between the inside and the outside, the censored and the uncensored, the one with the vocation and the one destined to other calls in life. The chaplain in *The Good Soldier*, on the contrary, is baring his stream of consciousness in a real-time speech to his listeners, just like Švejk does in everyday settings. From taproom to prison to courtroom to chapel, people in *The Good Soldier* express themselves in the same exterior monologues—from Švejk to chaplain, no one cares to censor their thoughts and divide the interior from the exterior.

The parallel between religious, private, and military life is further accentuated by the fact that the chaplain opens his sermon with "Attention!" (85) and closes it with "Dismiss!" (90). Unlike Father Arnall's speech, which is geared toward facilitating reflection and inducing confession, the garrison chaplain's speech is not about leading the inmates to God. In his speech, he paints a picture of a God surrounded by unforgiving helpers, who, like the chaplain himself, refuse to hand out forgiveness among the truly penitent. God's order is modeled upon the world of the monarchy—it is not earth that attempts to live according to the rules of the divine order, but religion itself abandons its higher aims to lower itself to the soulless methods of human punishment and discipline. Since there is no transcendence and no mercy, there is no point in introspection—hence the narrator preoccupies himself with the exterior happenings and abandons all attempts to present us with the interior reflections of his characters, who abandoned self-reflection in view of its futility in changing the course of their lives.

Hašek's refusal to engage modernist techniques of narration therefore is a conscious choice that reflects his view of the dialectic between his heroes and their reality underlying his work. Although *The Good Soldier* seems to share a great deal more of the characteristics Lukács associates with traditional realism (there is a definite narrator who addresses the reader in a preface and in an epilogue, the narrator seems to have the key to the whole life story of his characters, we are occasionally informed by his omniscience about the fate of the characters past the events portrayed in the novel), in its world view it is much more destructive than some of the authors Lukács singled out as illustrations for his discussion of "modernist nihilism." History does matter in *The Good Soldier* (after all, the events of the novel are set in motion by the assassination of Franz Ferdinand and the outbreak of the first World War) and actual local historical detail and politics enter the lives of the characters (as well as the pages of the book), but how Švejk and his bar fellows look at political and historical events bears no relation to the view of history in traditional realism (see in particular the conversation at The Chalice in chapter 1). History is no longer a predictable and workable tool in the hands of ordinary men, but the backcloth to the bungling of disillusioned heroes who have nothing to believe in. Stephen Dedalus may leave to forge in the smithy of his soul the uncreated consciousness of his race—Švejk would be incapable of even that much action, as that would require from a faith in at least artistic creation, a faith he grew quite incapable of, both in the traditional sense of religion and of political action.

In sum, I propose that it is time to explore the Central European modernist heritage with local continuities in mind, such as the connection between Hašek and his contemporary, Kafka, precisely in the context of a comparative Central European culture based in comparative cultural studies as proposed by Steven Tötösy (2002). I believe that while Lukács's explorations of the tension between modernism and historicism are useful and have informed many contemporary critical reevaluations of the modernist canon, we need to reassess his dialectic poles that pit Central European modernists against their West European contemporaries. We must question the evolutionist scheme that would posit Central European modernist writing as a throwback to some golden age and exclude them from the modernist canon. Instead of perpetuating an iron curtain between the "East" and the "West" of Europe and its cultures and literatures, an understanding and study of modernism including Central Europe will only enrich our knowledge about the varieties of literary, critical, political, and intellectual stances of the modernist period.

WORKS CITED

Auerbach, Erich. "The Brown Stocking." *Mimesis: The Representation of Reality in Western Literature*. 1946. By Erich Auerbach. Trans. Willard R. Trask. Princeton: Princeton UP, 1974. 525–54.

Berman, Marshall. *All That is Solid Melts into Air: The Experience of Modernity*. 1982. New York: Penguin Books, 1988.

Eidsvik, Charles. "Mock Realism: The Comedy of Futility in Eastern Europe." *Comedy/Cinema/Theory*. Ed. Andrew S. Horton. Berkeley: U of California P, 1991. 91-109.
Frank, Joseph. "Spatial Form in Modern Literature." 1945. *Essentials of the Theory of Fiction*. Ed. Michael J. Hoffman and Patrick D. Murphy. Durham: Duke UP, 1996. 63-76.
Goetz-Stankiewicz, Marketa. "Kafka and Hašek: Reflections on a Meeting in the House of Fiction." *Language and Literary Theory*. Ed. Benjamin Stolz, I. R. Titunik, and Lubomír Doležel. Ann Arbor: U of Michigan P, 1984. 339-54.
Hašek, Jaroslav. *The Good Soldier Švejk and His Fortunes in the World War*. 1923. Trans. Cecil Parrott. London: Penguin Books, 1974.
Jameson, Fredric. "Modernism and Imperialism." *Nationalism, Colonialism, and Literature*. Ed. Terry Eagleton. Minneapolis: U of Minnesota P, 1990. 43-66.
Joyce, James. *A Portrait of the Artist as a Young Man*. 1916. New York: Dover, 1994.
Kafka, Franz. *The Castle*. 1926. Trans. Mark Harman. New York: Shocken Books, 1998.
Konstantinović, Zoran. "Gibt es eine mitteleuropäische Literatur?" *Europa und Mitteleuropa. Eine Umschreibung Österreichs*. Ed. Andreas Pribersky. Wien: Böhlau, 1991. 201-12.
Kosik, Karel. "Hasek and Kafka." 1963. Trans. Karel Kovanda. *Telos: Quarterly Journal of Critical Thought* 23 (1975): 84-88.
Kundera, Milan. *The Art of the Novel*. 1986. Trans. Linda Asher. New York: Grove P, 1988.
Lukács, György. "The Ideology of Modernism." 1956. Trans. John Mander and Necke Mander. *The Critical Tradition: Classic Texts and Contemporary Trends*. Ed. David H. Richter. New York: St. Martin's P, 1989. 597-611.
Proust, Marcel. *Swann's Way*. 1913. Trans. C.K. Scott Moncrieff and Terence Kilmartin. New York: Vintage Books, 1989.
Tötösy de Zepetnek, Steven. "Comparative Cultural Studies and the Study of Central European Culture." *Comparative Central European Culture*. Ed. Steven Tötösy de Zepetnek. West Lafayette: Purdue UP, 2002. 1-32.
Tötösy de Zepetnek, Steven. "Selected Bibliography for the Study of Central European Culture." *Comparative Central European Culture*. Ed. Steven Tötösy de Zepetnek. West Lafayette: Purdue UP, 2002. 189-206.
Willett, John. "Is There a Central European Culture?" *Cross Currents: A Yearbook of Central European Culture* 10 (1991): 1-16.
Willet, John. *Art and Politics in the Weimar Period: The New Sobriety, 1917-1933*. New York: Pantheon Books, 1978.

Radnóti, Celan, and Aesthetic Shifts in Central European Holocaust Poetry

Zsuzsanna Ozsváth

Born in different times and different places, two great Central European poets of the Holocaust, Paul Celan and Miklós Radnóti, reveal essential commonalities that point toward a shared intellectual heritage. Striking among them is these poets' belief in the power of poetry, which Radnóti viewed as capable of controlling, perhaps even transcending, the peril that threatened the world and which young Celan saw as able to create a bridge between present and past. These beliefs were, of course, common in the Western literary tradition—although they have rarely surfaced with such intensity. Radnóti identified with the Hungarian legacy of the myth of the poet-hero who would save, and if need be die for, his country. He lived out his life, composed poetry, and marched to his own death, while still seeing himself an heir to this tradition. Antschel (Celan's family name until 1947) also looked upon literature and art as comprising his foundational ethos. But unlike Radnóti, he survived the Shoah and recognized its magnitude and consequences. Eventually, his experience during the Holocaust, the murder of his parents, and the loss of his community undermined his belief in poetry as a means of reaching the other. He started to doubt the potency of words to create a dialogue, to evoke and communicate the world of the past. So have the poets who walked in his paths. The poetry in Central Europe composed in the aftermath of the Holocaust would no longer rely on the myths that sustained the ethos of Radnóti and young Paul Celan.

Of course, the historical and cultural roots out of which Radnóti arose were different from those of Celan. Radnóti was born in 1909 into a Hungarian Jewish family, in Budapest, the Hungarian capital of the Austro-Hungarian empire. For many years, most Hungarian Jews had participated in, and benefited from, the fast-spreading emancipation and assimilation processes initiated in nineteenth-century Hungary. Protected by the law of 1867, giving them equal rights, and by that of 1895, giving them equal religious status, Jews started to live in considerable freedom in the Austro-Hungarian monarchy. Grateful for being tolerated, appreciated, even feeling wanted—unless, of course, they showed too deep an attachment to their religious or cultural past—masses of Hungarian Jews assimilated to the Hungarian way of life and became passionately patriotic. But their sense of security changed considerably after the first World War. The loss of that war, the subsequent violence created by the commissars of Hungary's Soviet Republic, the rise of the counter-revolutionary army and its pogroms, and the Trianon Peace Treaty, which excised two-thirds of Hungary's historical terrain, catapulted the country into ever new turmoil. Amid chaos and economic collapse, old ideals of liberalism disappeared and the nineteenth-century tolerance shown toward the Jews changed into hatred (see Braham 5–39). Living in a hostile world, young Radnóti experienced waves of discrimination. And the government did not try to relieve the tension. In fact, accepting the rhetoric of its murderous counter-revolutionary comrades-in-arms, the regime of Admiral Miklós Horthy decreed in 1920 the first anti-Jewish measure (the *numerus clausus* law) in twentieth-century Europe. This law not only reduced the number of Jewish students in Hungarian universities, it also resonated with both the ideas of the old-fashioned xenophobic right and those of the new anti-Semitic movement directed against the "Judeo-Bolshevists," conflating religious, racial, and ideological hatred (on the history of Hungarian Jews and Radnóti, see Ozsváth; see also Suleiman).

Neither was the Bukovina, part of Romania since 1919, where Paul Celan was born in 1920, free from nationalist, fascist or anti-Semitic outbreaks during the interwar period. But the history of the Jews in the region differed from that in Hungary, where Hungarian people, Hungarian culture, the consciousness of Hungarian history, and ancient Hungarian habits dominated. In the Bukovina, a multi-ethnic population, consisting of Russians, Poles, Romanians, Ruthenians, Germans, Jews, Armenians, Hungarians, Moldavians, Ukranians, and others, determined the region's diversity. This demographical difference also entailed significant cultural differences in the worlds of these two groups. Many Jews in the Bukovina had made their home in the area since the thirteenth century, when part of the region belonged to Poland, part to Moldavia. Living for generations in the same region and in tightly knit communities, by the end of the nineteenth century most Bukovinian Jews still cultivated their heritage and remained immersed in traditional Jewish learning. Although they absorbed German high culture and adapted to secular living, many of them felt free to retain their religious tradition. In Israel Chalfen's opinion, "they developed a novel sort of pragmatism that permitted them to be modern while retaining from Judaism the elements that gave their lives moral support and allowed them to safeguard their ethnic identity" (8). By the end of the nineteenth century, however, large segments of the Bukovinian Jewish community became absorbed by, and identified with, Austrian liberalism and Austrian culture in the context of German-language culture. As a result, many of them developed lifestyles and celebrated values that created a distinctly new cultural direction. Thus, while most Hungarian Jews identified themselves with their country's history and culture, becoming passionate Magyar patriots, most Jewish intellectuals in the Bukovina cultivated the German language, Austro-German art, and Austro-German liberal thought (for a parallel development see "Austroslovakism" in Peter Petro's study; see also John and Lichtblau). Even when the Jewish national movement, with its idea of a Jewish homeland began to gain momentum and push toward recognition of Jewish nationality as an official status, the admiration of the region's Jews for German high culture remained the same and even intensified during the interwar period. As Aharon Appelfeld, the Israeli writer from Czernowitz, recalls this extraordinary development: "In our house, German was insisted upon, as though it embodied everything good and beautiful" (Appelfeld, 50). Also Amy Colin emphasizes that "despite the Romanian rule, the growing nationalism, and the rise of fascism, the German Jewish component of Bukovinian culture reached its culmination precisely in the 1920s and 1930s" (xiii), that is, precisely during the years of Celan's childhood and youth.

Coming from a traditional Jewish family, Celan's father studied Hebrew, the Holy Scriptures, and the Talmud. He also went to public school, learned German, and trained for becoming a broker in the timber trade. Celan's mother, on the other hand, had acquired neither a religious nor a formal education. Despite this setback, or perhaps because of it, she spent much time reading the works of the great German classical writers and acquired a deep knowledge of German literature. Continuing to read intensely even after she married and had a family, she spoke high German at home, and set time aside for reading with her son the masterpieces of German literature. In this way, German became Celan's mother tongue and, although he wrote a few poems in Romanian, he made a conscious decision after the war to use German for expressing himself in poetry. This was a hard decision, however. Recalling it in his speech in Bremen, in 1959, he spoke of his awareness of the transformation the German language had to go through after the Holocaust. "Muted" and "answerless" at first, he said, it had to "pass through the thousand darknesses of death-bringing speech" (qtd. in Felstiner, *Selected Poems* 395). Noting both the pressure Celan felt to compose poetry and the urge to do so in German, once Celan wrote his friend and mentor Alfred Margul Sperber: "You do realize what I am attempting to tell you: there's nothing in the world for which a poet would give up composing poems, not even when he is a Jew and the language of his poems is German" (Rosenthal 403; my translation). The urgency to speak in a voice that came from his childhood and carried the echoes of the voice of his murdered mother, communicating feelings and visions, Celan felt, overrode all other considerations. This is the issue he touched upon in his essay about Edgar Jené, asking the question: how should the work succeed "when you ... never leave behind the deep but rather keep having a dialogue with the darkest sources?" (*Gesammelte Werke* 3, 157; my translation). Whatever had happened during the war, for Celan, the dialogue "with the darkest sources" was possible only in German.

Radnóti neither considered or even had any option other than expressing himself in Hungarian. Despite the fact that he learned several languages, Magyar was the language of his environment, the language of the great Hungarian poets, whom he loved and revered, the sound of his earliest nursery rhymes and the words of his lyrics. He expressed his joy and sorrow in Hungarian; he dreamt in Hungarian; Hungarian was the language of his people, whose fate and future he felt to be his own. He conflated his sense of being and identity with those of other Hungarian poets, and he understood his life in terms of the ethos and myths of his homeland. In fact, so passionately did he feel about the country of his birth and his own rootedness in its soil and culture, that when Aladár Komlós, one of Hungary's leading Jewish literary critics, invited him to be a contributor and editor to the *Ararát Almanach,* a publication of the Budapest Jewish Federation, Radnóti proudly rejected any forum other than the national, Hungarian public (*Napló* 210). No matter, he wrote Komlós, how anti-Semitic were the politicians of the day, or even some of his fellow literati, the heart and soul of Hungary, Radnóti insisted, did not exile him. Hence, to the heart and soul of Hungary, he was, and would remain to be, attached forever: "My 'homeland' doesn't scream at me from the bookshelves: 'go to hell wretched Jew,' but rather it opens its landscapes up to me; the bush does not tear a greater hole in me than on others; and the tree does not stand on tiptoes lest I reach its fruit. If I would experience anything of this sort, I would kill myself, because I couldn't live in ways other than I do; and I could neither believe nor think differently" (*Napló* 210; my translation). No matter what took place in Hungary, Radnóti's decision to demonstrate that he was the native son of his beloved homeland did not change.

Yet this could not have been an easy decision. By the time Radnóti wrote his letter to Komlós, Hungarian Jews had suffered the consequences of three pernicious anti-Jewish measures and Radnóti himself underwent his first three months of labor service. He knew about, and feared desperately, the draft for "work service," which had sent by April 1942, nearly 50,000 Jewish men to the Russian front. He saw and experienced that most Jewish breadwinners were squeezed out of their jobs and businesses (Braham 156–60). And he heard about the deportation of thousands of "foreign Jews" in the late summer of 1941, who were expelled from Hungary to Kemenets-Podolsk, where they were killed upon arrival. In addition, he was informed of the murder of more than 1,000 Jewish men, women, and children at Ujvidék in southern Hungary in January 1942, all of whom were shot into the Danube river by Hungarian military troops. Yet Radnóti's love for his country remained deep, unchanging, and unconditional. In fact, the more threatening the political circumstances, the more intensely he expressed his love and loyalty to his homeland. The intensity of this feeling is perhaps nowhere more passionately articulated than in his lyrics "I Know Not What . . . ," with the poem's emotionally loaded evocation of the tension among the country's lovely landscape, its culture, and the destruction threatening from the bombs of the airplane flying above: "I know not what to strangers this dear landscape might mean,/ to me it is my birthplace, this tiny spot of green;/ ringed now with fire, it was, once, my childhood rocking me;/ O may my body sink back to that life-giving soil (Ozsváth and Turner 171, 173). The "dear landscape" is the speaker's birthplace, his cradle and, as he hopes, his future and grave. He knows its bushes, its flowers, its people. He knows its "crickets, oxen, steeples, quiet farms," and he apprehends its "twittering orchards, vine props with their tended grapes,/ and the old granny in the graveyard where she weeps;" unlike the pilot who only sees the map and its "symbols and degrees" (see Ozsváth 188–89). Anguished by the conflict, Radnóti ends the poem, his last one he composed before the German occupation, with a plea for peace and mercy: "With great wings cover us, O guardian cloud of night." Of course, poems confessing deep devotion to the homeland have been part and parcel of most countries' culture. They have traditionally played an essential role in Hungarian poetry as well. But what makes Radnóti's poetic testimony in "I Know Not What . . ." unique among most patriotic poems is the context in which it was composed, the context that involved unimaginable atrocities aimed at people identified as Jews. Yet Radnóti was unable to face the reality of this rejection.

For Celan, during the war and shortly after, the language of poetry meant evocation and remembrance of a lost world, a process which Nelly Sachs once described as "we both live in the invisible home country" (*Paul Celan, Nelly Sachs* 69). To write poetry in German, to recall his murdered mother, to engrave himself into his "homeland"'s culture so that he would never again be viewed outside of it, never be exiled again, became Celan's goal and purpose. It is important to note that when he moved to France after the war, afar from the German-speaking countries as well as from the region of his birth, choosing to write poetry in German he acted upon a similar hope and a similar construction of the mind as once did his community. For neither did the Jews of the Bukovina, who identified themselves with German high culture, live in a country that had a German existence. Their world, too, was centered on memory, myth, and the imagination rather than on the living experience in, or the shared history of, an existing state or country. Although before the first World War, the area's administration and public education was conducted in German, the Bukovina had not sprang from a German-speaking land. With its poly-ethnic groups of people, it had been a region for many. Still, the German-speaking Jews relied on the values of German high culture, hoping to find in it their homeland, the place they had been searching for since ancient times, the place where they could belong. Did this fantasy interplay with an older dream? Was it more than a dream? Was it yet another expression of Jewish yearning for a homeland manifesting itself in attempts at replacement in their imagination and memory?

Radnóti, on the other hand, not only grew up in a country he felt was his homeland, but as a poet and Hungarian patriot, he also developed a compelling belief in a higher justice that would, he hoped, support the struggle of Hungarians against their enemies. Tapping an age-old tradition of poetic responses to the turmoil Hungary had to suffer at the hand of occupying armies and foreign governments, Radnóti appropriated the ethos virtually all Hungarian poets felt necessary to express in times of imminent national danger. He decided to follow in the footsteps of these poet-prophets and conflated the discrimination he had to suffer as a Jew with their struggle against oppression. The first conscious declaration of this ethos may be found in his early poem, "Like a Bull" (1933). With atrocity looming in the background, this piece was written several months after Hitler's take-over of Germany, almost a year after Gyula Gömbös became prime minister in Hungary, at a time when Jew beatings were practiced every day in Hungarian universities, among them in Szeged, where Radnóti himself was a student (see Csaplár 122–25). Although there is nothing concrete appearing in the poem that could be clearly related to events playing themselves out in the larger world, the images appearing in it gesture toward both the threat of murderous groups killings of the innocent and the speaker's decision on calling for life and justice. The piece captures a bucolic scene, with a galloping, playful bull in the circle of his cows. Suddenly, however, a pack of wolves threatens the idyll, and the persona observes the bull's response: "but the bull snorts and doesn't flee as the deer are/ fleeing, he fancies that when his hour comes round he'll fight,/ and fall, and the pack will scatter his bones all over the meadow" (Radnóti in Ozsváth and Turner 35). Rather than "snapping away with the wind" as the deer do, when sensing the scent of the wolves, the bull does not flee. "He'll fight," claims the speaker, his voice resonating with uncanny relevance: "Even so will I struggle and so will I die;/ still as a sign to posterity the fields will preserve my bones." These images presage then the death of innocent beings and the violence of the mob, images and perceptions that would be part of Radnóti's poetic themes and expressions from now until the end of his life. They also indicate his new ethos of resistance: "Even so will I struggle, and so will I die," says the speaker of the "bull poem," resounding yet another motif that would become a characteristic feature of the oeuvre of Radnóti. No matter what happens, the poet is aware of his role among his people. Innocent and pure as "baby Jesus in an icon," he would also become as strong and as hard as the great wolf who goes "bleeding through the snows" (Ozsváth and Turner 51).

In another poem, "Annotations to the Prophet Habakkuk," the speaker summons his biblical namesake to indict the Franco regime in Spain (Ozsváth and Turner 67). Thundering in the voice of the ancient prophet who fought against oppression, Radnóti's persona echoes the rage of the divine. The voice crying out from "Guard and Protect me," too, is that of the poet-hero (Ozsváth and Turner 71). He calls for courage so that he may remain true to the task given him: "let not the brownly-burning smoke of fear/ soil or besoot my word's white purity!" And in "Lines Written in a Copy of *Steep Road*," the speaker insists on seeing the portents of tomorrow (Ozsváth and Turner 89). He augurs that the poet, capturing the essence of things in the world, will be burned one day "because [he is] a witness to the truth." But poets of the time were not burned because they were "witness to the truth," but rather because they were Jews. Radnóti could not live with the reality of this rejection. His lyrics remain suffused by an ancient vision that projects the hero as a messenger of another world. "Smiling Empedocles," who ennobles death, is the hero of his poem "Palinode" (Ozsváth and Turner 102). And in "The Fourth Eclogue," the speaker appears as the instrument of divine will: "But let your wrath, in smoke, fly up among the stars/ And write, though all is broken, on the sky" (Ozsváth and Turner 151, 153). The poet-prophet knows that he must follow divine commandments, even when his people don't understand his message. His wrath rising up to the stars, he feels compelled to write on the sky so that what happened would be forever remembered.

When the Germans occupied Hungary on 19 March 1944, Radnóti's self-image as his country's speaker undergoes some shifts. In "O Ancient Prisons," the persona stares at a changed world, uttering, "all things fall apart./ He [the poet] sits and gazes, helpless at his heart." (Ozsváth and Turner 175) But then, in the April 30 poem, "Neither Memory Nor Magic," the persona's awareness of the impending disaster is bifurcated by the suggestion that despite imminent death, poetry has remained indestructible: "always the world rebuilds; though they forbid my song,/ in the new wall's foundations my word will sing and be" (Ozsváth and Turner 179). Visions of horror and abandonment notwithstanding,

Radnóti still believes that his poems will return from exile and that poetry can regenerate the world. In "The Seventh Eclogue" and "Letter to My Wife," it is no longer art or the artist that appear as guardians of memory and the past, but the beloved (Ozsváth and Turner 193, 195). And in "À la recherche . . . ," Radnóti uses pounding dactylic meter to show that the world of beauty and friendship is lost forever. "Verses swam in the lamplight; glimmering green/ adjectives danced on the froth and comb of the meter, and/ the dead were alive and the prisoners home, the missing/ belovedest friends so long ago fallen were writing" (Ozsváth and Turner 199, 201). Foreseeing the end of the world as he knew it, the speaker recognizes the portents and warnings of the imminent catastrophe. Yet he still attempts to re-create in meter and form the poetic images of the past, which, he believes, reach beyond the rim of the present, redeeming the future. Even in the first two "Razglednicas" (a series of poems), he gestures toward a region of transcendence (Ozsváth and Turner 211). But the last two pieces of the series are different from the rest of Radnóti's oeuvre: they point toward the ditch, beyond which no redemption beckons (Ozsváth and Turner 211, 213). Although both poems have preserved a rhyme scheme, the meter of the last one moves irregularly, and its images reflect a heretofore unimaginable reality: the mass grave. Until the moment he composed his last two poems, Radnóti believed in the myth of the poet's divine destination: to speak of the good and warn his people against wicked deeds and wicked choices.

In Celan's more complex, multi-lingual, poly-cultural environment, such beliefs would not have been possible. The constant change of linguistic and cultural leadership in the Bukovina did not make the development of a national concept of redemption possible; nor would Celan have wanted to identify with such concept. And yet, on another level, the cultural heritage with which he grew up and to which he wanted to remain dedicated shows common roots with that of Radnóti. Both poets held desperately fast on the hope to retain the homeland, which Radnóti found in Hungary and Celan in the German language: both structured their lives around, and defined themselves by, the ethos of high literature; and both saw the latter as the depository of the poet's memory of origins, and as the embodiment of civilization. In Czernowitz, young Celan was close to groups of Bukovinian poets, who found, "their models [in] Goethe, Heine, Uhland, and the aesthetic cult of the Munich School" (Colin 11). In fact, Amy Colin claims that Paul lived under the impact of the widely spread "belief [of] Bukovinian poets of Jewish descent in the existence of a holy and pure poetic German" (5). His ethos of high art, with its deeply rooted connections to the Jewish community of the Bukovina, is perhaps nowhere more movingly expressed than in his "Bremen Speech," the speech that gives a poetic account of the region where he was born, illuminating its high culture, the unspeakable horror committed against its Jews, and the world's ignorance of both. As he opens his statements: "The landscape from which I—by what detours! but are there such things: detours?—the landscape from which I come to you might be unfamiliar to most of you" (Felstiner, *Selected Poems* 395). Interrupted by two anguished dashes beyond which the ravished landscape of the Bukovina and the murdered Jewish community loom, the poet describes the area he came from as "a region in which human beings and books used to live." Summoning the great Jewish authors of the area and the role their books have played in culture, Celan points toward the irrecoverable loss. This once crowded place, with its extraordinary literary intensity, is now empty of both those books and those people.

The catastrophe struck early in the Bukovina: Celan could go home from Paris for a summer vacation in 1939; but he was unable to return to France because of the outbreak of the Second World War. Then, in accord with the Hitler-Stalin pact, the Soviets occupied and sealed off the city in June 1940. Later, the Germans overran the region in July 1941. Young Celan became a witness to unspeakable atrocities the Germans and their Romanian helpers committed against the Jewish community. The Great Temple of Czernowitz was set ablaze, its rabbi killed, in addition to thousands of Jews who were shot within the first six weeks (Chalfen 115). Surviving the first wave of murder, Celan and his family were forced to move to the ghetto. During that fall and winter, tens of thousands of people living in Czernowitz were deported to the area between the Dniester and the Bug rivers, where most of them died of torture, cold, shootings, and starvation. For the time being, Paul was taken to forced labor to the Prut bridge, while his parents remained in the Czernowitz ghetto. Soon after he returned, in June of 1942, deportations from the city started anew. Trying to flee from them, Paul found a place to hide. His parents, however, gave up the hope of escaping and remained in their apartment. Rounded up and shipped to Transistria, Paul's father died of typhus during the fall of 1942, and his mother was probably shot a few months later (Chalfen 126–29).

Taken to an area 250 miles south of Czernowitz to repair roads and bridges, Celan grows silent after his parents' deportation. Writing from the labor camp about his pain to Ruth (Lockner) Kraft, the woman he loved, he says: "You write that I should not despair. No Ruth, I don't despair. But my mother gives me such pain, she was so sick in the last days, she must always be wondering how I am, and now without ever saying goodbye, I'm gone, probably forever" (qtd. in Felstiner, *Paul Celan* 15). After a while, he regains his poetic voice and in a letter to Kraft, during the latter part of the summer of 1942, he speaks of his decision: "In my hands, I saw life transformed into much bitterness, but finally into a human quality [*Menschlichkeit*] that prescibed a path for me, a path I once tried to walk and which I will continue to walk, upright and convinced" (qtd. in Chalfen 149). Fighting against the blows he suffered, the loss of his parents and community, Celan continues to write poetry, attempting again and again to express himself, to evoke the past, remember his mother's voice, and remember the murdered Jews of Czernowitz.

Celan learns about the killing of his parents some time in December 1942 or January 1943. Probably around that time, he composed "Winter" (Felstiner, *Selected Poems* 9). The doubt which some of Celan's early lyrical idols, the great French and German poets of the time, had in the reliability of language does not appear to be a major concern in this poem. Naming the dead mother and the place where she died, Celan cries out in anguish: "It's falling, Mother, snow in the Ukraine." The poem opens and ends with the image of the murdered mother. In the second line, however, it evokes Christ and with him, as Felstiner says, the Jewish conflict: the millennial Christian persecution of the Jews, a theme which emerges frequently in Celan's early poetry. Appearing in four quatrains and showing an iambic pattern, five stresses, and a regular rhyme scheme, ABAB, "Winter" expresses itself in the form of traditional poetry—but it bears out both a weight and a set of associations that are new in the history of lyrics. Indeed, underlying the poem's classical structure is the image of the savage killing of the poet's mother, an image that invokes the blood-soaked landscape of the Ukraine with Germans and Romanians shooting Jews by thousands and ten thousands into mass graves. Yet despite the speaker's utterance of "torn strings" and a "discordant harp," the profoundly poignant lines of the poem lilt along smoothly, recalling old and beautiful songs. They also point toward Celan's premonition of his own future death: "What would come, Mother: wakening or wound —/ if I too sank in snows of the Ukraine?" Clearly, when 28 years later, Celan chose to take his own life, he would not sink in the snows of the Ukraine but in the waters of the Seine. As he projects that moment in one of his last poems: "heart-heavy/ azure rolls/ along over you" (Hamburger 340). Yet in light of his suicide, these verses show more than personal despair and more than poetic imagery; they reveal Celan's uncanny premonitory insight penetrating the region of time.

Other poems, probably written during the winter of 1942–1943, recall the murder of Celan's parents. Among them we find "Black Flakes," a rhymeless verse, yet flowing in the ancient dactylic measure, this piece also returns to the snow-blown scapes of the Ukraine: "Snow has fallen, with no light. A month/ has gone by now or two, since autumn in its monkish cowl/ brought tidings my way, a leaf from Ukrainian slopes" (Felstiner, *Selected Poems* 15). The poem contains images which, as most critics believe, return to the devastating experience Celan had when hearing about the murder of his parents. Its second stanza incorporates this information by summoning the letter the poet received—the only letter—his mother wrote him in the fall of 1942, from the concentration camp (Chalfen 154–55). With this heart-rending information moving the piece's poetic images, the words of the mother carry a weight of a previously unimaginable content: besides the father's death, they relate by implication the murder of thousands of people. Conflating the image of her shiver in the cold and her need for a shawl with the death of her husband, the voice describes the murder: "when snowdrift sifts your father's/ bones, hooves crushing/ the Song of the Cedar." Evoking the crushed body of the Paul's father, the poem echoes old Antschel's Zionist beliefs by associating him with the Zionist tune "Song of the Cedar." Her voice trembling in the cold, the mother begs for a shawl: "Oh for a cloth child,/ to wrap myself when it's flashing with helmets " Her shawl would not only be warm; it also would defend her from the killers wearing their "flashing helmets." And then, for the third time, the voice reiterates her wish, "a shawl, just a thin little shawl, so I keep/ by my side, now you're learning to weep, this anguish,/ this world that will never turn green, my child, for your child!" The voice foretells the future, auguring that those who saw the world turn into a "black winter" would never see it change into spring again. Ultimately, in the last four lines, the son speaks: "Autumn bled all away, Mother, snow burned me through:/ I sought out my heart so it might weep, I found—oh the summer's breath,/ it was like you./ Then came my tears. I wove the shawl." Celan would weave that shawl of anguish and the poems of anguish for as long as he lived.

The other famous lyrics Celan composed in 1943 under the impact of his mother's murder is "Nearness of Graves" (Felstiner, *Selected Poems* 11). Written in couplets and driven by a plaintive lyricism and an almost unbearable longing, this poem touches upon issues that are essential for understanding Celan's life life and work alike:

> Still do the southerly Bug waters know,
> Mother, the wave whose blows wounded you so?
>
> Still does the field with those windmills remember
> how gently your heart to its angels surrendered?
>
> Can none of the aspens and none of the willows
> allow you their solace, remove all your sorrows?

> And does not the god with his blossoming wand
> go up in the hills climbing hither and yon?
>
> And can you bear, Mother, as once on a time,
> the gentle, the German, the pain-laden rhyme?
>
> *(Felstiner, Selected Poems 11)*

Recalling the place of his mother's death, the images of the first two lines conjure up the river's waves giving her wounding blows. With each couplet resounding in a beautiful melodious tune and moving ennobling grace, the poem summons the famous German lyrics coming from an age drastically different from that in which Celan lived: "The Song of Mignon" from Goethe's *Wilhelm Meister*. This parallel consists not only in both poems' opening question about a faraway land but also in their lines' tuneful flow and in their meters' dactylic rhythmic structures. Yet despite the parallels, the landscape Celan's poem evokes shows no similarity to that of Goethe's. Rather than portraying the blue skies and green hills of beautiful Italy, Celan recalls the violated world of the Ukraine with its waters, hills, and fields soaked by blood. In fact, while each first line of Celan's couplet refers to what could be seen in a flash as an idyllic image of a faraway land, each second line points to the desecration of the earth by torture and death.

The second couplet of Celan's poem moves away from the river Bug to evoke yet another side of the landscape: the lovely fields and mills which frame the murderous attack against Jewish life, all of which remained silent and disengaged while his mother died. Thus, the next two lines capture the trees and the meadows as bystanders, failing to help and relieve her suffering. And the seventh and eighth lines project a mighty but remote spring god ruling over the bud-covered hills of the region, while the ninth and tenth lines of the poem utter a crucial question: "And can you bear, Mother, as once on a time,/ the gentle, the German, the pain-laden rhyme?" Can the past be resurrected? Can it be repeated? Can it be re lived? And can the poet do this by using methods and approaches of the past, creating with them contemporary artistic productions that are capable of communicating both that art and that past? Would his mother, who taught him to speak, bear his use of German as if nothing had happened, as if those who killed her would be other than German? Can he still believe in the humanizing power of poetry as the great German lyricists did for centuries? Can he continue to speak and make verses, to sing, and conjure up lyrical images in a language whose speakers have erased all previously held values? He decided that he can, that he must. "There is nothing in the world" he said, as cited earlier, "for which a poet would give up writing, not even when he is a Jew and the language of his poems is German" (qtd. in Rosenthal 403). While Celan's language would remain German, his poetic style and approach underwent essential changes. Most poems he composed in the Bukovina during the war are rhymed and appear in traditional structures, although we may detect in some of them Celan's growing interest in, and search for, formal changes (Wiedemann-Wolf 155–72). Moving to Bucharest, however, he left behind "the German, the pain-laden rhyme," the beautiful, ancient structures, the meter, assonance, and harmony of classical poetry, all of which he found increasingly unusable after the Holocaust—and barring a few exceptions, he would never make use of them in the future.

To be sure, Radnóti, too, had moments of recognition of the world that had changed essentially, with its continuity broken forever. In Yugoslavia, in the labor camp, separated from everything and everyone he loved, he composes "À la Recherche . . . ," a poem expressing a "search of time lost" (Ozsváth and Turner 199, 201). Of course, worlds apart from, and in another context than, Proust's novel, Radnóti gropes, like Celan, for the past, recalling the nights when "verses swam in the lamplight; glimmering green adjectives danced on the froth and comb of the meter," when "poets and young wives garlanded" set around the "glittering table," and "quickened companions would pledge/ their friend the Grey Friar from the slender goldeneyed glasses" (Ozsváth 207–08). Summoning all that glitter and glimmer, while aware of the murder of most of his friends and "brother-poets," Radnóti beheld the future: "That night will never return," says the speaker with anguished certainty, "for what happened takes on from death another perspective." Yet despite this farewell to the past, and that night which "will never return," in his next lyrics, written six days after "À la Recherche . . ." in the camp in Yugoslavia, he reached back to the eclogue, the Virgilian structure and rigor, with its thundering classical hexameter, to the formal style and approach of poetry. Likewise, he used in "Forced March" the structure which not only scans like, but also re-creates the ancient visual design of, the Nibelungen line—a pattern, curiously, also used by Celan in his lyrics "Russian Spring," written just like "Forced March," toward the end of the war (see Helzel 313–23; Weidemann-Wolf 171; Felstiner, *Paul Celan* 24–25). And although it is Radnóti's understanding of imminent death that drives the last two "Razglednicas," the enormous care he demonstrates in writing down his poetry, and the precaution he takes to save his notebook from death and decay, reaffirm his unchanging belief in the redemptive power of poetry.

Celan, on the other hand, stopped composing poems written in the formal mode of the tradition. Moving from the Bukovina to Bucharest in April 1945, he started to open himself up to the influence of a group of surrealist literati. Although surrealist streaks appear in Celan's early poetry, it is in Bucharest that he expressly appropriates that style and approach. By the time he leaves Bucharest for Vienna and moves further on to Paris, he uses more and more irregular rhythms, innovative stanza structures, and shorter lines in his lyrics, developing his own style, his own language, writing his own dazzlingly beautiful, path-breaking compositions. But over the years, his verse turned increasingly dark, more complex, more fractured, and more cryptic. And it is not only his poetic approach that changes. His very belief in the power of poetry changes as well. He becomes less and less able to believe that the lyrical enterprise can conjure up the past, that it can move toward anything else but silence. In fact, over the years, Celan felt ever more intensely that the region he spoke of in his 1959 acceptance speech in Bremen, the culture in which once "human beings and books used to live" can neither be recalled nor will it be remembered. As a matter of fact, he feared that what is "at stake in a poem" the reaching out, the moving "toward an addressable Thou, toward an addressable reality" is no longer reachable and no longer addressable (Felstiner, *Selected Poems* 396). And the more despondent Celan grows in light of the impossibility of "reaching out," of creating a dialogue between the "Thou" and the poem, the tighter and more interlocked his words turn, the shorter his lines appear. He drowns himself in the Seine on or around the 20th of April, 1970.

The wounds the Holocaust burned into the flesh of civilization seem to have made the continuity between the present and the past almost impossible. Not that all Jewish poets have given up traditional forms and poetic meter. But the new generations of Central European lyricists have not been able to follow Radnóti's path and believe in the redemptive power of poetry; neither have they followed the early Celan and come to believe in the possibility of "continuing a dialogue." The "pain-laden line" has become so unbearably anguished that it has been broken off in the aftermath of the Holocaust.

WORKS CITED

Appelfeld, Aharon. "Buried Homeland." *The New Yorker* (23 November 1998): 48–61.
Braham, Randolph L. *The Politics of Genocide: The Holocaust in Hungary.* 2nd ed. New York: Columbia UP, 1994. 2 vols.
Celan, Paul. *Gesammelte Werke.* Frankfurt: Suhrkamp, 1983. 5 vols.
Chalfen, Israel. *Paul Celan: A Biography of His Youth.* Trans. Maximilian Bleyleben. New York: Persea Books, 1991.
Colin, Amy. *Paul Celan: Holograms of Darkness.* Bloomington: Indiana UP, 1991.
Csaplár, Ferenc. *A szegedi fiatalok művészeti kollégiuma.* Budapest: Akadémiai, 1961.
Felstiner, John, trans. *Selected Poems and Prose of Paul Celan.* New York: W.W. Norton, 2001.
Felstiner, John. *Paul Celan: Poet, Survivor, Jew.* New Haven: Yale UP, 1995.
Hamburger, Michael, trans. *Poems of Paul Celan.* New York: Persea Books, 1988.
Helzel, Frank. "Nibelungische Echos." *Zeitschrift für deutsches Altertum und deutsche Literatur* 128.3 (1999): 309–36.

John, Michael, and Albert Lichtblau. "Jewries in Galicia and Bukovina, in Lemberg and Czernovitz: Two Divergent Examples of Jewish Communities in the Far East of the Austro-Hungarian Monarchy." *Jewries at the Frontiers*. Ed. Sander Gilman and Milton Shain. Urbana and Chicago: U of Illinois P, 1999. 29–66.

Ozsváth, Zsuzsanna. *In the Footsteps of Orpheus: The Life and Times of Miklós Radnóti*. Bloomington: Indiana UP, 2000.

Ozsváth, Zsuzsanna, and Frederick Turner, trans. *Foamy Sky: The Major Poems of Miklós Radnóti*. 2nd ed. Budapest: Corvina, 2000.

Paul Celan, Nelly Sachs: Correspondence. Trans. Christopher Clark. Riverdale: The Sheep Meadow P, 1995.

Petro, Peter. "Austroslovakism in Anton Hykisch's Novel about Maria Theresa." *Comparative Central European Culture*. Ed. Steven Tötösy de Zepetnek. West Lafayette: Purdue UP, 2001. 91–102.

Radnóti, Mikós. *Napló*. Budapest: Magvető, 1989.

Rosenthal, Bianca. "Quellen zum frühen Celan." *Monatshefte* 75.4 (1983): 393–404.

Suleiman, Susan Rubin. "Central Europe, Jewish Family History, and *Sunshine*." *Comparative Central European Culture*. Ed. Steven Tötösy de Zepetnek. West Lafayette: Purdue UP, 2002. 169–88.

Wiedemann-Wolf, Barbara. *Antschel Paul—Paul Celan. Studien zum Frühwerk*. Tübingen: Max Niemeyer, 1985.

Comparative Central European Culture: Gender in Literature and Film

Anikó Imre

There is a conspicuous similarity between the gender structures that underlie the modern nation and the modernist love lyric. Western feminist critics have begun to expose the transcendence and transparence associated with poetry in general, and the gender politics of the love lyric in particular. Rachel Blau DuPlessis identifies the cluster of foundational materials upon which the lyric is traditionally built. Gender is identified as the thread that weaves (through) them: Lyric, love, beauty, and woman—the four elements of the cluster—inseparably interweave and naturalize one another: "Certainly poetry is always to be beautiful, and in these beauties linked to the beauties of Woman. And Woman must be beautiful—soft and peerless and deep, even if raving, angry, hysterical. . . . Love will be poetic. Poetry will concern love; love will suggest sex, or at least forms of desirous imprisoning, loving predation, capture of richness. To be in love, to possess that beauty, is to be inspired to write. And willy-nilly, the whole cluster is reaffirmed" (DuPlessis 72).

The inequality of sexual power that maintains both poetry and nationalism has been pointed out by feminist critics of nationalism and feminist critics of literature, respectively. However, the two paths have rarely been consciously connected, despite the fact that some historical situations beg for a joint reconsideration of nationalism and poetry in terms of gender and sexuality. The ongoing transitions from state socialism to global capitalism in Central and East Europe provide especially rewarding opportunities for such feminist intervention.

Central and East European nationalisms undeniably exhibit symptoms of postcolonial nationalisms—a continued mimicry of the colonizer(s), self-deprecation, economic dependence, and the insistence on "good" nationalism as the small nation's rightful protection. From the very limited number of theoretical frameworks dealing with this matter I regard Alexandar Kiossev's and Steven Tötösy de Zepetnek's framework useful. Kiossev uses the notion of "self-colonization" to describe Central and East European nations' voluntary acceptance and mimicry of European values. Tötösy applies (post)colonial studies to the cultures of the region based on the proposition that the region has been colonized, historically, by the West (e.g., Germany) and in the last forty years by the Soviet Union and communist ideology and he proposes the notion of "in-between peripherality" in order to describe the postcolonial locus of the region where repeated political and cultural subjugation coincides with cultural self-referentiality (see Tötösy, "Post-Colonialities," "Urbanity," "Cultures," Configurations," "Comparative Cultural").

While I consider the postcolonial analogy indispensable to a discussion of Central and East European nationalized sexualities, I use the term "(post)colonial" with reservations, partly because of Central and East Europeans' own resistance to it, partly because it would gloss over precisely those East Central European peculiarities that, I argue, make the region such an important in-between location for theory per se. The most significant such difference has to do with race. Racial difference silently continues to confirm Central and East Europeans' alleged superiority to racialized others, those in the Third World and mainstream postcolonial countries. "Eurocentrism" would be a more appropriate term to characterize Central and East Europe's voluntary submission to Europe, to distinguish the process from the domination that Central and East Europeans have endured from "non-European" empires such as Russia (the debate about Russia and Europe is of course an important one I am not able to discuss here; see, e.g., Neumann; for a discussion of testimonial poetry in post-communist society, see Lutzkanova-Vassileva).

Tellingly, the concept of Eurocentrism is free of negative connotations in Central and East European scholarship and public discourse. Ironically, the insistence on the linguistic-cultural identity of the nation is another trait that Central and East European nations share with many post-colonial nations. According to John Hutchinson's binary typology of "cultural" and "political" nations, grounding nascent national unity in language and culture—as opposed to locating them within political traditions and institutions—was a major drive in late nineteenth-century India and China (130) as well as in early-nineteenth-century Poland, Ukraine, or Slovakia (123–26).

In what follows, I examine examples of literary and cinematic manifestations of "poetic nationalism" and gender during the transitional period of the 1980s and 1990s in Hungary, in the comparative cultural context of Central and East European and Third World points of reference. It has been well established that, since the fall of state socialism, Central and East European intellectuals have rapidly lost the prestige they had traditionally enjoyed, as a result of losing their dissident political status (see, for example, Deltcheva 1999.)

Simultaneously, Western scholarly interest in Central and East European literature and film has declined, revealing the fact that it had been nurtured by Cold War political considerations as much as by genuine curiosity towards little-known cultures. Since 1989, most academic inquiries, along with Western media, have directed their attention toward ethnic conflicts and economic transitions. As a result, Central and East European nationalisms are generally approached in terms of categories such as "ethnic" and "political," as if they were "coherent and programmatic discourses with internal rationality" (Kennedy 4). At the same time, individual and collective desire remain the hidden, private elements of Central and East European lives, and the question which identities are centered in nationalistic discourses and which are marginalized is regarded as irrelevant by most native and Western observers. This is not to say that there has been no interest in the "oppressed." On the contrary, a wealth of social science literature has emerged in the last ten years about the situation of Central and East European women (see the collections by Berry; Funk and Mueller; Rai, Pilkington and Phizacklea; Gal and Kligman). However, as Slavenka Drakulić puts it, Western feminists' "cold, artificial, slippery questions" about the "position of East European women" do not touch her reality (132). Instead, I propose an anti-essentialist and at the same time feminist approach that allows to go beyond women's economic conditions and political representation and that takes into account their desires in relation to national cultures. The problem, I argue, needs to be able to address women who are socialized, from the cradle, to love and cherish their nation through loving and cherishing its poetic culture, and who are unanimously prejudiced against all forms of feminism and socialist politics. While this may appear to be a utopian task, I am convinced that any approach dealing with the cultures of Central and East Europe that does not consider women's erotic attachment to their nation will not be able to convince them that their ultimate interests might not coincide with those of male national and intellectual elites. Poststructuralist theorists of coloniality, women of color, and (post)-Third-Worldist feminists have successfully de-essentialized the nation to show that it is "an evolving, imaginary construct rather than an originary essence" (Shohat 190). Yet, Central and East European nationalisms are still regularly left out of these analyses, bound as they are to their First-Third World binary framework.

A feminist analysis of Central and East European cultures can only be effective if it is able to critique the essentialist sexual division that both poetry and nationalism insist on. Therefore, instead of victimizing the women in these cultures, I read male intellectuals' insistence on sexual essentialism as attempts to naturalize certain desirable masculinities. Following the postcolonial analogy I set up above, I argue that socialist/communist oppression and post-communist inferiority to (West) Europe—which have perpetuated a recurring national failure to be "fully" European—register in the sexual identity of Central and East European men as a form of emasculation. This requires a compensatory infliction of sexual violation on the internal colonized: on women and other national minorities. While economic and social accounts gloss over the sexual effects of the transition altogether, it is easy to see that the current general uprooting of norms and expectations has also revealed a crisis of traditional forms of masculinity. As in the case of postcolonial nativisms (see Mama 54–46; Heng 30–32), women and femininity are currently mobilized throughout the region to re-anchor national and sexual essentialisms. I propose that Hungarian literature and film of the 1980s and 1990s provide a unique opportunity for such anti-essentialist, feminist, and postcolonial readings of "poetic nationalism" for several reasons. The aesthetic trend that emerged in Hungarian literature and cinema in the late 1970s has shown a marked departure from the engagement with socialist realism, a requirement of an earlier period. A new mode of literary and cinematic communication developed, often in the course of collaborations between writers and filmmakers (see Szegedy-Maszák 430; Bodnár 61–62). These works presented themselves in terms of the liberation of the individual from the "super-politicized communication" of "really existing socialism," and from the Lukácsian concept of "aesthetic reflection"—the pivotal notion of the centrally prescribed relationship between socialist art and cultural politics (see Töttössy 882–83). The literary and cinematic works that result from this break with socialist realism share many of the aesthetic features of Western postmodernist literature—intertextuality, subversion and the mixing of genres, the questioning of grand narratives. In Hungary, going far beyond being a stylistic fashion, postmodern culture has functioned as an "elite communicative model," where "the 'elite' consists of the *literati*: Writers, critics, filmmakers, university students" (Töttössy 884). These changes were thoroughly linked to the emergence of capitalist forms of economy within state socialism, allowing citizens relative prosperity within the "second economy" under the Kádár regime (see Kolosi and Rose; Kapitány and Kapitány). Hungary—owing to the economic reforms of János Kádár's "goulash communism"—was considered to be the "happiest barracks" of the socialist camp from the late 1970s through the 1980s (see Arpad; Kuczi; Kolosi and Rose; Lengyel; Hankiss). Sygmunt Bauman refers to similar developments all over Central and East Europe as the "postmodern stage" of state socialism and communism.

The contradiction between the lingering official communist rhetoric and the realities that defied it at every moment made it impossible to separate truth from lies in the countries formerly under communist ideology and Soviet colonization. Cynicism and fantasy, which had already been important modes of expression as a result of decades of public communication in which "information [was] the most valuable article of commerce" (Arpad 22), became indispensable resources of survival. Intellectuals' escape from oppositional politics into "pure poetry" and postmodern play afforded them a relatively safe place "beyond ideology," where they were able to continue the allegorical discourse of the "we" without having to take full political responsibility for it. What I emphasize here is that literary and cinematic representations of this transitional period registered political and social changes that were not representable at the time by any other means. To borrow Fredric Jameson's terminology, rather than being instruments of a new, non-collective self-consciousness, these cultural representations were symptoms and signs of emerging collective self-consciousnesses that only blossomed into quantifiable forms after 1989. These self-consciousnesses are not present in the works' overt messages or in the authors' declared intentions (the liberation of the individual from politics), but, rather, in the "raw material:" in the inadvertent formal contradictions which, as Jameson asserts, the reading/viewing public is always sensitive to. Rather than reading the overt messages of these "postmodern" works and the declared intentions of their authors, which criticism on both sides of the late Iron Curtain has been invested in decoding, I read them through the inadvertent cracks and fissures of those intentions. Nowhere are the cracks and fissures more self-revealing, nowhere lie the contradictions more on the surface than in the representation of gender and sexuality.

The majority of these postmodernist texts exhibit a striking thematic concern with femininity and the female body (see Tötösy, "Configurations" 96–99). Many of them employ female protagonists as the male intellectual's, and, on a larger scale, as the nation's, representatives. These women are all beautiful—often racialized, ravenously sexual but, at the same time, submissive and nurturing, victimized and idealized. They embody the "postmodern" intellectual's attempts to preserve his own absolute identity with the help of the "natural" female body and, at the same time, to extend his own metaphorical freedom through the performativity of the feminine and the playfulness of postmodernist aesthetics. These—ostensively depoliticized—representations are markedly re-poeticized.

The prototype, and a much revered example of Hungarian postmodernist literary works in which "men write in the feminine" is Sándor Weöres's cycle of poems, entitled "Psyché" ("Psyche"), written, in segments, throughout the 1970s. The protagonist and narrator is a fictional nineteenth-century Hungarian poetess, Erzsébet Lónyai, here named Psyché. Generically, "Psyché" is a combination of memoir, diary, lyric poems, translations, and letters, accompanied by a fictive biographical study by one of Psyché's imaginary contemporaries, and by a real critic's review. It is written in almost untranslatable, artificial, and archaic Hungarian. Psyché herself is the adopted daughter of a Hungarian count and the natural daughter of a Gypsy woman. According to a typical Hungarian critical account Psyché's Gypsy ancestry explains her propensity to "extremes," "adventure," and "amours" in spite of the convent education she received as a result of her more distinguished paternal heritage (Vajda 1988, 18). This description of Psyché's extremisms is euphemistic: in the narrative she appears simply, biologically, promiscuous. She makes contact with outstanding European male artists of the age—Goethe, Hölderlin, Beethoven—but this intellectual "elevation" of her character only slightly counterbalances her inability to resist sexuality and her almost predatory seductiveness. Vajda's comment on Weöres's text illustrates the broader interpretive context where "'Psyché' goes beyond the display of Weöres's empathy and love of games and turns into a feat of psychological transvestism as well. We experience the lives, loves, maturation into a woman and later mother, the happiness and sufferings of a real woman. . . . Psyché is the virtual creation of a life style and a new possibility for life. The dream of a late rococo, early Biedermeier literature in an independent and free Hungary, where poets are not burdened by the need to express the crucial problems of society and the nation but are free to devote themselves to the common manifestations of love, joy, and sorrow: this is the dream of a Hungarian literature, European in character, one that could afford the luxury of being Hungarian in language and not necessarily in subject" (Vajda 1988, 20; my translation). This interpretation is typical of the way in which gender is invariably excluded from among valid categories of politics and criticism. The transcendence of female experience is not rendered problematic in the national imaginary, because it is made clear that Psyché is not a real woman. She is an allegory of the Hungarian male intellectual who is castrated by political oppression. He wishes to transcend the binding political tasks of a national artist by elevating Hungarian literature to the level of "Europeanness," which is co-terminous with "human." The paradox that this transcendence of the national is conditioned on the gender privileges of the Hungarian male artist is effaced in the absence of real gender difference, which, in turn, characterizes the sphere of poetry.

Based on Jenny Sharpe's feminist work on allegory and postcolonial violence, Monique Tschofen argues that—even though the trope of rape is not identical with literal rape—the two are situated along a continuum. Rape encompasses a spectrum of represented sexual relations that signify violence, violation, and domination. Rape can occur even when the dominated woman is supposedly willing and desiring (Tschofen 503–05). In her readings of postcolonial novels, Tschofen wishes to "undermine and unravel the typology that makes it possible for this mode of allegorical signification to challenge and resist colonial power structures and yet reinforce patriarchal power relations" (503–4). Tschofen shows, for instance, that the literal and symbolic levels are inseparable in the Sudanese author's, Taleb Salih's novel, *Season of Migration to the North* (1966); there is a constant slippage between the two. Even though the English women who are violated by the colonized protagonist yearning for mastery are supposed to be metonymical, they are still being raped. "The personal is steeped with political meaning, sexual relations become a way of waging war, and the woman's body is a battle field: a territory to be scouted, fought over, and possessed, a fertile semiotic field upon which layers of meaning can be projected" (506). The similarities between such postcolonial texts and "Psyché" are unmistakable. There is a complex allegorical contract at work between the text and its readers, specific to the conditions of decaying state socialism. On the one hand, it issues the "hermeneutical imperative" of national allegory, that "crucial aspect of the liberating and resisting imperative of postcolonial writing" (Tschofen 501). On the other hand, it is also understood that Psyché's fickle, ironic postmodernism is a rightful refusal of the expectation of naive representational realism prescribed by socialist realist aesthetics. According to György Konrád such a refusal justifies, in an "artistic society" (37), a certain kind of hermeneutic nihilism. The duality of these liberties provides unlimited representational freedom over the female body. The traditional entitlement to national representation, and the simultaneous release from the responsibility of representation, makes it very difficult for a potential feminist effort to foreground the continuity between the textual and the sexual.

Such an effort is prevented in several ways: Psyché is the author's invention. She is removed from the contemporary and the familiar to a mythic past, which is, at the same time, a nostalgically evoked part of national history, embedded in a coveted European cultural context. This era is represented in a language that is at once real and fictional. Psyché's Gypsy blood, which, in the biological essentialism of the national imagination, is solely responsible for her excesses, is not the blood of real Gypsies, but of exotic, free, art-loving creatures: products of the Eurocentric, orientalizing fantasy that the Hungarian artist mimics. She is worlds apart from real, contemporary Roma who are being blatantly marginalized throughout Central and East Europe. Significantly, Psyché, is half-Gypsy, half "poet-nobleman": a perfect allegory of the feminized, but beautiful and rebellious, "noble" artist, whose masculinity is clearly tied to her intellect, which, in turn, easily sheds the guise of fictional femininity. One the one hand, Psyché is a woman forged out of the two man-made stereotypes that have been endlessly employed in European arts to contain the threatening, castrating aspects of women's sexuality: she is a whore who becomes a mother by the end. This duality is a strategy to keep a safe distance from the female-ness that the feminine image necessarily implies. On the other hand, and unlike "real women," Psyché' is a creative intellectual whose promiscuity is determined by external factors that are beyond her control. As an allegory, she is for and about men with maternal productive talent in a politically prostituting, feminizing historical situation.

Two questions emerge at this point: can male intellectuals, Psyché's allegorical referents, emerge from this risky play with a female persona unharmed, untainted by femininity? And, how are women expected to, and allowed to, identify with such androgynous images? The answer to both questions depends, to a great extent, on the historical and social context in which the reception takes place. In the 1980s of Central and East Europe, when intellectuals still enjoyed at least nominally the protective shield of their high modernist cultural privilege and dissident status, putting on a female mask was a much less risky act than it has appeared to be since 1989. DuPlessis's description aptly describes the mechanism when she claims that the postmodern poet remains the "third term" of modernist poetry, "mediating between the polarized sexes," in the spiritual realm where men and women are equal in the spirit of "psychic and intellectual androgyny" (*Writing* 74). The voluntary revelation of the fractured basis of his work provides him with a degree of "femininity," but it is strictly metaphorical, easily contained. As for the second question, it is not likely that women who have read Psyché found anything objectionable in its gender scheme. A thorough training in reading "their" culture through the filter of national allegory teaches women to identify with the point of view of their internal colonizer, while they suppress or are ashamed of ambivalent emotions. The claim that Hungarian nationalism is "transcendent" creates a make-believe common ground that includes women. Thus, the centrality of the female image must have even reinforced women's false sense of inclusion in the national collective, while it has modeled and naturalized male-dependent heterosexuality.

The way in which "erotic" postmodernist works have provided a bridge in this transition is best illustrated by comparing Péter Esterházy's pre-1989 book *Kis magyar pornográfia* (*Little Hungarian Pornography*) and his post-1989 *Egy nö* (*A Woman*, translated as *She Loves Me*): the former, an ironic set of anecdotes in which the political and the personal/sexual inseparably interweave, relies on women and the feminine to convey a collective and gender-neutral powerlessness. Esterházy introduces the book this way: "This is the author's most East-European book, and his most helpless, too. It was written in 1982–1983, in the overripe period of the Kádár era, under small, Hungarian, pornographic circumstances where pornography should be understood as meaning lies, the lies of the body, the lies of the soul, our lies. Let us imagine, if we can, a country where everything is a lie, where the lack of democracy is called socialist democracy, economic chaos socialist economy, revolution anti-revolution, and so on. . . . Such a total, all-encompassing lie, when from history through green-pea soup, when from our father's eyebrows and our lover's lap everything is a lie, not to mention this theoretical yet very tangible presence of threat, all this makes for a highly poetic situation" (v–vi). While, according to this, the national "we" is being corrupted by communist oppression, in the book it is only the prostitution of women's bodies that is depicted as "natural" and morally deplorable. Men's prostitution by other men always appears in invisible quotation marks; it is metaphorical, tragic, temporary, and it ennobles through the suffering imposed. It appears as if women's "natural" prostitution were necessary, precisely, to protect the boundaries of the male body and poetic soul from contamination with the performativity of the feminine. The implied audience of Esterházy's preface is a masculine political subject who is familiar with the "absolute" meaning of "democracy." The appeal is to the idealized European Man whom the feminized, East Central European man emulates in a subtle version of colonial mimicry.

In contrast with *Little Hungarian Pornography*, Esterházy's postcommunist novel in the Hungarian original, *Egy nö*, appears without a preface. The cover features a naked arse, part of an unspecified Egon

Schiele painting. The image combines a clever marketing strategy with an allusion to the book's European high modernist pretensions. It is also a visual commentary on the book's obvious intention to celebrate the freedom of calling everything by its name. The text wallows in destroying taboos but, while there is still the resonance of something vaguely political about this triumph over the shadow of censorship, the now attained freedom of speech seems to translate into unlimited liberties to name women's most intimate body parts and sexual acts. National allegory, or the right to undifferentiated representation, does not disappear altogether in Esterházy's work in the historical and aesthetic transition between *Little Hungarian Pornography* and *She Loves Me*. In the latter, erotic and pornographic descriptions continue to mix with details of life under communism and post-communism. Communism continues to function in Hungarian culture of the 1990s as a referent evoked with a mixture of bitterness, humor, and nostalgia, a very real extension of the political, social, and cultural impact of communist rule and Soviet hegemony over the region. The triviality of the "us" versus "them" binary opposition is evident in its very projection into everyday sexual situations. Yet, the text also reveals the eagerness to continue the allegorical game, partly because it has been a source of pleasure, partly because it is as familiar, available, and safe as women's bodies, unlike the much more inscrutable rules of post-communist games.

The intellectual, however, retains the right to analyze the transition and tries to affirm his artistic autonomy through indispensable references to the feminine. The reliance on the female and the feminine in representation not only does not register as political, but even provides naturalizing imagery for the triviality of politics. On the one hand, Esterházy dismisses the earlier, allegorical politics of the "we" in sarcastic terms: "Perhaps the most egotistic society in history built itself here on constant reference to this virtual we" (*Elefántcsonttoronyból* 144). At the same time, his entitlement to a position outside of the "we" remains unquestionable even after the transition. As in his novels, he asserts his "natural" place in the family of male Hungarian poets and writers, thereby justifying his birth right to a politically neutral status. "I am an indebted and grateful son and product of Hungarian literature, and, at the same time, I am someone who is indifferent to some of the important traditions of this literature; for instance, that fact that it makes the collective its central value. I am not attracted by the heroism that follows from this. Then I would rather be a woman writer than a real man" (77). And this stand, as Tötösy argues, occurs in the work and postures of Endre Kukorelly, another Hungarian postmodernist writer, whose poetic texts circle "around and about relationships with women, interweaving the national and the political contexts in the personal one" and while Kukorelly's reliance on the female and the feminine is "profoundly patriarchal" and male-oriented, Kukorelly calls himself without blushing a "feminist" (Tötösy "Configurations" 97–98; see also "Cultures" 139–40).

The crisis of nationally privileged masculinities has provoked defensive attempts, throughout Central and East Europe, to coerce women into remaining faithful resources for the nation state. This general antifeminist backlash has blamed women for the emasculation of men and the abandonment of family priorities (see Occhipinti; Mihancsik; Goven; Eisenstein "East European"; Dolby). The demonization of "monstrous" women in Hungary already started in the 1980s, condemning women who had made an alleged alliance with the communist state against men. Spokespersons of the electronic and media campaign—among them leading dissidents writers and journalists—have accused women of destroying the nation by refusing to bear children and by abandoning their husbands; of following their insatiable sexual appetites, and of neglecting their natural duty of nurturing children (see Goven 224–35; Kürti 276–77). The analogy with women's situations in postcolonial nations is impossible to miss. Amina Mama claims that, in emerging nations of Africa, the masculinity of nationalist discourses is a source of male bias. While nationalisms always call on "the new woman," postcolonial leaders such as Kwame Nkrumah are unable to view women beyond reproductive and nurturing roles (54–55). Zillah Eisenstein levels similar charges against Václav Havel and Mikhail Gorbachev ("East European" 312–14). This hostile atmosphere explains why Central and

East European women have been so cautious to associate themselves with feminism. They have perfectly internalized the guilt and the shame of the colonized, transferred to them by men whose colonized masculinities are permanently insecure. Unlike Renata Salecl, who faults post-communist women for not being able to see femininity as a performance (5), I think that most women's choices in the region are extremely limited unless they are willing to face complete alienation from their environment. Most women, especially in positions of relative empowerment, opt to perform a masquerade: they identify, or pretend to identify, with the masculine viewpoint, conform to the sexual roles approved by the national imagination, and never address gender as a political matter (see Mihancsik). Thus, in the Hungarian antifeminist campaign, such politically active and publicly present women as Kata Beke and Magda Gubi joined the woman-bashing chorus, implicitly distinguishing themselves from "bad" women (see Goven).

How can feminism make a meaningful intervention in a situation where women have gone from communist-nationalist colonization straight to post-communist-nationalist demonization? As a first step, gender should present itself as an issue; it should have a name; it should be possible to separate it from the sexual essentialisms in which it is firmly grounded, and from the nationalistic discourses that daily confirm this grounding. The hermeneutic project of reading through the inadvertent and intentional ruptures of reifying national discourses has just barely begun in Central and East Europe. As Susan Rubin Suleiman argues, politics does not reside in texts themselves, but in the ways they are read. They are what they do for a community at a particular place and time (53). Or, Judith Butler suggests that feminists should read pornographic texts "against themselves" not as constitutive of or representative of what women really are, but as allegories of "masculine willfulness and feminine submission", as expressions of a desire that "repeatedly and anxiously rehearses its own unrealizability" (68).

From this theoretical position, the apparently disconnected phenomena of Hungarian—and Central and East European—postmodern art's aesthetic (ab)use of the feminine, the current anti-feminist backlash, and the invasion of pornography, can be read and critiqued as thoroughly interrelated processes. Recent Central and East European, "feminized" (post)communist and (post)modernist texts provide many opportunities for such deconstructive critiques. Such analyses would counter the "plural text" with an analysis of the "political status of the plural self" (Suleiman 53). Textuality does not help explain the killing in Bosnia, writes Suleiman (53). But violence occurs not only in its most horrific version, in war; there is the textual rape of women I am discussing here. And as Chela Sandoval urges, such violence can only be opposed by another kind of violence, the "violent shattering of the unitary sense of self, as the skill which allows a mobile identity to form takes hold" (23).

NOTE

This paper is adapted from an earlier version, Anikó Imre, "Gender, Literature, and Film in Contemporary East Central European Culture," *CLCWeb: Comparative Literature and Culture: A WWWeb Journal* 3.1 (2001): <http://clcwebjournal.lib.purdue.edu/clcweb01-1/imre01.html>.

WORKS CITED

Anderson, Benedict. *Imagined Communities: Reflection on the Origin and Spread of Nationalism.* London: Verso, 1983.
Arpad, Joseph T. "The Question of Hungarian Popular Culture." *Journal of Popular Culture* 29 (1995): 9–31.
Bassnett, Susan. "Crossing Cultural Boundaries, Or How I Became an Expert on East European Women Overnight." *Women's Studies International Forum* 15 (1992): 11–15.
Bauman, Zygmunt. *Intimations of Postmodernity.* Routledge: London, 1992.
Berry, Ellen E., ed. *Postcommunism and the Body Politic.* New York: New York UP, 1995.
Bhabha, Homi. "Of Mimicry and Man: The Ambivalence of Colonial Discourse." *October* 28 (1984): 317–25.

Bodnár, György. "Literature and Film: Hungarian Experiments in an International Context." *Yearbook of Comparative and General Literature* 32 (1983): 61–66.
Butler, Judith. *Excitable Speech: A Politics of the Performative*. New York: Routledge, 1997.
Csepeli, György. "Competing Patterns of National Identity in Postcommunist Hungary." *Media, Culture, and Society* 13 (1991): 325–39.
Deltcheva, Roumiana. "East Central Europe as a Politically Correct Scapegoat: The Case of Bulgaria." *CLCWeb: Comparative Literature and Culture: A WWWeb Journal* 1.2 (1999): <http://clcwebjournal.lib.purdue.edu/clcweb99-2/deltcheva99.html>.
Deltcheva, Roumiana. "Post-Totalitarian Tendencies in Bulgarian Literature." *Postcolonial Literatures: Theory and Practice/Les Littératures post-coloniales. Théories et réalisations*. Ed. Steven Tötösy de Zepetnek and Sneja Gunew. Thematic Issue of *Canadian Review of Comparative Literature/Revue Canadienne de Littérature Comparée* 22.3–4 (1995): 853–65.
Dolby, Laura M. "Pornography in Hungary: Ambiguity of the Female Image in a Time of Change," *Journal of Popular Culture* 29 (1995): 119–27.
Drakulić, Slavenka. *How We Survived Communism and Even Laughed*. New York: Harper Perennial, 1993.
DuPlessis, Rachel Blau. "'Corpses of Poesy': Some Modern Poets and Some Gender Ideologies of Lyric." *Feminist Measures: Soundings in Theory and Poetry*. Ed. Lynn Keller and Cristanne Miller. Ann Arbor: Michigan UP, 1994. 69–95.
DuPlessis, Rachel Blau. *Writing Beyond the Ending*. Bloomington: Indiana UP, 1985.
Eisenstein, Zillah. "Eastern European Male Democracies: A Problem of Unequal Equality." *Gender Politics and Post-Communism*. Ed. Nanette Funk and Magda Mueller. New York: Routledge, 1993. 303–30.
Esterházy, Péter. *She Loves Me*. Trans. Judith Sollosy. Evanston: Northwestern UP, 1997.
Esterházy, Péter. *A Little Hungarian Pornography*. Trans. Judith Sollosy. New York: Quartet Books, 1995.
Esterházy, Péter. *Az elefántcsonttoronyból (From the Ivory Tower)*. Budapest: Magvető, 1991.
Funk, Nanette, and Magda Mueller, eds. *Gender Politics and Post-Communism: Reflections from Eastern Europe*. London: Verso, 1993.
Gal, Susan, and Gail Kligman, eds. *Reproducing Gender: Politics, Publics, and Everyday Life after Socialism*. Princeton: Princeton UP, 2000.
Goven, Joanna. "Gender Politics in Hungary: Autonomy and Antifeminism." *Gender Politics and Post-Communism: Reflections from Eastern Europe*.

Ed. Nanette Funk and Magda Mueller. New York: Routledge, 1993. 224–40.
Hankiss, Elemér. *East European Alternatives*. Oxford: Clarendon, 1990.
Heng, Geraldine. "A Great Way to Fly: Nationalism, the State, and the Varieties of Third-World Feminism." *Feminist Genealogies, Colonial Legacies, Democratic Futures*. Ed. M. Jacqui Alexander and Chandra T. Mohanty. New York: Routledge, 1997. 30–45.
Hutchinson, John. "Cultural Nationalism and Moral Regeneration." *Nationalism*. Ed. Hutchinson and Anthony D. Smith. Oxford: Oxford UP, 1994. 122–31.
Jameson, Fredric. "Class and Allegory in Contemporary Mass Culture: Dog Day Afternoon as a Political Film." *Movies and Methods*. Ed. Bill Nichols. Berkeley: U of California P, 1985. 715–33.
Kapitány, Gábor, and Ágnes Kapitány. "Changing World-Views in Hungary, 1945–1980." *Journal of Popular Culture* 29.2 (1995): 33–43.
Kennedy, Michael D. "An Introduction to East European Ideology and Identity in Transformation." *Envisioning Eastern Europe: Postcommunist Cultural Studies*. Ed. Michael D. Kennedy. Ann Arbor: U of Michigan P, 1994. 1–45.
Kiossev, Aleksandar. "Megjegyzések az önkolonizáló kultúrákról" ("Notes on Self-Colonizing Cultures"). *Magyar Lettre Internationale* 37 (2000): 7–10.
Kolosi, Tamás, Rudolf Andorka, Richard Rose, and György Vukovich, eds. *A Society Transformed: Hungary in Time-Space Perspective*. Budapest: Central European UP, 1999.
Kolosi, Tamás, and Richard Rose. "Introduction: Scaling Change in Hungary." *Hungary in Time-Space Perspective*. Ed. Rudolf Andorka, Tamás Kolosi, Richard Rose, and György Vukovich. Budapest: Central European UP, 1999. 1–20.
Konrád, György. *The Melancholy of Rebirth: Essays from Post-Communist Central Europe, 1989–1994*. Trans. Michael Henry Heim. New York: Harcourt Brace, 1995.
Konrád, György. *Az autonómia kísértése (The Specters of Autonomy)*. Paris: Magyar Füzetek, 1980.
Kuczi, Tibor. "Szalai Erzsébet: Vadkeleti metszetek" ("Erzsébet Szalai: Images from the Wild East"). *Kritika* 11 (1998): 40–41.
Kürti, László. "The Wingless Eros of Socialism: Nationalism and Sexuality in Hungary." *The Curtain Rises: Rethinking Culture, Ideology, and the State in Eastern Europe*. Ed. Hermine G. de Soto and David G. Anderson. New Jersey: Humanities Press International, 1993. 266–87.
Lengyel, György. "The Post-Communist Economic Elite." *A Society Transformed*. Ed. Rudolf Andorka, Tamás Kolosi, Richard Rose, and György Vukovich. Budapest: Central UP, 1999. 85–96.

Lutzkanova-Vassileva, Albena. "Testimonial Poetry in East European Post-Totalitarian Literature." *CLCWeb: Comparative Literature and Culture: A WWWeb Journal* 3.1 (2001): <http://clcwebjournal.lib.purdue.edu/clcweb01-1/lutzkanovavassileva01.html>.
Mama, Amina. "Heroes and Villains: Conceptualizing Colonial and Contemporary Violence against Women in Africa." *Feminist Genealogies, Colonial Legacies, Democratic Futures.* Ed. Jacqui Alexander and Chandra T. Mohanty. New York: Routledge, 1997. 46–62.
McClintock, Anne. *Imperial Leather: Race, Gender and Sexuality in the Colonial Context.* London: Routledge, 1995.
Mihancsik, Zsófia. "A láthatatlan nem: magyar nök filmen" ("Invisible Gender: Hungarian Women in Film"). *Filmvilág* 47.7 (1999): 16–21.
Mosse, George L. *Nationalism and Sexuality: Middle-Class Morality and Sexual Norms in Modern Europe.* Madison: U of Wisconsin P, 1985.
Neuberger, Benyamin. "State and Nation in African Thought." *Nationalism.* Ed. John Hutchinson and Anthony D. Smith. Oxford: Oxford UP, 1994. 231–35.
Nowicki, Joanna. "Közép-kelet-európai sztereotípiák: vonzalom, gyanakvás és identitás" ("East Central European Stereotypes: Sympathy, Suspicion, and Identity"). *Regio* 1.1-2 (1995): 8–24.
Occhipinti, Laurie. "Two Steps Back? Anti-Feminism in Eastern Europe." *Anthropology Today* 12.6 (1996): 13–18.
Parker, Andrew, Mary Russo, Doris Sommer, and Patricia Yaeger, eds. *Nationalisms and Sexualities.* London: Routledge, 1992.
Paul, David W., ed. *Politics, Art and Commitment in the East European Cinema.* New York: St. Martin's, 1983.
Quart, Barbara. "A Few Short Takes on Eastern European Film." *Cinéaste* 19.4 (1993): 63–64.
Rai, Shirin, Hilary Pilkington, and Annie Phizacklea, eds. *Women in the Face of Change: The Soviet Union, Eastern Europe, and China.* New York: Routledge, 1992.
Sandoval, Chela. "U.S. Third World Feminism: The Theory and Method of Oppositional Consciousness in the Postmodern World." *Genders* 10 (1991): 1–25.
Sharpe, Jenny. *Allegories of Empire: The Figure of the Woman in the Colonial Text.* Minneapolis: U of Minnesota P, 1993.
Shohat, Ella. "Post-Third-Worldist Culture: Gender, Nation, and the Cinema." *Feminist Genealogies.* Ed. Jacqui Alexander and Chandra T. Mohanty. New York: Routledge, 1997. 183–209.
Suleiman, Susan Rubin. "The Politics of Postmodernism after the Wall (Or, What Do We Do When the 'Ethnic Cleansing' Starts?)." *International Postmodernism: Theory and Literary Practice.* Ed. Hans Bertens and Douwe Fokkema. Amsterdam: John Benjamins, 1997. 50–64.

Szegedy-Maszák, Mihály. "Postmodernism in Hungarian Literature." *International Postmodernisms: Theory and Literary Practice*. Ed. Hans Bertens and Douwe Fokkema. Amsterdam: John Benjamins, 1997. 429–33.
Tötösy de Zepetnek, Steven. "Comparative Cultural Studies and the Study of Central European Culture." *Comparative Central European Culture.* Ed. Steven Tötösy de Zepetnek. West Lafayette: Purdue UP, 2002. 1–32.
Tötösy de Zepetnek, Steven. "Configurations of Postcoloniality and National Identity: Inbetween Peripherality and Narratives of Change." *The Comparatist: Journal of the Southern Comparative Literature Association* 23 (1999): 89–110.
Tötösy de Zepetnek, Steven. "Cultures, Peripheralities, and Comparative Literature." *Comparative Literature: Theory, Method, Application*. By Steven Tötösy de Zepetnek. Amsterdam/Atlanta, GA: Rodopi, 1998. 121–72.
Tötösy de Zepetnek, Steven. "Urbanity and Postmodern Sensuality: The 'Post-Magyar' Endre Kukorelly." *World Literature Today* 70.2 (1996): 289–94.
Tötösy de Zepetnek, Steven. "Post-Colonialities: The 'Other,' the System, and a Personal Perspective, or, This (Too) Is Comparative Literature." *Postcolonial Literatures: Theory and Practice/Les Littératures post-coloniales. Théories et réalisations*. Ed. Steven Tötösy de Zepetnek and Sneja Gunew. Thematic Issue of *Canadian Review of Comparative Literature/Revue Canadienne de Littérature Comparée* 22.3–4 (1995): 399–407.
Töttössy, Beatrice. "Hungarian Postmodernity and Postcoloniality: The Epistemology of a Literature." *Postcolonial Literatures: Theory and Practice/Les Littératures post-coloniales. Théories et réalisations*. Ed. Steven Tötösy de Zepetnek and Sneja Gunew. Thematic Issue of *Canadian Review of Comparative Literature/Revue Canadienne de Littérature Comparée* 22.3–4 (1995): 881–91.
Tschofen, Monique Y. "Post-Colonial Allegory and the Empire of Rape." *Postcolonial Literatures: Theory and Practice/Les Littératures post-coloniales. Théories et réalisations*. Ed. Steven Tötösy de Zepetnek and Sneja Gunew. Thematic Issue of *Canadian Review of Comparative Literature/Revue Canadienne de Littérature Comparée* 22.3–4 (1995): 501–05.
Vajda, Miklós. "Introduction." *Eternal Moment: Sándor Weöres*. London: Anvil, 1988. 13–19.

Austroslovakism in Anton Hykisch's Novel about Maria Theresa

Peter Petro

Anton Hykisch is one of Slovakia's major writers today. He was also the first ambassador of Slovakia to Canada after the country separated from Czechoslovakia in 1993. His early work, for example his book of travels in Canada—*Canada Is Not a Joke* (1968)—is an open confrontation with the world he glimpsed at the occasion of the Montréal Expo in 1967. His debut in the 1960s was connected to the flourishing of literary experimentation that one can designate as the "decade of experimentation," possible by the gradual relaxation of the communist party's control at the time (see Petro 1982–83; see also Petro 1999, 1995). In this promising period, Hykisch publishes his novel *Nadia* in 1963 and introduces himself an author whose interests include European culture and intellectual history in general and Central European culture in particular. Hykisch follows *Nadia* with a novel in 1965 describing the travails of his generation, *Námestie v Mähringu* (*A Square in Mähring*) and where he focuses on an autobiographical event, his unsuccessful attempt to leave Czechoslovakia. The novel is also a fictional account of reflections on the difficulties of émigré and refugee life.

As an author with penchant for history in the period of communism where a simulacrum of history took the center stage, Hykisch searched for the topic and angle that would enable him to write in a manner which would free him from the simulacrum dictated by socialist realism. His historical novels *Čas majstrov* (1977) (*The Age of the Masters*) and *Milujte kráľovnú* (*Long Live the Queen*) (1984) not only continue in the direction he initiated in his first published work, but present a creative solution on several levels. This is particularly so with his historical novel, *Long Live the Queen*. The novel was not only a critical success story in then communist Czechoslovakia, it was also a publishing event: its first edition of ten-thousand copies was sold in one day and soon the novel appeared in Croatian, German, and Romanian translation. In criticism, reviews of the novel were overwhelmingly positive right after the novel's first edition and throughout the three editions following. For example, one of the most prominent critics at the time, Vladimír Petrík, in his comments stressed that "Hykisch managed to highlight equally well the political movements of the age as he did the conditions in such fields as philosophy, contemporary economics, literature, arts, and so on. The reader will get a novel that is not a novel of adventure, but because of its artistic and philosophical qualities, is an adventure in getting to know an age" (qtd. in Jurík 12; my translation). Following the novel's German translation in two editions, the German reviews were also complementary although less effusive (see Busch).

Long Live the Queen represents Hykisch's excursion into the past of his own country, inextricably connected to Vienna, the Austro-Hungarian empire, the Habsburgs, and to Maria Theresa. Prior to the arrival of the Hungarians (*Magyars*) in the ninth century, Slovaks lived in the Great Moravian empire. In the tenth century the territories of present-day Slovakia became part of the Kingdom of Hungary until 1918. At the time of the novel's period, the present capital of Slovakia, Bratislava (Pozsony in Hungarian and Pressburg in German) was also the capital of Hungary. That was why Maria Theresa was crowned in this city Queen of Hungary. Hykisch chose for a specific reason the period in question: the period of Maria Theresa occurs after the wars of the Reformation and after the Ottoman empire is defeated and the Turks are no longer occupying the territories of Habsburg lands. Most importantly, the period occurs before Romanticism and the nationalist fervor that wreaks havoc in the realm of the Habsburgs. At the time of the writing of the novel, this period of history was insufficiently appreciated or even known by not only Hykisch's contemporaries but by the younger and considerably brainwashed generation in particular. Brainwashed not merely by the twenty years of totalitarian propaganda; there was also the propaganda of the two previous regimes of Czechoslovakia, namely the Masaryk-Beneš periods of 1918 to 1938 and 1945 to 1948 and the proto-Nazi period of Jozef Tiso from 1939 to 1945. A positive, let alone fact-based, historical consideration of the Habsburg rule was hardly conceivable at the time when the new Czechoslovak Republic was basing its legitimacy on distancing itself from the Habsburgs who were, consequently, systemically demonized. Nor was the situation much better during the Second World War in Slovakia that, as a vassal state of Nazi Germany, served under the ideology of the *Drang nach dem Osten.*

By the time the communist system collapsed in 1989–1990, the Austro-Hungarian past has undergone a marvelous transformation. One heard of the Hungarian government's overtures to Otto von Habsburg, one could see in Budapest the popularity of the many publications devoted to the artistic restoration of images of the era before 1914, etc. But all this happened after the collapse of the Soviet empire and the re-emergence of Central Europe in 1989–1990. Hykisch's novel was published in 1984, during the time of "Normalization" and the "Biafra of the Spirit" (the consequence of the Warsaw Pact invasion of 1968), none of which, incidentally, can be detected in the novel. That during this time of communist dictatorship an independent and intellectually and artistically free text appears in print is in itself a considerable accomplishment. In addition to the contextual implications of the novel and the historical period it narrates, the novel is a testimonial to the author's independence, his inner freedom, and this is of interest not only as an attempt to look with fresh eyes at a neglected historical period; it is a rich and formidable narrative fashioned in an imaginative manner. It is also is a text imbued with a belief system of Catholicism, a text written from the point of view of a modern and critically astute individual of the Catholic faith. It is, above all, a remarkable testimonial to tolerance in an intolerant age. One wonders if today, when "inclusivity" is so valued, a novel could appear treating its subject with the understanding and tolerance of Hykisch's novel. But this is the genius of the author: he chose for his novel the age of Maria Theresa and the age, as depicted by Hykisch, was an age of tolerance, indeed.

It is here that the concept of "Austroslovakism" in Hykisch's text becomes relevant. He presents in his novel a Slovak version of the wider concept of "Austroslavism," an ideological and political orientation of Slavs of Austrian lands and that denoted the wish to align the interests of the Slavs of the empire with the interests of the Habsburgs (this orientation at times included German-language culture, similar to the situation of German-language culture and Bukovina Jews; see Ozsváth). Originally, Austroslovakism refered to a petition of the Slovak National Council taken to emperor Franz Josef in March 1849. While the emperor was willing to consider the independence of Slovakia, events unfolded and Hungary itself demanded independence from Austria, only to suffer, after defeating the Austrians, military defeat by the Russian army the emperor asked for help. The defeat of the Hungarians brought the Austrian willingness to isolate Hungary to an end. Thus, Austroslovakism is a notion that denotes an attempt to forge some kind of alliance between Slovakia and Austria (see Kirschbaum 118–21). Ultimately, as we well know, Hungary forged an alliance with the Austrians by 1867 and the Austro-Hungarian empire came into existence where nationalities within the kingdom of Hungary received little recognition.

Hykisch takes as his point of departure the story of Maria Theresa, empress of Austria and Queen of Bohemia (the Czech lands) and Hungary who ruled from 1740 to 1780. The novel begins and ends with the queen's death while an epilogue instead of prologue allows the author to use the conclusion for the meditative narrative of a final judgment. Hykisch's narrative method is reminiscent of Mikhail Bulgakov's conclusion in his *The Master and Margarita;* like Bulgakov, Hykisch allows his characters to view their lives *sub specie aeternitatis*. The novel is layered in a complex structure of the social standing, ethnic differences between Austrians, Czechs, Hungarians, Serbs, Slovaks, and other nationalities of the empire, and religious professions. Perhaps the most successful accomplishment of Hykisch is his fictional rendition of the main character in his novel, Maria Theresa. She is depicted as an attractive human being whose intelligence and determination has no equal in her realm. We follow her progress from a talented young woman, inexperienced in statecraft, but not shy to rule and a quick study and a great judge of character of her rather uninspiring group of courtiers whose advice and services she would have to use. She is gradually transformed to a formidable powerhouse respected by friend and foe alike. A particular talent of Maria Theresa revealed here is her ability to gather a group of capable advisors and listen critically to their suggestions in order to choose the best possible course of action. The narrative switches between the traditional omniscient third person and the first person narrative. As an example of the narrative, here is an excerpt, the queen's deathbed meditation from the "Epilogue instead of a Prologue," wherein we get a sample of Maria Theresa's dispassionate judgment:

> Yesterday and today I turned away all my daughters. They don't have to see how the once most beautiful ruler of Europe wreathes in spasms and helpless coughing and how her fat body shakes in the black robes, without make-up, exhausted, with a double chin, thinning hair, swollen eyes, a mass of powerless, superfluous body. Only Joseph II, my son and co-ruler, and since my death the only sovereign of a spacious empire from Cheb to Cracow, from Trieste to Košice, from Milano to Belgrade, from Brussels to Temesvár has to hear out his mother and rival. We have only two days left, according to divine and human judgment. These are my last days to deal, between my fits, windows open, with everything that still bothers me. Just the two of us. We went through many files, I appended a codicil to my testament, I left money to hundreds

of schools that I founded. Now we can continue working. We mentioned dozens of names, evaluated their position, whether friend or foe, crowned heads or peasants. There was Louis XVI, the husband of my light-headed Marie Antoinette; then the opinion of the Pope and the Russian Empress, the King of England, the Kurfürst of Bavaria, the Prussian King Frederick (he survived me by six years); Jews and Freemasons, Jesuits and Jansenists, the dead Voltaire (he died a horrible death and I am happy I did not die the way he did). Then the Cardinal Migazzi, the Esterházys, Pálffys, Kinskys, Harrachs, Nostitzes, all those who are trembling ever since I died for fear how Joseph II will treat them, once his hands are untied, since they were tied by me, my fat little hands. From tomorrow, Thursday, a new age will dawn in the countries of our realm. My son, rapacious and dissatisfied, will prepare it. ("I am only Joseph II, but I want to be called the Great.") I will not be called the Great. They say the Russian Empress Catherine is already Great. The godless Voltaire termed her, sycophantically, Semiramis of the North. I will not become Great in history. I did not bed my courtiers and did not murder my husband. I have been and I will remain only Maria Theresa, perhaps a good mother. I will remain on the medals and will be buried in the Kapuziner crypt. Will I remain anywhere else? (7; this and all subsequent translations are mine)

Beginning from about the time of Maria Theresa's accession to the throne, the highpoints of her forty-year-long rule are intermingled with the stories of a formidable, but not overwhelming, list of characters both noble and common from a variety of countries. Chief among them is her nemesis, Prussian king Frederick II the Great (1712–1786), whose conquest of Silesia led to a cycle of war that marred, on and off, half of Maria Theresa's reign. Despite this fact, Frederick is not cast as a villain, but as a shrewd, if emotionally damaged, monarch, whose learning path tends toward wisdom rather than futility. Frederick's celebrated correspondent, mentor, and sometime friend, Voltaire, on the other hand, emerges as a questionable opportunist whose machinations fool neither Frederick nor Maria Theresa. The story of the wooing of Voltaire by Frederick the Great and his subsequent disenchantment with the philosopher is one of the most entertaining and amusing sections of the novel. Here, Hykisch makes a fresh departure from the canonical depiction of the freethinker Voltaire by emphasizing his human qualities that seem less impressive than his written work, endowing the portrait with an immediacy and authenticity the great man lacks in standard treatments.

At the other end of the social spectrum is Ignác Kollár, a soldier from Terchová, a village in the mountains of Slovakia, whose brother Adam František (Franz) Kollár (1718–1783) makes a spectacular career. He begins as a Jesuit student of languages and law who leaves the Society of Jesus and ends as a custodian and then head of the court's library in Vienna, ennobled by the queen with the predicate of nobility of "von Kereszten." This meteoric rise is an example of the enlightened reign of the queen who preferred men with abilities rather than such simply well born. Upward mobility of men from such modest backgrounds was impossible without the scholarly order of the Jesuits who encouraged learning even among the most disadvantaged. This, too, must have been an eye-opener to those brainwashed to see the Roman Catholic church as only an oppressor of people. One wonders: at the time of the novel's publication in Czechoslovakia, where were the ever-watchful eyes of the state censors? Much of the political tension and dramatic action moves between the cities of Vienna and Bratislava. About thirty miles from Vienna, perched on the border with Austria and Hungary, Bratislava—then called Pressburg and Pozsony, in German and Hungarian, respectively—is today the capital of Slovakia. Bratislava is as unlikely a capital, as Vienna: both are uncomfortably close to borders. However, at the time of the novel, Bratislava is also the capital of Hungary, since the Hungarian Diet resided there ever since the Ottoman Turks occupied the greater part of Hungary (since the sixteenth century). The history and politics of Austria, Hungary, the Czech lands, and the Ottoman conquest of much of Hungary all converge at the coronation of Maria Theresa as Queen of Hungary in Pressburg/Pozsony/

Bratislava. This event allows Hykisch to describe his beloved city to both his immediate Czech and Slovak readership and to his wider audience such as his German readership.

Austrians and Germans visiting Bratislava today tour St. Martin's Cathedral where Maria Theresa was crowned or the Old City Hall, where she held court after the coronation. Hykisch invokes the poet Ján Kollár who mused about this event and its significance for Slovaks a century after the coronation: "Look at the castle! Was it not the residence of the ancient kings of Great Moravia? And now the coronation: Where are the ancient symbols of our ancestors? Is not true that today's Hungary is not only the result of eight hundred years' toils of the Magyar nobility but also by the Slovaks who live in today's Hungary and have lived in Pannonia long before the arrival of the Magyars, the German colonists, and the Czech Hussites?" (186). Hykisch then relates the tragedy of the nobility of Slovakia to the events of the queen's story: the nobility of Slovakia perished "during the fights on behalf of the Hungarian kings that lasted hundreds of years, or did not consider it proper to mention its origin and its tongue. It blended with the *natio hungarica*. Accepting Latin, it forgot its mother tongue and this tongue is not considered developed enough to express lofty ideas" (186).

Hykisch, differently from the usual patriotic or nationalist nostalgia in Slovak literature, makes his Slovak characters harbingers of the progressive movement championed by the queen against the resistance from the nobility in her lands and he uses the story and history of Kollár to illustrate and describe his point. Thus, Kollár's enlightened views on the issue of church property and the lack of division between state and church anger the leaders of the Diet who, stubbornly resisting the reforms already applied in the lands of Austria and Bohemia, attack Kollár. He is seen as the mouthpiece of Maria Theresa not only by the palatine (the Hungarian viceroy) and the primate (the Hungarian Roman Catholic Church leader), but also by the queen herself. Through Kollár, Hykisch introduces the "Slovak" theme in his novel by reference to a group of scholars—all historical figures—such as Matej Bel (1684–1749; Mátyás Bél in Hungarian) a polyhistor and the publisher of the first newspaper in the Kingdom of Hungary, *Nova Posoniensia* (1722), the astronomer Maximilian Hell (1720–1792) who was the head of the Imperial Observatory in Vienna and son of the great inventor in mining, Matej Hell (1653–1743) from Bánska Štiavnica (Hykisch's own place of birth), Jozef Ignác Bajza (1755–1836) the author of the first Slovak novel, *The Adventures and Experiences of Young Renée* (1784), and Juraj Fándly (1750–1811), the most prolific Slovak author of his generation.

Hykisch reserves most of his sympathies and empathy for the queen, who, awed by the task ahead of her, reflects during her first sitting of the Privy Council:

> How to unify this mixture of countries, grand duchies, kingdoms, which found itself under one common ruler some two hundred years ago? How to rule in a conglomerate where for the Austrian lands I am the Archduchess with one set of laws and for Bohemia, Moravia, and Silesia I am the Czech Queen and have to deal with the Land Assemblies. For Hungary I am again a Queen, but I have to listen to the powerful Palatine, of a country with utterly different laws and rights, an ambitious Diet, with almost independent counties, and I cannot change an iota in the ancient privileges of the Hungarian nobility. And then there is the Archduchy of Tuscany and the Provinces of the Netherlands. Everywhere there are archdukes, governors, other nations, languages, and mores. Will these different scenes of the hastily stitched picture not tear under the first blow and will they, like poorly stitched clothing, not come apart? (90)

But how is Maria Theresa seen from the outside by her subjects when she acts as their new ruler for the first time? In Hykisch's fictional rendition she appears as an attractive and "sexy" woman and accessible ruler who establishes an immediate rapport with her subjects: "By golly, she is beautiful, this young woman, thousands will realize. The men can't take their eyes off her, checking her out from both sides of the street, they make noises, they whistle and shout. She is not fragile. Not at all! She's no violet. She is well developed like a fully matured bunch of grapes. Her hair falls in two lockets on her shoulders, just begging to be caressed and set right . . . Well, this is what she looks like, our new one. She's a beauty, the devil take it, one has to admit that" (127).

Are, then, any bad characters in this story? Strangely, even Maria Theresa's conflict with the Hungarian Diet over taxation does not really qualify as the author's intent to describe the nobles and their resistance to change negatively. Instead, it is the unwieldy bureaucracy of the empire Franz Kafka so well describes, the government, that is criticized when the queen is forced by circumstances to agree to the use of forced labor when the serfs, driven to despair by their avaricious masters, are unable to pay their taxes. At the same time, Hykisch makes the point that such practices existed throughout all lands of the empire despite the queen's efforts "to improve the lot of the Hungarian serfs," as in the case of Hungary (see, e.g., Endrey 280).

This is a novel that is not really programmatically against something as much as it is *pro*-Maria Theresa, and therefore pro-Central Europe, pro-Austria, and pro-Habsburg, since Vienna is seen as the focus and initiator of reforms for the empire and its peoples. Thus it is my contention that Hykisch's novel is an example of twentieth-century Austroslovakism. In the nineteenth century, the concept invested Austria with the ability of progressive leadership as well as the protector of the interests of Slovakia within a Central Europe. As I mentioned earlier, the notion goes back to the frustrated expectations of Slovaks during the revolutionary years following 1848 when, fearing Hungarian nationalism, they put their trust in Vienna. However, when for economic as well as political reasons Vienna made a deal with Hungary, this resulted in the oppression of Slovaks along with all the other nationalities living in the kingdom of Hungary, now an equal partner with Austria. From a historical point of view, Austroslovakism bore little fruit either in the nineteenth century or at any other time since. What makes Hykisch's rendition and his revival of the concept in a novel written during communism interesting is the prescient sensibility of the author and the fact that fifteen years after the writing of the novel Austria again plays a significant role in Central European affairs. Hykisch has one of Maria Theresa's counselors, Count Kaunitz, say the following: "Our former orientation towards the seafaring powers, England and the Netherlands, is unsupportable from the point of view of our monarchy's interests. Our realm had become a Central European state where the center of gravity oscillates around Danubian lands. The recent wars have shown that the fate of the Habsburg empire is decided between the Rhine, the Vistula, and the Danube. England and the Netherlands have no significance for our continentality" (250).

Unequivocally Central European without the soul-searchings and controversies of a Milan Kundera (see Pichova), Hykisch's novel represents a realization of the "continentality" of the Habsburg lands. Hykisch proposed before it happened the reassessment of the concept of a Central European space, a political, economic, and cultural space that is a truly multiculturally united mini-Europe and that represents a model for the future. While it also makes us aware, acutely, of the slowness and dragging of feet of the European Union and its admitting of Central European states to its membership, Hykisch's Austroslovakism could be read as well as exploited for the constructing and advancing of a Central European identity and culture. This is a space where many nations and creeds once shared to mutual advantages: by not negating but rather by putting aside the disadvantages which also existed in the history of the Central European space, the revival of the region's cultural cohesion would serve well not only those who live in the region but also a new united Europe as well (see also Tötösy). Hykisch's novel as a prescient text that turned into a at this time yet to be realized possibility represents one of those rare texts which bridge fiction and history in a way that allows the promise of a better reality.

WORKS CITED

Busch, Ulrich. "Eine kühne Persönlichkeit." *National-Zeitung* (22 May 1989): 8.

Endrey, Anthony. *Hungarian History.* Melbourne: The Hungarian Institute, 1982.
Hykisch, Anton. *Milujte kráľovnú* (*Long Live the Queen*). Bratislava: Slovenský spisovateľ, 1998.
Hykisch, Anton. *Es lebe die Königin.* Trans. Gustav Just. 1988. Berlin: Aufbau, 1998.
Kirschbaum, Stanislav J. *A History of Slovakia: The Struggle for Survival.* New York: St. Martin's P, 1995.
Ozsváth, Zsuzsanna. "Radnóti, Celan, and Aesthetic Shifts in Central European Holocaust Poetry." *Comparative Central European Culture.* Ed. Steven Tötösy de Zepetnek. West Lafayette: Purdue UP, 2002. 51–70.
Petro, Peter. *Critical Essays on Milan Kundera.* New York: G.K Hall, 1999.
Petro, Peter. *History of Slovak Literature.* Montréal: McGill-Queen's UP, 1995.
Petro, Peter, "Modern Slovak Fiction: The Sixties, a Decade of Experimentation." *Slovakia* 30 (1982–83): 153–64.
Pichova, Hana. "Milan Kundera and the Identity of Central Europe." *Comparative Central European Culture.* Ed. Steven Tötösy de Zepetnek. West Lafayette: Purdue UP, 2002. 103–14.
Tötösy de Zepetnek, Steven. "Comparative Cultural Studies and the Study of Central European Culture." *Comparative Central European Culture.* Ed. Steven Tötösy de Zepetnek. West Lafayette: Purdue UP, 2002. 1–32.

Milan Kundera and the Identity of Central Europe

Hana Pichova

The identity of Central Europe has been a problem for Milan Kundera since his adolescence; it gave birth to a theme with many variations," writes Ladislav Matějka (127). The "variations" are reflected throughout Kundera's public, private, political, and literary life; for example, in his involvement with the Communist Party, his expulsion from the party, his exile in 1975, his statements about the impact of Soviet culture on Czechoslovakia, his criticism of Dostoevsky, and his fictional accounts of recent historical events (for a recent volume on Kundera, see Petro). Kundera's variations have provoked an array of responses from many prominent intellectuals of our day and these responses have resulted in political/literary polemics that not only add to the theme's "heaviness," to borrow the author's term for meaning, but reflect the problematic quest for a political and aesthetic identity of Central Europe today. Not surprisingly, Kundera's role is no less prominent today than in the past, he has put forth yet another variation in his latest novel befittingly entitled *Identity*.

Before turning to the present, to the most recent variation, a detour into the polemics of the past will prove useful. I will not discuss here the famous and certainly crucial debate between Kundera and Brodsky regarding Dostoevsky and Western culture. Rather, my intention is to the less known but closer to home debates, among Czech intellectuals themselves and that reflect a political and literary split, one that persists in the Czech Republic and one that has an impact on the shaping of a Central European identity in the Czech lands today. In 1968 then two principal literary figures of Czechoslovakia, Milan Kundera and Václav Havel, began a polemic which addressed the question of national, individual, and a writer's identity in historically volatile times. A few months after the Soviet invasion in 1968, still at a time of relaxed censorship, Kundera published an essay, "Český úděl"("Czech Destiny") in which he discusses the fate of small nations. A fate that he sees simultaneously as grand and precarious: grand because, "by their incessant search for their own identity and by their fight for survival, the small nations resist the terrifying push toward uniformity on this earth, making it glitter with a wealth of traditions and customs, so that human individualism, marvel and originality can find a home in this world" (Kundera 1968, 4). And this world, Kundera adds, in which voices of small nations are heard as much as those of their large counter points, would be a better and a happier one. However, he warns, because small nations have to create, continuously, and worry about, self relevance—if they stop, they may fall into lethargy and dreaminess, but, unlike large nations' dreams, theirs may end up in a state of never waking up—their fate is indeed precarious (Kundera 1968, 4).

Since Kundera's thoughts on the destiny of small countries and cultures appeared at a time of great political turmoil and uncertainty, it is not surprising that these thoughts provoked controversy among Czechoslovak intellectuals. For example, Havel retorted to Kundera's text sharply with his own "Český úděl?" ("Czech Destiny?"), the question mark added. He accused Kundera of escapism, of dreaming about greatness and destiny, at a time, when one ought to resist and to dissent. Havel called for shedding illusions about the historical role of a small nation and to gather the courage to face reality. Kundera was able to publish his rebuttal in his "Radikalismus a exhibicionismus" ("Radicalism and

Exhibitionism"), that happens to be one of his last texts published in Czechoslovakia in the aftermath of the Soviet invasion. Here, Kundera criticizes Havel for moralistic exhibitionism and he decries Havel's call for active resistance when faced with no hope of success.

The exchange anticipates the split of the unofficial line of Czechoslovak intellectuals and letters into two groups. Predictably, Havel became a dissident, spent years in prison, wrote absurdist plays and philosophical essays such as "Moc bezmocných" ("Power of the Powerless"). His voice from prison came in the form of *Letters to Olga,* a translated document, yet one that is limited to a national audience. Kundera, on the other hand, became an exile, settled in France and produced fictional and essayistic variations on the Soviet and communist destruction of Central Europe. His novels, *The Book of Laughter and Forgetting* and *The Unbearable Lightness of Being,* international bestsellers, weave politics and love themes into a web that has raised more attention in the West about the repressive regime in Central Europe than political newscasts could and his texts created an audience and interest in the culture and history of a small country in the heart of Europe. Rather than closing the gap between the two unofficial groups of Czechoslovak letters, Kundera's novels created another polemic. In the 1980s, smuggled back to their homeland, they met with an unexpected reception from a prominent dissident literary critic, Milan Jungmann. Although his article, "Kunderovské paradoxy" ("Kundera's Paradoxes"), was extremely disparaging, it could not appear officially in Czechoslovakia, for both critic and author were personae non gratae. In turn, Jungmann's article was smuggled to the West and published in the émigré journal *Svědectví* where it launched a heated debate between émigrés and dissidents, a debate that questions the very function of literature as well as the role and responsibility of a Central European writer.

Jungmann begins with a premise that the dual reception Kundera's works elicits—undifferentiated and uncritical reception in the West including the émigré readership versus embarrassed and perplexed silence by Czechoslovak dissidents—reflects two cultural environments that assign different meaning, function, and responsibility to literature. That is, incongruous ideas on how literature and art should manifest freedom and morality produced this wide gap in readers' response. Kundera's work consequently becomes the focal point for the problematics of two notions in Czechoslovak culture, namely, exilic and dissident. This alone, argues Jungman, merits our attention. Indeed, Jungmann the dissident critic devotes twenty pages to what he defines as aesthetic and ideological conflicts he has with Kundera. For example, Jungmann sees Kundera's presentation of sexual themes as meaninglessly pornographic and he views philosophical discussions as deliberately reductive, all for the sole purpose of achieving popularity and easy readability. Jungmann's most interesting critical point, however, concerns his analysis of Kundera's fictional depiction of historical realities. For instance, in *The Unbearable Lightness of Being*, Tomas, a physician, who, after his return from exile after the Soviet invasion of Chechoslovakia because of an article he published before the Soviet invasion becomes a window washer, a common occupation of dissidents. Impossible, argues Jungmann, doctors who fell out of favor with the system were only downgraded because the shortage of doctors prevented the government to punish a much needed professional for a minor offense such as a critical article. Thus, Tomas' fate, one characterized by a free-spirited existence of daily sexual encounters with his window clients, portrays an unrealistic picture that may lead to the Western readers' idealization of dissidents' lives under totalitarianism, argues Jungmann. Furthermore, echoing Havel, he also criticizes Kundera for depicting the protagonist Tomas' inability to see the power of the powerless, in other words, to acknowledge the dissidents' belief in acts, no matter how insignificant these may seem. Implicit in Jungmann's argumentation is a view of the Western reader as naive and shallow, unable to distinguish between historical realities and fiction. To underscore this viewpoint, Jungmann openly reproaches Western criticism for lack of rigor, skepticism, and questioning in regards to Kundera. All of these qualities, one is lead to assume by Jungmann, are inherently and evidently present in the readership behind the iron curtain.

Certainly, Jungmann's essay is the most disparaging I have read to this day about the work of Kundera. Predictably, it produced a heated response from émigrés such as Květoslav Chvatík (Germany), Josef Škvorecký (Canada), and Petr Král (France). Their defense of Kundera appeared in the same journal, *Svědectví*, only two issues later, and it emphasized several points: the right of fiction to deviate from historical truth that is a prerogative of literature and has a long tradition also in Czech and Slovak literature. Further, they argue that steamy sexual scenes and the use of philosophical discussions are hardly an effective means of gaining a wide readership. The émigrés also differed with Jungmann on the subject of Kundera's reception in the West. They point out that although popular among intellectuals and students of literature, Kundera's work has not captured the general masses nor has it gained an equivocally positive response from the Western critics as Jungmann seems to believe.

It is this last point, namely Jungmann's low opinion of Western readership that merits further discussion in light of the Central European writer's position today, a position that is fully dependent on a reader (and if it happens to be a foreign one, all the better). Jungmann's assertion that Kundera caters to his Western reader is partially true. The author of bestsellers translated into more languages than one can remember does not hide the fact that his linguistic eloquence underwent a certain amount of simplification for the sake translations. In addition, the dictionary of misunderstood words in his *The Art of the Novel* reflects a desire to at least somewhat eliminate cultural barriers. So perhaps there is something to learn here. After all, as Havel notes about Czech and Slovak writers, not much literary fame has been achieved outside of their borders owing to the fact that Czech and Slovak literature is not only difficult to translate but to digest: "It does not display the easy virtuosity of global literature. It is too heavy" (127–28). Certainly, all literatures of Central Europe carry the burden of historical complexities and "heaviness." Yet, Jungmann's presumption that Kundera is successful because he eliminates this heaviness partially by reducing his aesthetic, moral, and cultural standards reveals an elitist attitude. In essence, the Central European writer is positioned into a liminal space beyond which lurks misunderstanding. And the Western reader, who is quite unknown, is not given the benefit of doubt. Although I would argue that heaviness can become a source of pleasure to a foreign reader—even if some of the texts' cultural implications are oblique—Jungmann's criticism is important not because he is right about Kundera but because his analysis recalls, ironically, Kundera's own warning against that "terrifying push toward uniformity on this earth which must be avoided in order to preserve the small nation's traditions and customs" (Kundera 1968, 4).

To preserve the culturally unique is perhaps not a challenging issue for a Central European writer; however, what to do with politics which dominated the literary scene for the last forty years is (on the problematics of Soviet and communist colonialism and Central Europe, see Moore; Tötösy). Ladislav Matějka poses this question: "so what is literature's future when the political relevance of the Central European theme and of Russian evil is no longer germane" (134) And in a country where writers become presidents, where literature, history, and politics were at times indistinguishably entwined, one wonders. Today, Czech writers wonder as well. In 1991, at an international festival of writers supported by the English magazine *Bookseller,* the theme was politics, more precisely, the discussion centered on fear that politics and literature may get separated. This presents a rather ironic twist because in the 1960s the call was for freeing literature from overpowering by politics. Yet, the fear is justified. Jungmann questions the very function of literature by posing the questions of why does literature begin, what is its meaning, and what is the purpose of writing? The answers Jungmann provides reflect the Central European dilemma: the written text that cannot find a reader is dead, or only a comfort to the writer's soul. Nonetheless, the artistic word desires to be a message to the world. Only the coexistence of the written and the reader brings to life a text's spiritual power as an irreplaceable value confirming the identity of national being. A society that does not need self-reflection of its condition—which is provided by literature and art—could be fulfilled by consumerism, but would waste away spiritually. Czech literature today fortunately no longer needs to fulfill the role of a prosecutor of a ruffian power, but it ought to keep its national consciousness in the minds of most Czech writers and artists. Jungmann argues that if the delicate balance between politics as a process of national development and culture as its living consciousness is disrupted either by politics not allowing culture its basic possibilities of development or if culture turns away from its responsibility of preserving the laws of ethics in its national organism, there would be neither politics only politicking nor culture except one that finds expression in glossy magazines and escapism only (1997, 77–79).

In this journey for a balance between politics and literature, between the past and present, where do we locate Kundera and his Central European theme? As mentioned previously, this most prominent of Czech writers has not been embraced in his native land after the Velvet Revolution. His appearances are rare and he seldom grants interviews. He visits his homeland incognito (for example by comporting a false moustache) and, overall, the reception of his work has been lukewarm at best. Many of his recent novels have not been published in the Czech Republic, a list that includes *The Unbearable Lightness of Being*. Some critics go as far as to consider him a French writer. Ironically, it is Jungmann who had come to Kundera's defense and publicly argued for his place in Czech literature. Kundera's precarious position in Czech letters says much about the difficulty of uniting the two groups of once unofficial literature, of exiles and dissidents, and about the past and politics. His situation may be also a reflection of Central European self-reflective behavior according to which most cultures of the region discount diaspora and émigré authors and do not include such in the canon of the national literature.

Since 1989 new writers have appeared on the scene, some have even been translated into foreign languages. Jáchym Topol and Michal Viewegh are perhaps the most read and translated, yet their works are not bestsellers outside of the Czech borders. This lack of international success is not owing to the "heaviness" of their works. Instead, their themes are very much oriented toward contemporary Czech society. For example, Topol captures in his novels the emotional dislocation that followed the Velvet Revolution of 1989 and Viewegh returns to his country's communist past in one of his first novels, *Báječný život pod psa,* but now concentrates on the everyday lives of Czechs, on divorce, vacations, love and so on. Since both writers are talented, the potential is there and one hopes that one of their works will receive international acclaim. Many former dissidents have published their works, but most of these are located in a very specific time and place, the totalitarian years, and contemporary relevance into the present seems difficult. A few writers such as Ludvík Vaculík, Václav Havel, and Ivan Klíma have achieved certain level of international recognition, yet their readership is limited. Exile writers such as Josef Škvorecký and Jan Novák have mostly remained in their adopted homelands and, in a reverse context, are considered ethnic/minority authors in their adopted cultures. Thus, at present it is still Kundera whose voice transcends boundaries and whose work invites and achieves international recognition.

In his recent writing, Kundera does not abandon the theme of Central European identity. One of his recent novels, *Identity* (1997), can be read as another variation on what seems an inexhaustible subject. Recalling Kundera's 1968 essay "Czech Destiny" and his call for the need to preserve the identity of small nations "so that human individualism, marvel and originality can find a home in this world" (4), we recognize this idea posed thirty years later. Although in identity Central Europe is nowhere discussed, human individualism is. And perhaps it is the identity of an individual, of a Central European, which is the crucial and no less complicated issue today. Relinquishing the usual grandiose scope of his previous novels—an exception is *Slowness* which directly precedes *Identity*—Kundera strips his fictional world of all historical and political events. Absent are borders separating Central Europe from the Western world, gone are philosophical discussions about eternal return, warnings about totalitarianism, demystifications of "truths," poignant descriptions of loss, and diatribes about kitsch and cultural wastelands. In *Identity* all is centered around the individual and the rest is spare, as are the setting, the action, and the narrative techniques. The plot is perhaps even too modest.

The novel opens up with a scene from a vacation. Jean-Marc does not recognize his lover Chantal while walking on the beach. Meanwhile,

Chantal, also walking on the beach, notices that men no longer turn to look at her. This brief episode foreshadows the central themes of the novel; the misunderstanding among the two lovers, the questioning of who the other is, as well as the pondering of one's own identity. More involved feelings occur upon their return to Paris when Chantal begins to receive love letters from a mysterious admirer. Keeping them secret from Jean-Marc, these letters eventually have a destructive effect on their relationship. Chantal suddenly realizes that the letters are from no other but her lover. Why would he send them? To "trap her" (94)? But why? So that he could leave her since he was the younger of the two? Chantal's deduction, an obvious misreading of intensions, leaves her feeling deceived. Without hesitation, she takes a train to London where she then finds herself in midst of an orgy in a house with red curtains. Meanwhile, Jean-Marc who followed but lost her, finds himself on a bench in front of this very house. The reader now suspects that at some point reality was suspended. This suspicion is confirmed with Jean-Marc's exclamation: "Wake up! It's not real!" (167). The novel could effectively end here, yet there are few more pages dedicated to the dream. Although the dream has a distinct end, its beginning is blurred. The narrator underscores this ambiguity with his incessant questioning: "And I ask myself: who was dreaming? Who dreamed this story? Who imagined it? She? He? Both of them? Each one for the other? And starting when did their real life change into this treacherous fantasy? When the train drove down under the Channel? Earlier? The morning she announced her departure for London? Even earlier than that? ... At what exact moment did the real turn into the unreal, reality into reverie? Where was the border? Where is the border?" (167).

These questions along with the lovers' tender middle-of-the-night dialogue close the novel. It is the end of *Identity*, more precisely the two sentences: "Where was the border?" and "Where is the border?" which brings us back to Kundera's variations on Central European identity and identity per se. Although the technique of blurring the border between dream and fictional reality is not unique to this novel—one only has to recall Tamina's escape to a children's island in *The Book of Laughter and*

Forgetting and in which the last chapter is entitled "The Border"—the idea of border as a physical and political entity is presented differently. *Identity* is the author's borderless novel par excellence. Characters move fluidly from a beach in the South of France, to Paris, then to London, then back, or perhaps they don't move at all, which ultimately would be of little consequence. There are no political barriers, no barbed wires. There is no mention of another country closed off from the rest of the world. Juxtaposing this with *The Book of Laughter and Forgetting*—as well as the rest of his novels with the exception of *Immortality*—the tragedy of Tamina is based precisely on closed borders, in more general terms, of Central Europeans denied freedom.

Stripped of political and historical burden symbolized by the border, the characters are not only able to move physically wherever they desire, but they have no external forces (usually of totalitarian nature) to overwhelm or crush them. It is the mundane existence of boring jobs, of obnoxious relatives, and of a few memories from the past (even the death of a child is minimalized) that preoccupy Chantal and Jean-Marc. By abandoning the historical/political setting, by abolishing borders, Kundera creates space for the exploration of the individual. For Kundera now, a decade after the borders of Central Europe had opened up, it is any individual, French or Central European, who tackles the problem of how to relate to the other, how to differentiate ourselves from others, what is the meaning of friendship and life, and what are one's possibilities in this world.

In "Notes Inspired by *The Sleepwalkers*," Kundera writes, "The Great Central European novelists ask themselves what man's possibilities are in a world that has become a trap" (48). Kundera's reply to himself and to his readers before came in the form of *The Unbearable Lightness of Being* and *The Book of Laughter and Forgetting*. In contrast, today one can rephrase the proposition: "The Great Central European novelists ask themselves what man's possibilities are in a world that has opened its trap." Kundera offers *Identity*, a text that can be read as an exploration of the individual's secrets and as a search of the human spirit. And here, unexpectedly, Havel's words come to mind. When asked about the future of Central European culture without the burden of politics, Havel refused to participate in any predictions: "The secrets of culture's future are a reflection of the very secrets of the human spirit" (*Living in Truth* 124). My own reading of Kundera and Havel is that these two prominent representatives of that difficult to define concept, Central European culture, may just have arrived at a juncture and Kundera's novel, *Identity,* represents the global or at least European Central European . . . .

WORKS CITED

Bock, Ivo, Květoslav Chvatík, Petr Král, and Josef Škvorecký. "Ještě of románech. Milana Kundery" ("Still More about Milan Kundera's Novels") *Svědectví* 20 (1986): 614–33.

Havel, Václav. *Living in Truth*. Ed. Jan Vladislav. London: Faber and Faber, 1989.

Havel, Václav. *Letters to Olga*. Trans. Paul Wilson. New York: Knopf, 1988.

Havel, Václav. "Moc bezmocných" ("Power of the Powerless"). *O lidskou identitu* (*Concerning Human Identity*). By Václav Havel. London: Svědectví, 1984. 55–133.

Havel, Václav. "Český úděl?" ("Czech Fate?"). *O lidskou identitu* (*Concerning Human Identity*). By Václav Havel. London: Svědectví, 1984. 193–200.

Jungmann, Milan. *V obklíčení příběhu* (*Besieged by Tales*). Brno: Atlantis, 1997.

Jungmann, Milan. "Kunderovské paradoxy" ("Kundera's Paradoxes"). *Svědectví* 20 (1986): 135–62.

Kundera, Milan. *Identity*. Trans. Linda Asher. New York: Harper Perennial, 1997.

Kundera, Milan. *The Art of the Novel*. Trans. Linda Asher. New York: Grove P, 1988.

Kundera, Milan. "Notes Inspired by *The Sleepwalkers*." *The Art of the Novel*. By Milan Kundera. Trans. Linda Asher. New York: Grove P, 1988. 47–67.

Kundera, Milan. "Radikalismus a exhibicionismus" ("Radicalism and Exhibitionism"). *Host do domu* 15 (1969): no pag.

Kundera, Milan. "Český úděl" ("Czech Fate"). *Listy* (19 December 1968): n.pag.

Matějka, Ladislav. "Milan Kundera's Central Europe." *Cross Currents: A Yearbook of Central European Culture* 9 (1990): 127–34.

Moore, David Chioni. "Is the Post- in Postcolonial the Post- in Post-Soviet? Toward a Global Postcolonial Critique." *PMLA: Publications of the Modern Language Association of America* 116.1 (2001): 111–28.

Petro, Peter. *Critical Essays on Milan Kundera*. New York: G.K Hall, 1999.

Tötösy de Zepetnek, Steven. "Comparative Cultural Studies and the Study of Central European Culture." *Comparative Central European Culture*. Ed. Steven Tötösy de Zepetnek. West Lafayette: Purdue UP, 2002. 1–32.

Politics, History, and Public Intellectuals in Central Europe after 1989

Katherine Arens

In what follows, I trace a recent—and very old—configuration of Austria's "imagined Europe"—to coin a term from Benedict Anderson's "imagined communities"—yet far outside his project of nationalism. To do so, I begin with a hegemonic, if not entirely Austrian, voice joining Austria's past with Europe's future, Otto von Habsburg, heir to the throne of Austria-Hungary, and representative to the European Union (EU) who carries a German passport, to outline how he uses this map of Europe for the present political climate. After that, two particularly visible authors of "mixed" Austrian heritage, Peter Handke and Milo Dor, travel through the periphery of this redefined Europe to provide commentary on the post-1989 Balkans. Their "travel literature," journalism designed to appeal to the popular imagination, ties the Balkans to Europe in a way not known to the Cold War powers, who follow the convention that the Balkans are not part of Europe, a notion that has been in place as long as Rebecca West's *Black Lamb and Grey Falcon: A Journey through Yugoslavia* (1940).

In an era of political alignment, Dor and Handke espouse the position that the Balkans do indeed start in the western districts of Vienna, but that those Balkans are part of Europe, part of the traditional European bulwark against the non-civilized, and never defined in light of the NATO west, or as part of a mythical Central Europe. That is, their "imagined Balkans" and Austria function not only as "the heart of Europe," as a tourist bumper sticker of a decade ago had it, but as Europe's *chora,* a space upon which various legislations are imposed, a potentially resistant substrate that is shaped by the dominant order, but which can never exhaust it.

Otto von Habsburg, politician of the "European idea" and long-time worker for the European Parliament, has, for at least twenty years, taken it as his particular mission to resist the map of Europe used by the so-called great powers since the Second World War. Even before the fall of the wall in 1989, for instance, the national designations "East Germany" or the "German Democratic Republic" (GDR; DDR in German abreviation) did not exist in his personal political dictionary. These "East" Germans were actually *Mitteldeutsche,* the Germans in the middle between the West Germans and those lost into the historical mists of the East Bloc: *"das 'DDR' genannte Mitteldeutschland"* (Habsburg, *Zurück* 9). In Habsburg's account, the wall between East and West Europe did not fall in November 1989, when the physical brick and mortar of the barrier between two parts of Berlin were chipped away by crowds, flood-lit under the Brandenburg Gate. Instead, the "East Bloc" actually fell on 19 August 1989 at Sopron/Ödenburg, at the Austrian-Hungarian border, "When 661 'Central Germans' [GDR citizens] cut through the barbed wire and stormed through the open gate to Austria, and then there occurred the greatest mass flight of Germans out of the GDR since the erection of the wall 28 years earlier, then the 'Iron Curtain' was no longer sustainable, not even in world politics . . . the wall and the fall of the red tyrants from the Baltic to the Adriatic . . . but the picnic proved to be the spark in the dry wood of the Yalta system of injustice" (Habsburg, *Return* 14; the opening of the border occurred with the understanding of the then still communist Hungarian government of Gyula Horn). Here, Habsburg harks back to a European rhetoric much older than himself. He is not simply claiming dynastic privilege, but is also reaching back to the early nineteenth century, before the map of Europe became almost uniformly nationalist. His Europe resists division according to the East-West compass points that have been the West's reference point and line of demarcation since the Second World War. He is more inclined to divide Europe north from south, according to life styles. Thus it is no surprise that, in August 1989, Habsburg was accused of luring innocent Germans who were on "vacation" in Hungary across the border. His version is that the event was simply Europe restoring itself: "Paneuropa is all of Europe" (Habsburg, *Return* 19). Reinforcing this map of Europe, in the individual chapters of his *Return to the Center* Habsburg rewrites the histories of the successor states of Central and East Europe, each in its own national voice. Each of Habsburg's essays in his 1991 book uses one of the individual histories of the region to draw a line from a separate national history into a unified Europe to which it belongs. His own Austria, for example, was threatened with extinction in the occupations during the second World War: "Vienna seemed just as condemned to extinction as did Berlin in Germany, with its wall" (*Return* 20). It survived then, but now one must ask: "Does Austria Have a Future?" (*Return* 24). His European map includes, for instance, Bavaria as a province even while he valorizes it as one of the loci of European Christianity (*Return* 31). Yet overall, Habsburg's Europe is, not surprisingly, also the Europe of the Habsburgs, looking North and East, part of a Europe that exists up to the national borders of the continent.

Habsburg fears the rhetoric used around reunited Germany. The new Germany, he feels, is looking to redefine itself in the outdated nationalist mode, which is unacceptable to the future of the continent. That nationalist Germany is a historical aberration, while reunited Germany has a chance to join Europe. A better model for post-wall Europe, in his opinion, can be found in the Habsburg past, which had a tradition of freedom and federalism in the European states. That heritage is shared by the rest of what had been framed as the "East Bloc" during the Cold War. Thus Habsburg's Czech Republic can celebrate Jan Hus; Slovakia is the land of Masaryk and Beneš; the Croatians and Slovenians are "coming home" after Tito's demise. He tours the rest of the "rebirth of the

Balkans" (*Return* 86) in a similar voice, as the rebirth of a European civilization. He includes Europe up to the Baltic in a future map that would reflect Europe's restoration to itself: "Estonians, Latvians, and Lithuanians put their hopes in us. Europe would be incomplete without these peoples who have suffered more than others for their membership in Europe" (*Return* 102). Habsburg's solution is humanist (and utopian): that the political resolution of that war will necessarily rest with the politicians and functionaries, while the true politics of the region lies with its civilians, never with their ex-governments. Here, again, Habsburg's rhetoric consciously echoes the Nazi period as part of an unacceptable alternative to the future he prefers: "It is a property of modern, or purportedly modern, politics, that one has theoretically condemned blood guilt, but continuously practices it. That is a return to barbarism" (*Return* 152). Even a country like the GDR is a primary victim of such logic. Habsburg warns of the psychological consequences of not distinguishing between what governments enacted through force, and what the people in those countries did. Without this optic, the East Block's successor states will be a long-term series of disasters, because the people will blame themselves for not resisting the regimes. He thus rejects collective guilt out of hand—the West must not blame victims, but root out the *Bonzen*, the party bosses who exploited them. Habsburg's Europe, then, is a state of mind that must be cured. Habsburg always remains ecumenical, however. Not wanting to offend the self-satisfaction of the traditional Western powers, he still argues for Paris as a cultural center of Europe, because it is not provincial. Yet Habsburg's future Europe will be federated, with many centers, not centralized. National tensions that accompany centralization will be the downfall of the idea of a continent united (*Return* 165). New nation-states will not solve the problems remaining on Europe's map, since Europe can only exist as a macro region, not as micro states—*grossräumig,* as a zone of cooperation that has existed since the Holy Roman Empire (*Return* 167, 171). He thus advocates persistently self-determination in the region, as a *Gesamteuropa* (*Zurück* 173) that is, moreover, resolutely Christian (*Return*

232–33). Only near the end of the volume does the historical term "Central Europe" (*Mitteleuropa*) reemerge as a guidepost.

Herein lies the particular onus of Central Europe. It is no accident that meditations back on the spiritual center of Europe—our Christian heritage and our imperial-federal tradition—fall together with the freeing of our geographical center of our part of the globe. . . . The Paneuropean idea originated on the soil of the old Danube Monarchy. Now, all of Europe must renew itself on the basis of its geographic, historical, and spiritual center. Therein lies our challenge for the years to the millennium. Only then will we do justice to our worldwide responsibility that will determine the start of the next millennium (*Return* 248). This is the "paneuropäische Idee" that Habsburg adopts as the title of his more recent book, where he argues that Europe has to be more than an economic union, it must be a cultural one, as well (*Mémoires* 135). While the utopianism of such pronouncements remains evident, one should never underestimate the calculation of Habsburg's rhetoric—he is an exemplary historical-publicity-agent. In a set of interviews given in French, for example, he spins his model Europe in a framing that more closely reflects Central Europe's imperial past rather than to the humanist-democratic ideal represented in *Return to the Center*. An emperor, he notes, can be seen as an exemplary federalist: "The emperor does not belong to a single one of his nations" (*Mémoires* 205). And more importantly, he argues for a trinitarian unity in multiplicity for the political faces he assumes in his political career: "As a legitimist . . . I am, for instance, republican in Switzerland and monarchist in England" (*Mémoires* 267). Such a perspective, reflecting regional historical traditions as well as the coming European federation, would, for example, legitimize both Serbian and Croatian self-determination (*Friedensmacht* 77), as it would the historical claims of most of the globe's major flashpoints (*Paneuropäische Idee* 234). Habsburg's political calculation evokes a warm image, an almost Josephinian humanism of a continent freeing its political serfs. No matter his distinct politics, it is crucial to note that close parallels to his Paneuropean rhetoric recur throughout

Austria's journalistic rhetoric on the "new Europe." As does a more self-consciously internationalist literary voices, Peter Handke and Milo Dor will share this map, although by no means the political motivations behind Habsburg's specific targets.

Peter Handke is Austrian by passport who has often lived and worked in Paris; he is also typically Austrian in being of mixed ethnic heritage, of Slovene descent. Since the fall of the Wall and the various Balkan offensives, he has written a number of controversial newspaper essays that have turned into slender volumes, each evoking firestorms of reaction (including from Milo Dor). One of the earliest of these essays was called *Abschied des Träumers vom Neunten Land,* after a Slovene legend; it was published in the *Süddeutsche Zeitung* in 1991, on the occasion of the first nationalist battles in the Balkans. He is careful not to purport to speak for the Slovenes, although he shares their ancestry. More significant for the present purpose is, however, his clear anti-nationalist rhetoric, shared with my other two test cases, Dor and Habsburg: "And I see no rationale for the state of Slovenia" (*Abschied* 7). Where Handke diverges from his compatriots, however, is in his steadfast refusal to explore the representative politics of nation-states and their preferred historical images, preferring to discuss the Balkans as part of the life-world of a Europe that needs restoration. That non-existent nation-state of Slovenia is his homeland, but it cannot and should not be defined as a political entity. For Handke, Slovenia is a homeland only in his experience, the only place where things feel substantial to him, where he feels he is a "guest of reality" (*Abschied* 15): "And in spite of all this, I have never in my life felt so at home as a foreigner as in the land of Slovenia" (*Abschied* 11). The actual political border between Italy and Slovenia emerges to him not as a mythical place, but as a real place beyond political history, a geographical unit in the particular karst landscape that is more defining than its historical belonging to Austro-Hungary. In this gesture, Handke underscores the arbitrariness of political labels to a greater degree even more than Habsburg, since he stresses that even the politically amorphous term *Mitteleuropa* is an identity written only late onto this landscape (*Abschied* 22), one story among many that can enforce particular historical points of view, enacting explicit agendas. Those agendas do not, however, correspond to the experience of the country that he shares with his translator, Zarko Radoković (*Abschied* 26). At best, shifting political allegiances evidence a North-South border for European prejudice. Handke characterizes the everyday stereotypes enforcing this line: no true European wants to be a member of the purportedly lazy South. Yet Handke clearly believes in the legitimacy of a history of shared experience, even if he does not believe in the persistence of political history: "I ask: is it possible, no, even necessary, for a country and a people nowadays to declare itself immediately to a state formation (with all the trappings, coats of arms, flags, holidays and border crossing gates), if that state hasn't come to that point by itself, but only as a reaction against something—and in addition, against something from without, and also something that is sometimes annoying or tedious, not actually pressing or crying out for redress?" (*Abschied* 42).

Politically, the Slovenia that Handke saw in 1991 was simply an accident of history, a group of people talked into being a small state, despite how much they share with the rest of ex-Yugoslavia (*Abschied* 44). This country was seduced from outside into creating borders that he calls *"Unwirklichkeitsstreifen"* ("stripes of un-realities"), borders that have not grown naturally out of the region or its history, and so feel strange (*Abschied* 45). Handke would again use such *ad hominem* judgments about what is "natural" to a region in 1996, for another series in the *Süddeutsche Zeitung*, and his intervention would not be received well. The culprit this time was a travel narrative entitled *A Journey to the Rivers* (*Eine winterliche Reise zu den Flüssen Donau, Save, Morawa und Drina, oder Gerechtigkeit für Serbien*). The English edition has a preface telling Handke's version of the story:

> This text, appearing on two weekends at the onset of 1996 in the *Süddeutsche Zeitung,* caused some commotion in the European press. Immediately after publication of the first part, I was designated a terrorist in the *Corriere della Sera,* and *Libération* revealed that I was, first of all, amused that there

were so few victims in the Slovenian war of 1991, and that I was exhibiting, second, "doubtful taste" in discussing the various ways of presenting this or that victim of the Yugoslavian wars in the Western Media. In *Le Monde* I was then called a "pro-Serbian advocate," and in the *Journal du Dimanche* there was talk of "pro-Serbian agitation." And so it continued until *El Pais* even read into my text a sanction of the Šrebrenica massacre. (*Journey* vii)

Handke asserts that his essay's goal was not political. He simply sought "aesthetic veracity" in expressing his experiences of the Balkans (*Reise* viii). He had, he claims, long wanted to visit the Balkans, then once had the chance to appear at a Belgrade theater festival. From that visit, he remembered only the country's rivers. In 1996, he wanted to find that land of the rivers, to return to the Balkans, and move behind what the media were making of the Balkans: "I felt the need to go behind the mirror" (*Journey* 2)—behind the "looking glass," and behind the screen imposed on the region by news media. The result was a trip, an essay, and great public outcry: "And whoever is thinking now: Aha, pro-Serbia! or Aha! Yugophile!—the latter a *Spiegel* [the German newsmagazine] word—need read no further" (*Journey* 2–3).

To penetrate behind the media, Handke did not wish to visit the country officially, or even as an acknowledged tourist. He hoped to blend in, with the aid of his guides, Zarko Radaković, his translator, and the author, Zlatko B. (pseudonym, Adrian Brouwer). They set off in October 1995. Handke's only preparation involved seeing a film, Emir Kusturica's *Underground,* which had been panned by many political critics (most notably by the philosopher Alain Finkielkraut) even before they had seen it. The trip is narrated in an egregiously faux-naïve tone that is at great pains to underscore only what he sees, feels, and thinks about, not any of the images that might have been inserted in his consciousness by the media. In the area of the first Yugoslav war, therefore, he muses about why the Serbs and the Croats were involved, and how he would behave in such a situation: "Thus a part of me could not take sides, much less judge" (*Journey* 21). The press tableaux through which he purportedly "knew" the region seem to avoid the realities of the issue: "Who will someday write this history differently" (*Journey* 26). The established images need to be redone, if the region is to have a future. But those experiences are occluded by established images, and so, if they are to be reclaimed, he has to find counter-images of Serbia from its own ground. To reenter what Dilthey called the life-world of this country, he interviews people on the Belgrade street about what they consider their own history, and what they felt Serbs' future would be. But threaded into the answers he receives, he finds trances of normalcy, of music—and a pervasive black market. He does not hold himself aloof, but rather trades stories with his interlocutors, such as that about his Slovenian grandfather in Carinthia who had voted for unification with Yugoslavia in 1920. His life as a European thus has links with these people. One interviewee, a country man, seeks to engage Handke in complaints about his leaders, who purportedly caused the people's suffering. Handke, however, persists in seeking a Yugoslavia outside the official one. Even though the Dayton talks were in progress at the time of his walk, Handke refuses to be engaged in political judgments about a situation which he does not yet understand experientially.

The second part of Handke's trip leads him to another river, to the Drina, in Bosnia, where he concentrations of soldiers for the first time, and realizes what is being done to the life-world of the Serbians. He realizes that they are not in a particular state, but they are in a state of mind that characterizes them: "There remains for me, precisely in the crystal-sharp isolation of almost everyone there, for the first time a sense of something like a *Volk*, otherwise rightly long since declared dead: conceivable because this people so visibly dwells in the diaspora in its own country, each in an intensely personal disjunction" (*Journey* 70). When, one day, he finally manages to be alone in Serbia, he reports in the Epilogue, he meditates on how easily reporters falsify this life world. Those who should be chronicling the world are only falsifying it; these "false ones" have the hubris to assert their grasp of Serbia's truth. He blasts specifically the *Spiegel* magazine and its "Balkan experts" for official reporting that becomes what he calls describes as poisoned words. Significantly, this "official" reporting is also the German point of view that keeps Yugoslavia from burying its dead. The world has accused Serbia of paranoia, but Handke finds a very different life-world, a nation of orphaned, abandoned children, who follow the beacon of the *Volk* to alleviate their isolation and distress—a psychological state that will condition individuals' political responses for generations. If the Serbian situation is to be alleviated, Europe has to operate against this state of psychological derangement: "To grow up, to do justice to, to not only embody a reaction to the century's night and thus add to the darkening, but to break out of this night" (*Journey* 81). This cultural therapy will not be popular, Handke knows, since it does not correspond with the official political line. He is proposing a human solution rather than a political one, a poetic second childhood for Europe. With this call, Handke reverts to an enlightenment image of Europe, calling on us to remember the experiences of a shared western childhood, rather than the press images that have done everything they could to block any possibility of Serbia's return to normalcy.

After his first meditations from 27 November to 11 December 1995, Handke returns six months later to the former Yugoslavia and updates his essays in the *Summer's Appendix to a Winter's Journey* (*Sommerlicher Nachtrag zu einer winterlichen Reise*). The trip was occasioned by the translation of his earlier essay into Serbian. His new, more official, role does, however, make him nervous, because his *Winterliche Reise* has been misunderstood, that he might have "done something incorrect, wrong, unjust by writing" (*Summer's* 18–19). He has even been confronted by some Serbians who say he has reported details wrong—a raft of "factual corrections" that are imposed on his experience, his story. The people of this Serbia are somehow still trapped in media images. Thus he tries to leave his official role, and to go out into the landscape and experience the things of Serbia rather than its people. The result is an odd, depopulated set of images of Yugoslavia's landscapes, and another level of memory and experience about the country.

Far out in the country, finally, he finds a church, which leads him to meditations about the differences between Islam and Catholicism. And he hears tales told with many tears by Bosnian country people who need us to listen. His trip to the hinterlands is by no means a trip out of history. One may, he believes, still inquire of the Serbs why they committed atrocities and started a new war, having clearly not learned from the region's history. Yet here, again, history can also be a frozen picture, and so to judge the Serbs from that perspective alone would be another kind of foolishness. The West thinks it knows this history of Bosnian oppression since the Turks, but it is wrong. The region's memory is not that of the rest of the West; he has found clear traces of that other history in the back country, away from the Western media, on his road to Belgrade. But any such history must be integrated with current experience. Handke closes on a note of regret that such histories must always be written to emphasize official enemies. Again, he demands that a new history of the region be told, not to vindicate the Serbs, but so that the region's state and its state of mind be brought into some kind of correspondence. In this demand, he shares a map of the Balkans with Habsburg, in that both agree that the region's identity does not correspond with nationalist images, or with what the Western media tries to make of it. Handke also believes in the interconnections between this region and what has traditionally be called Europe, although he refuses to think through the political implications of that connection, preferring instead to emphasize the region's need to reconcile its experience of itself and its history with its present-day course. Yet to ignore the persistence and predominance of political histories imposed from without, as Handke does, is a quixotic gesture, a utopian gesture, that cannot pass without contradiction. To believe that it is possible to retreat behind the media, behind the front lines, and find an untouched land is naïve—and, to Handke's credit, his *Sommerlicher Nachtrag* acknowledges precisely those dashed hopes. Yet he continues to assert the value of witnessing in a way that others do not.

Not surprisingly, Handke's meditations about the limits of media coverage *vis-à-vis* Serbia were received less than salutoriously and taken as -

pro-Serbian or simply naïve. Among the most vociferous reactions was that of Milo Dor, in *Farewell, Yugoslavia* (*Leb Wohl, Jugoslawien*), essays dating from 1990 to 1996. Dor was born of Serbian parents in Budapest, grew up in the Banat and Batschka and Belgrade, and worked in a forced labor camp during the second World War. He thus embodies the map of Europe as a part of the one-time *Vielvölkerstaat* of Central Europe, as he characterized it already in 1977 (*Mitteleuropa* 10–11). Dor's *Mitteleuropa* is, not surprisingly, multi-ethnic and multicultural; it represents a state of being, a shared experience of history and interconnected destinies: "If one travels through the space of the so-called Central Europe, one notices clearly that a certain feeling of belonging together is not only a myth, but a tangible reality whose roots reach far back. Disputes with the one-time Austrian colonial power have receded to the background, so that, finally, one can speak freely and without restraint about relations and commonalties, commonalties that make us into an important connecting member in the association of all European peoples" (*Mitteleuropa* 19).

It is crucial to note that Dor's map of Central Europe still reaches into the heart of Vienna, to the near side of the *Gürtel* (the boulevard circling the city). Dor writes from the heart of old Vienna, from the Eighth District, Josefstadt, named after the Emperor who freed the serfs, a part of Vienna he calls "our urban village" (*Leb Wohl* 7), yet an area with international chic. His apartment superintendent is Serbian, his greengrocer is Greek, an Italian runs the ice cream store. This is the world of Dor's own heritage. His father was born in the Banat before the turn of the century and he knew many of the languages of the monarchy. From this venue, Dor has watched Serbs and Croats playing out an international game of nationalism on the basis of imagined historical slights and utopian national destinies. The historical substance of the Balkans war is, he feels, is less than it is made out to be, not even enough material for a "usable one-act play" (*Leb Wohl* 13). Some arbitrary "national rights" have been made into excuses for national, in a gesture that runs against the trend of Europe. Dor, too, moves into a utopian discourse about Europe, but his image retains full view of the links between imagined nation-states, states of mind, and day-to-day politics: "What, in fact, still remains to us, if we don't simply want to look on helplessly as our vision of a confederation of the free people of Europe, equal before the law, disappears once and for all into the fog of aggressive, self-righteous nationalisms?" (*Leb Wohl* 18).

Dor named his collection after a 1912–1913 popular song "Leb wohl," a link he uses to speak of the region as experiencing a time out of joint. On the one hand, there seems to be an ancient destiny playing itself out in the Balkans, a tragedy of present nationalism that actually functions much like the postwar era's socialism that these states purport to be overcoming. And Dor agrees with Handke that the Western press is in a kind of feeding frenzy over the bones of the region, which is again being termed a prison. Yet Dor underscores the active historical dimension of these conflicts, especially how the real tragedy of the twentieth century, fascism, is still being played out in Yugoslavia, as it has since the Ustascha (*Leb Wohl* 29): "A spectre is haunting Europe. It is not the spectre of communism, with which Marx and Engels tried, 150 years ago, tried to scare and terrify the owners of our continent, but rather the spectre of nationalism, of intolerance, of xenophobia, and of the more or less hidden battle for spheres of influence—in a word, the spectre of fascism which, lightly disguised in pseudo-democratic phrases, has begun to spook around again in European regions" (*Leb Wohl* 26). Dor points to the 1991 PEN declaration about Croatia as exemplary of the West's inadequate historical knowledge of the region. That declaration states simply that nothing justifies the aggression in Croatia or its violation of minority rights. Such statements, in Dor's view, ignore the most dangerous legacy of the West that was imposed on the region, and now needs to be accommodated: nationalism. Like Handke and Habsburg, Dor detests this political "solution" which does not fit the region, at all.

Where Dor diverges from Handke is his willingness to undertake an overt political dissection. Like Habsburg, he knows the absurdities of the region's histories in great detail. He explains, for instance, that 29 June is Serbia's national holiday, commemorating a battle lost to the Turks, the start of national oppression in his country. His own ancestors trekked (his verb) to Austria in the wake of these invasions in 1691. Like Handke, he stresses the psychological fallout of this history in the region, but drawing more overt political consequences, such as recommending that the Serbs take political responsibility for their own situation. Where Handke and Habsburg speak for the region by proxy and lineage, however, Dor speaks as a resident, owner of a summer house in Rovin, in Istria. He has experienced the war directly, as he ended up barricaded on an isthmus in the middle of a battle that ruined his family's summer season. That personal inconvenience is not, however, allowed to take center stage, since Dor has found many more significant casualties of war, such as the Bosnian writer Ivo Andrić, who died in 1972. The region's history is still too palpably linked to the Second World War, he notes as he visits Tito's palace. Neither Austria nor Germany behaved well in the region; neither Serbia nor Croatia is democratic; war crimes on all sides remain active in memory, hidden under the use of the word *Volk*. And today, the West prolongs that agony by acting on nationalistic principles rather than rethinking the region. Serbian deserters from the army, for instance, will be repatriated out of Vienna, without being able to claim asylum rights (*Leb Wohl* 144).

The original 1993 version of *Leb Wohl* ended with an open letter to Rade (Radomir) Marković (former head of Serbian State Security, the secret police organization). The later editions include, first, the letters that were Marković's response and Dor's rejoinder to it. In the latest version, Dor adds an essay, "Sarajewo Must Not Die," in which he calls the war in Serbia a war against the civilian population. Dor, however, confesses his own burnout, his own inability to stem the tide as threats of nationalist revenge rise again: "Nationalism in itself is a spiritual disease that occasionally besets all the residents of a state" (*Leb Wohl* 167). Given the distinct political turn of Dor's work, it is no wonder that he has also added an essay on Handke, who has, in his account, suddenly taken it into his head to "leave his ivory tower" as a "late entry" and enjoin the Yugoslavia situation (*Leb Wohl* 172). Dor thinks Handke's motives were less than pure and authentic, and that Handke was trying to be an *engagé* intellectual like the French philosophers, who take it as their right to judge what they do not know. Handke takes off like Don Quixote, tilting after the windmills of the mass media, and programmatically detesting journalists. Dor suspects Handke, a latecomer, "fighting for imaginary justice" (*Leb Wohl* 173). Dor's Handke simply went to Belgrade and let himself be led around, proving himself "completely devoid of feeling and tact" (*Leb Wohl* 174). More centrally, Handke's Yugoslavia is mythical, since he never even met many in the region working against neofascism, or the "Belgrade Circle" of 100 intellectuals who were trying to do better by the region's history (*Leb Wohl* 174). Handke, in short, misses what is going on as he gives a vision of a Balkans without the homeless and with no refugees. Dor does not believe that a psychological assessment of the region will suffice. Instead, there must be a rectification of the situation, an elimination of the nationalist inheritance from the Second World War and the Cold War. Handke errs fundamentally in assuming that Serbia still exists as a state of mind; Dor prefers to cast the region as part of the legacy of the West, as Habsburg did in his own way. Dor's Europe is, however, considerably less benevolent, less humanist that Habsburg's, although he agrees that the Balkans are, indeed, part of that Europe.

That three writers of very different political stripes and goals choose to share a common map of Europe and its history is a significant index of the public discourse of their part of Europe. Even though they evaluate and use that map differently, they speak in very parallel frameworks to their journalistic publics. Their common judgments about the Balkans, are significant, outside the framework of the North American Treaty Organization (NATO) and the West. They challenge the map of Europe that has been in place for most of the twentieth century.

Just like after the First World War and after the Second World War, the end of the Cold War did not result in a map that includes Central Europe; instead, it formalized tensions that had existed in the region for centuries, especially nationalist sentiments. but instead formalized tensions that had existed in the region for centuries, especially nationalist sentiments. A nationalist map failed in all three of these earlier eras, and so to presume success for them now is merely to prolong the nationalist genocide of the twentieth century in a region that is part of Europe, but which has been carefully cordoned off as not sufficiently European.

Second, the region is part of Europe, by custom, usage, and mutual determination, and has been for the millennium (whether that millennium is the international Christian one, Austria's 1996, or the Hungarian millennium of its Christianization). The Balkans do indeed begin at the *Gürtel* in Vienna—not as Europe's traditional power centers, but as one of those suburbs perpetually determining of European policy and politics. This is also a region whose interests always get spoken for by the European powers. The Greeks would call it a *chora:* an outpost of colonization, nominally under Europe's regency, but never under its control.

Third, the Balkans are the *chora* of Europe in an additional way, that used by Julia Kristeva in her work since *Revolution in Poetic Language:* That is, it is an order, an organized way of life that is shared and which underlies all overt politics of the region. In particular, one has traditionally called the Balkans the place where the order of civilization meets the order of chaos—civilization meets the barbarians. But that designation is political, since who the barbarians are changes in each case. In this way, the Balkans are a *limes*, a defense perimeter against the inhuman, but also a space where Europe's history is challenged by the non-European, the invaders, be they the Turkish empire of yore, Islamic warriors battling Christians, nationalists of the Nazi or Cold War era, or now the media. Recognizing this tie, this strategic territorialization (in Deleuze and Guattari's sense) is a key to European consciousness and self-definition, particularly to the persistent inadequacy of designations like "Central," "Eastern," "East Central," and other "European" sub-entities (see, e.g., Deltcheva; Tötösy).

Historiographically, the Balkans are also the region where national narratives meet and break down as they face the resistance of a landscape that did not nurture nationalist illusions of similarity and national identity, because they have perpetually been multicultural, multilingual, and shifting. In one sense, all three authors use this Balkan-Europe to evoke images of conservative, traditional humanism, but that undervalues the political weight of their image. If one would add a text like Claudio

Magris's *Danubio* to the mix, one would see the region as a different kind of test case: Not, as Karl Kraus called the dying Austro-Hungarian empire, a "proving-ground for world destruction," but rather a region that puts Western identity, Europe's identity, to the test—a region that ought to be taken seriously as the conscience and the unconscious of Europe's identity (a subject *en procés*). This is the region that resists co-optation by too-simple historical narratives, be they heroic, ethnic, nationalist, religious, or economic. In my reading, then, "Austrian" intellectuals after 1989, in their journalistic incarnations, share much in common with "Austrian" diplomats since Metternich: a sense of the region's over-arching history and significant, and a map that has largely resisted being rewritten by the Western narratives of world wars and cold wars. The "Paneuropa Picnic," Habsburg's leak in the barbed wire that was a line in the sand for the Cold War (a psychological barrier and a political one), thus deserves perhaps even more note than the pickaxes taken to the Berlin Wall: that event, like these three sets of meditations on what cannot be called "Central Europe" shows the psychological barriers to a new/old Europe, the real life habits, not the official narratives, that need to be identified and perhaps overcome if a new, more humanitarian (if not humanist) Europe is to exist in the next millennium.

The danger of this vision is its ignoring the Nazi era, Soviet colonialism after its end, and the disregarding of the economic scripts that reinforce particular nationalisms (allowing, for example, Germany to purvey arms into the Balkans as somehow "not us"). Its strength is its ability to keep focus away from the official, largely political histories of the region (which Habsburg outlined so effectively), and away from the more personal narratives denying the region's belonging to other entities (Handke's problem). Instead, this discourse of Balkans-as-Europe offers a new vision of statehood and of European integration that can accommodate difference and not level "the West" to a single state of being. Whatever their individual political agendas, Habsburg and Dor make an integrated vision of politics, economics, and humanity possible. Their Europe has multiple, decentered centers instead of a monolithic West. Despite his arguable shortcomings in dividing art from politics in the seemingly disingenuous way he does here, Handke contributes at least to the deconstruction of the nationalist narratives that Habsburg and Dor try to circumvent, if not to a reconstructed vision of the Balkans. These three very difficult intellectuals are, in short, decisively not Germans or Americans—not reflecting the ego or rhetoric of the dominant powers of the West that have caused trouble for at least a century.

WORKS CITED

Anderson, Benedict. *Imagined Communities: Reflection on the Origin and Spread of Nationalism*. London: Verso, 1991.
Deltcheva, Roumiana. "Comparative Central European Culture: Displacements and Peripheralities." *Comparative Central European Culture*. Ed. Steven Tötösy de Zepetnek. West Lafayette: Purdue UP, 2002. 149–68.
Dor, Milo. *Leb wohl, Jugoslawien. Protokolle eines Zerfalls*. 1993. 3rd ed. Salzburg: Otto Müller, 1996.
Dor, Milo. *Mitteleuropa, Mythos oder Wirklichkeit. Auf der Suche nach der größeren Heimat*. Salzburg: O. Müller, 1996.
Habsburg, Otto von. *Die Paneuropäische Idee. Eine Vision wird Wirklichkeit*. Wien: Amalthea, 1999.
Habsburg, Otto von. *Friedensmacht Europa. Sternstunden und Finsternis*. Wien: Amalthea, 1995.
Habsburg, Otto von. *Mémoires d'Europe. Entretiens*. Paris: Criterion, 1994.
Habsburg, Otto von. *Return to the Center*. Trans. Carvel de Bussy. Riverside: Ariadne P, 1993.
Habsburg, Otto von. *Zurück zur Mitte*. Wien: Amalthea, 1991.
Handke, Peter. *A Journey to the Rivers: Justice for Serbia*. Trans. Scott Abbott. New York: Viking, 1997.
Handke, Peter. *Eine winterliche Reise zu den Flüssen Donau, Save, Morawa und Drina, oder Gerechtigkeit für Serbien*. Frankfurt: Suhrkamp, 1996.
Handke, Peter. *Sommerlicher Nachtrag zu einer winterlichen Reise*. Frankfurt: Suhrkamp, 1996.
Handke, Peter. *Abschied des Träumers vom Neunten Land. Eine Wirklichkeit, die vergangen ist. Erinnerung an Slowenien*. Frankfurt: Suhrkamp, 1991.
Tötösy de Zepetnek, Steven. "Comparative Cultural Studies and the Study of Central European Culture." *Comparative Central European Culture*. Ed. Steven Tötösy de Zepetnek. West Lafayette: Purdue UP, 2002. 1–32.
West, Rebecca. *Black Lamb and Grey Falcon: A Journey through Yugoslavia*. 1940. New York: Penguin, 1982.

Comparative Central European Culture: Austrian and Hungarian Cinema Today

Catherine Portuges

More than a decade has passed since the fall of the Berlin Wall, offering a timely moment to reflect on the changes wrought by the post-communist transition in Central European cinema. Alongside radical transformations arising from the privatization of film studios and funding structures for co-productions taking place in the European market are thematic concerns in current cinema that revisit aspects of Habsburg history, particularly the inscriptions of nation, gender, and generation. In the post-transition era, the cultures of cinema in the region have been proportionately—yet individually—affected in fundamental ways by the seismic upheavals of the past decade. Within the framework of socialism, these cinemas played a vital role in international visual culture; at present, some may experience and express nostalgia for the former regimes that enabled filmmakers to depend upon regular production through a planned economy, in contrast with the uncertainties of the 1990s which have seen the emergence of new, often fragile, structures through privatization and globalization. For in the absence of state socialism and its neo-Stalinist variants, it was feared that Central and East European world of cinema would lose its much-vaunted critical prowess, its distinctive esthetic modes of ironic and allegorical expression, and hence its role as a site of interest to the international film community.

However, these concerns soon proved to have been a catalyst for innovative film production in highly original works whose subject is often the vicissitudes of the transition itself. Dramatically insistent, engaging questions of national identity within the framework of trans-national and global cinema, these films confront such contemporary subjects as the resurgence of ethnic nationalism; the re-emergence of communism as a potent political force; the debate over struggles to establish "civil society" and market economy in the face of authoritarian resistance and criminal opportunism; the eruption of interethnic warfare in the former Yugoslavia and the former Soviet Union; and the social unrest and despair that arise from widespread economic dislocation, suffering and alienation. These and other developments are increasingly the focus of a growing number of internationally acclaimed films from the region that at once critique and interpret their national cultures in cinematic texts of startling originality, post-modern film language, and symbolically transformative cinematic expression (see Portuges 2001; see also Deltcheva).

The re-making of identity is considered in relation to this changing visual, political and psychological landscape in tendencies evident in the restoration, conservation and destruction of socialist entities. It should be noted that by "transition" I mean to suggest the moment of passage from euphoria to disillusionment, and its accompanying rhetorical shift from "East" to "Central" Europe. For such a term is inevitably fraught with contradiction: a musical metaphor, for instance, might articulate "transition" as suggestive of modulation from one key to another. Here, I invoke it not as a masking strategy nor, for that matter, an evasion of responsibility for taking a stance (as was sometimes the case in the early 1990s disparaging term "transitology"), but rather in its most dynamic sense: that is, as a focus on the epic events of this epoch, now a part of history—on the relationships between past and present as represented cinematographically, from the vantage point of over ten years after the fall of the Berlin Wall.

The upheavals of the past decade have fostered a reconsideration of urban space, communist history and politics, as well as minority, ethnic, and gender identities within broader cultural and social contexts represented in contemporary film and video, including fiction, experimental, documentary, and avant-garde forms. In the context of Steven Tötösy's comparative cultural studies as applied to the study of Central European culture, the present paper offers a comparative perspective on selected works from the region that foreground these transitional phenomena situated in the contemporary landscape of a globalized film economy, with its concomitant border crossings, migrations, intergenerational reconfigurations and millennial echoes. By brief descriptions of selected recent films from Austria and Hungary—premiered at the 24th Toronto International Festival (September 1999), each of which invokes the passing century within its own perspective, I hope to suggest a number of theoretical concerns represented in cinematic practice from the region during the post-communist transition. In the past year alone, Austrian filmmaking has experienced exceptional vitality: the most prestigious festivals—Cannes, Berlin, Rotterdam, and Le Cinema du Réel in Paris— have put the spotlight on a number of new films, enabling them to gain international recognition. For instance *Nordrand,* by the promising director Barbara Albert and a European community co-production among Austria, Switzerland, and Germany, had its world premiere in Venice in August 1999, as the only German-language film selected for the competition program. Two other Austrian co-productions also appeared in that festival, *Luna Papa,* by the Tajik-born Bakhtiar Khudojnazarov, with an Austrian production company as majority producer and Robert Dornheim's *The Venice Project.* From there, *Nordrand* and *Luna Papa* traveled directly to Toronto in September 1999, the most important festival in the North American market. Also premiering in Toronto were Austrian Diego Donnhjofer's *The Virgin* and *Pripyat,* a film by Austria's foremost documentarian, Nikolaus Geyrhalter, completed in January 1999 and scheduled for screening later that year at the New York Film Festival.

An important aspect of the recent interest in and successes of films by Central and East European film makers is a lacking historical perspective in North American filmography. Indeed, it should be noted that a significant portion of Hollywood and European cinema history rests on the talents of Austrians and Hungarians (see Portuges 1996–1997). Marking the recent centennial anniversary of the invention of the motion picture, it seems especially fitting to invoke the horizons of cinema beyond the influence of Hollywood—beyond, as well as within, separate national borders. From the era of its earliest pioneers to that of its most recent post-communist émigrés, the culture of Hollywood has tended to characterize its product as an un-equivocally and un-problematically "American" phenomenon. The 1886 arrival in New York of the French cameraman Félix Mesguich, for example, dispatched from Paris to demonstrate the brand-new Lumière Cinematograph, prompted some to insist that cinema may have been born French, only to grow up American (see Boujut 7). As national rhetorics competed to claim the movies for their own in this anniversary year, and in spite of its all-too-real status as commodity and industry, the realm of cinema remains in some sense an "imagined community," defined by artists whose cultural diversity traverses geography and language, production and performance, spectatorship and reception. Constructed variously as national allegory, colonizing oppressor of difference, or glamorous dream factory, its gaze is said to be located perpetually in the present, even the present of history: like that of the traveler, the filmgoer's world may be read as a deterritorialized zone that at once invites and refuses the impulse toward temporal or spatial grounding. Instead, akin to childhood memory, cinema's very un-attainability lies beyond reach, fleeting when grasped, as the first spectators of the Lumière brothers' home movies discovered when they sought to enter or flee the physical reality of the screen itself (see Portuges 1997).

This elusive transnationality, this counter-hegemonic spirit in fact resists the stamp of any single nation, group, style, or movement. Yet, as international celebrations of cinema's first century drew to a close, the extraordinary contributions of its Central and East European artists remained largely hidden from view, and, with notable exceptions, absent from its many histories. They are, it seems to me, nonetheless worthy of renewed attention, perhaps all the more so today when global film industries compete for dominance at the expense of so-called "minor cinemas." Prior to the international acclaim accorded *Nordrand,* her first feature, a director of award-winning short subjects, Barbara Albert, has enjoyed international recognition from the start of her career at the Saarbrücken festival in 1994, in Locarno in 1997, and in Rotterdam in 1999. *Slidin'— Alles bunt und wunderbar,* an episodic milieu study narrated through snapshots from the everyday lives of two friends, credits the director as screenwriter of the first of three segments, while *Nachtschwalben* won the 1994 Max Opuls Prize. The latter film was followed by a 27-minute investigation of the fantasies of a nine-year-old girl in *Die Frucht deines Leibes,* a film that earned an invitation to Venice and a Leopard of Tomorrow prize at the Locarno Film Festival.

Nordrand is the story of five young people from different social and ethnic backgrounds who meet in Vienna in 1995, seeking a measure of hope and stability in their otherwise dislocated lives. Under the strain of seemingly perpetual migration, exile, war and exclusion, these young refugees from areas of the former Yugoslavia have, in a sense, become victims of circumstance: Tamara, Jasmin, Valentin, Senad, and Roman live near the northern border of Austria, their lives repeatedly intersecting and drifting apart. The Austrian Jasmin and the Serb Tamara both face unwanted pregnancies; meeting at an abortion clinic they endure their traumatic experience together and then part ways. Valentin, a Romanian who dreams of going to America meets Tamara by chance in a bus station café. Senad, a Bosnian Muslim refugee, stumbles across Jasmin on the frozen banks of the Danube, unconscious after a drunken binge, while Tamara and her lover Roman experience an increasingly tumultuous, volatile, and intermittent relationship. It is worth noting that within the past decade, a number of important films have been produced within wartime conditions in and about Bosnia, most under the most difficult imaginable circumstances. Many seek to foreground the experiences of ordinary people caught in the fray; among them, several have emerged to succeed in international competition, and have obtained limited distribution with the support of co-producers. They succeed, often admirably, in providing a historical framework as a backdrop to the nightmare conditions of the Bosnian war, while at the same time representing vibrant characters of uncontestable humanity. In so doing, they manage to create artistically viable, challenging, yet beautifully produced films that invite the audience to move beyond conventional Western attitudes of incomprehension or helplessness with regard to the tragic events they portray (see also Deltcheva; Portuges 1999).

Emotional uncertainties, fear of the unknown and an inevitable loss of purpose in their inhospitable, temporary environment create conditions of friendship, exploitation and conflict, contextualized by identities rendered problematic by their status as exiles, emigrés, sojourners and refugees, and shared by those in similar situations throughout the New Europe. A network of intimacy based on mutual attraction and adversity catapults them into existential circumstances in which the primary topic of discussion is persistent anxiety and ambivalence about the future; frequently framed by Albert's unsentimental camera angles as desolate, isolated figures from what not long ago was known as the "other Europe," strolling with a deceptively casual demeanor through the cafés and train stations of this multicultural landscape, their discourse is marked by a subtext of constant longing for a better job, a visa to a another country or a dream of return from exile. The prospect of short-term affection or a passing sexual encounter seems to motivate their actions as they collectively and individually repress the lacerating impact of war and alienation, seeking moral force and community together in an indifferent, if not openly hostile, environment. The protagonists, all in their early twenties, confront wrenching life decisions without family support, some, for that matter, in the face of emotional and physical abuse. "The important thing for me," says the director, "is . . . the loss of childhood" (Press Conference, Toronto International Film Festival, September 1999).

The mélange of ethnic cultures and linguistic identities reflects the increasingly multicultural character of Vienna where they live—and, indeed, the situation is not much different in Budapest or Prague—providing a dynamic interrogation of those who support crypto-fascist suspicions of foreigners. And shortly after the premiere of *Nordrand* Jörg Haider's Freedom Party had mounted posters around the capital in the weeks preceding the Austrian national elections, promising to put a stop to "over-foreignization" and "misuse of asylum," both phrases widely understood as code words promoting a cessation of immigration (see "Anti-Immigrant"). Haider's argument rests on the perception and reality of a country where native citizens fear the increase of low-wage earners, criminals, and others considered to be undesirables from Eastern Europe and the Balkans. Today, Vienna encompasses some 200,000 from the various regions of former Yugoslavia in a city of 1.7 million inhabitants, most of whom arrived during the 1970s and thus by now giving rise to a large second-generation community. While in more recent migrations, Austria accepted a substantial number of refugees during the war in Bosnia, many of whom have since returned or have been deported to their former republics, an ethnically diverse population from Eastern Europe, Turkey, and the Middle East is inevitably a significant element of the picture: "I find it strange that there are so few Austrian films with foreigners as protagonists," suggested Albert at the press conference of the Toronto festival. Her own film features a number of languages spoken by the protagonists on camera, from Tamara's Serbian conversations with her family to Valentin's dialogue in Romanian and Senad's in Bosnian. The actress Edita Malovcic, who plays Tamara, was born in Austria of a Serbian mother and a Bosnian father and the actor who plays Senad from Bosnia is an ethnic Albanian Kosovar. The Kosovo conflict in fact coincided with the post-production process of *Nordrand;* NATO bombing began just after shooting was terminated and was suspended the day after editing was completed. Synchronization was accomplished on the first day of bombing, with most of the cast present. One senses the portentousness of these events in the film's culminating scene on New Year's Eve, as the protagonists both experience and momentarily transcend interethnic, class, and political conflicts, embodied by an embrace between the Serb Tamara and the Bosnian Muslim Senad.

"It is a sad ending," says Albert, "as the protagonists split up, accepting the fact that they will go their own ways in opposite directions, leaving youth behind. . . . Yet no matter how bad things are for her at home, there is something very much alive about Jasmin's family," she adds, a comment that would seem to elide references to Jasmin's father's sexual abuse of her younger sister, an abuse countenanced by their mother's silent complicity, all of which take place in the family's bleak apartment in one of the immense concrete blocks on the outskirts of Vienna's urban core (Press Conference, Toronto International Film Festival, September 1999). The title *Nordrand,* in English "Northern Edge," the "wrong side of the tracks" of working-class neighborhoods, evokes a particular meaning for the director of the film, for in addition to its association with a marginalized society, she has a personal connection to a similar apartment complex on the northern edge of the city in the working-class 21st district of Vienna on the "other side" of the Danube, where she grew up: "A family where all the kids were either in prison or beaten regularly by their father—that was my neighborhood. But I liked growing up there because it allowed me to feel a proximity to real life . . . everyone always knew what was going on . . . the 1970s were very exciting in these new housing projects . . . there was an atmosphere of approaching a happier future, which had to do with the political situation during those years, when the socialists under Bruno Kreisky were very strong. . . . But in the late 1970s and early 1980s, crime and drugs rose considerably in the neighborhood. And now teenagers from those times live in those apartment blocks with their families" (Press Conference, Toronto International Film Festival, September 1999). In many ways, *Nordrand* also evokes the wintry, desolate landscape of the Albert's narrative and its accompanying search for refuge from the cold—psychologically, culturally, politically, economically. Yet in another sense the North becomes at once destination and object of desire for Albert's characters from Southeastern Europe, as Vienna is, obviously, farther North than West for them; North may be read as a point on a compass, recalling the obsession with the West depicted in many Central European films of the early 1990s.

"The main themes are place, origin, countries, and homeland," states Albert, "and I'm quite fond of the North. . . . For me, the 1990s have been a time of major political change in Eastern Europe, of people from those countries coming to the West to try their luck. Also a time of the war in ex-Yugoslavia, and of the expansion of right-wing parties, but also a time of clubbing, parades and fun, when one seemed freer than before. . . . The borders seemed to allow more movement than before" (Press Conference, Toronto International Film Festival, September 1999). Albert's focus intersects with that of many other young European film makers in their concerns for portraying contemporary youth, immigration, and border crossings in an urban framework, a preoccupation exemplified in film such as the award-winning Hungarian director Ibolya Fekete's *Bolshe Vita* (Hungary 1995), based on documentary footage of the period immediately following the fall of the wall. In the film's opening sequence set in Vladivostok, migrants from Russia and former Yugoslavia wonder "where does the West begin?" (see, in particular, Roumiana Deltcheva's discussion of the metaphor of travel and the road as a theme in Central and East European cinema; see also Portuges 1997).

A specific Central European issue, that of the environment, is Nikolaus Geyrhalter's *Pripyat* (Austria 1999). The film is set in an ominously abandoned apartment complex, a soccer field suffocated by gnarled weeds, and abounds in references to "strontium levels" and "gamma-spectrometric primary analysis," which might otherwise suggest a science fiction film (see "Press Note"). But this lost world, a "zone of alienation," in the words of a local official, does indeed exist: a poisoned province extending from the Chernobyl nuclear power plant in Eastern Ukraine deep into Belarus. Prior to 1986, the settlement of Pripyat, five kilometers from Chernobyl, had a population of 50,000. Thirteen years after the disaster, only 15,000 live or work there. Focusing on the lives of those who have returned to their hometown, Geyrhalter offers a document and a passionate and humane perspective on current debates about nuclear energy, ecology, and the environment. In 1997, the young director responded to the confusion of information about the Balkan war with his own observations made over the course of four seasons in *The Year after Dayton*. While shooting *Pripyat,* he spent twelve weeks in the restricted area surrounding the Chernobyl nuclear power station, creating an even-handed portrayal of everyday life after the accident. The administrative term for its residents—"autonomous returnees"—is only one of many indications that *Pripyat's* vacancy rate will remain high for a century or so. Preparing a meal of fish from the contaminated river, an elderly man winks as he offers an appetizer of mushrooms and then qualifies the suggestion: mushrooms, the Ministry of Disaster Relief has warned, are basically radiation sponges. Still, a few should be okay, he surmises. While the locals appear to shrug off the dire consequences of these living conditions, it is painfully clear that their pragmatism, like the protective black sarcophagus over Chernobyl's fatal Unit 4 reactor, is a strategy of survival. Participants in a cruel, negligent experiment, both workers and residents remain largely uninformed about the long-term effects of radiation. Monitoring and containment efforts seem to remain at a token level, with defeated scientists acknowledging that many questions remain, but few answers. The barbed-wire fences that enclose the "zone" do little if anything to remove the threat to local populations. Derived from the Russian word for "five," Pripyat is the nexus for five rivers (recalling the five estuaries of the Ota river of Hiroshima as portrayed in Alain Resnais' 1959 film *Hiroshima mon amour,* originally conceptualized as an anti-atomic bomb documentary) and a vast network of marshlands. A long food chain, combined with the vagrancy of wind and precipitation patterns, have extended the danger of radiation poisoning across space and time. Filmed in black and white, *Pripyat* is an eloquent, poignant exposé of the irreparable damage instigated by reckless technological progress while it is also a powerful millennial statement. Geyrhalter's next project, his most ambitious to date, in fact focuses on the millennium. *Anderswo. Fernab des Millenniums (Elsewhere: Far from the Millennium)* documents a year-long search for human communities with perceptions of time far removed from that of the Gregorian calendar—people, according to the director, "living on the edge of globalization, on the brink of extinction, documenting ways of life that will not survive the new millennium in their present form" ("Real to Reel" 9).

Turning next to recent filmmaking in Hungary, István Szabó, one of the leading directors of the post-war generation of both Hungarian and international film makers, has won throughout his prolific career over sixty major international awards, including an Academy Award for Best Foreign Film for *Mephisto* (1981), directing, among other distinguished films, *Father* (1966), *Love Film* (1970), *Confidence* (1979), *Colonel Redl* (1985), *Hanussen* (1988), *Meeting Venus* (1991), and *Offenbach's Secret* (1996). His most recent production, *Sunshine,* is a millennial work of sweeping ambition and creativity, an epic chronicle of the fortunes of three generations of the Sonnenschein family, set against the shifting backdrop of Central Europe throughout the twentieth century. The story of this family of Hungarian Jews whose fate is inevitably linked with Central Europe and the Habsburg monarchy, revolutions, the Holocaust, and totalitarian regimes, is elegantly told by the narrator, Iván Sonnenschein, the last surviving member of the dynasty. The narrative begins with Iván's great-grandfather, Manó, the son of a publican who leaves his village at the age of twelve to make his fortune in the city, carrying in his pocket a book of recipes inherited from his father containing the secret ingredients of an herbal liqueur. The drink he manufactures, a "taste of Sunshine" (*Sonnenschein* in German and the surname of the family, and *a napfény íze* in Hungarian) becomes widely popular and provides a stable foundation for the family's wealth and gradual elevation into the upper bourgeoisie, financially as well as culturally. Manó's son, Ignác, comes of age in the Austro-Hungarian empire and enjoys a brilliant career as a lawyer and judge in emperor Franz Joseph's liberal monarchy. Ignác balances his professional responsibilities with his love for his first cousin, Valéria, whom he eventually marries and they have two sons, István and Ádám (Ralph Fiennes plays the role of the first son in each generation). In the film, the family's history is played out in the patriarchal line with the grandfather, Ignác (a pragmatic lawyer), the father Ádám (the champion fencer), and the son Iván, with whom the story ends. Each is faced with a complex set of crises that threaten to betray the promise of the family name and bring about the loss of the Sonnenscheins' rich heritage, both cultural and financial. Ádám becomes a world-class fencer who represents his country during the 1936 Olympics in Munich but his triumph there carries little weight when anti-Semitic policies are introduced in Hungary and culminating in the occupation of Hungary by Germany in 1944. Ádám's victory as a "Christian" olympic gold medalist—Ádám had converted to the country's dominant religion to further his fencing career—is stirring, while his shocking fate—captured by the Hungarian Nazis, the Arrow Cross militia and subsequent murder in Auschwitz while defending his "Hungarian" honor—leaves the viewer caught in history's arc of nightmares. Ádám's son, Iván, survives the death camps and makes his own career in Stalinist Hungary, only to become part of the generation forced to come to terms with the nation's postwar communist legacy (for a recent analysis of the film, see also Suleiman).

Screened at the 1999 24th Toronto International Film Festival and the 2000 31st Hungarian Film Week in Budapest, *Sunshine* has garnered both criticism and acclaim, including awards from the European Film Academy (for best screenplay, cinematographer, and actor), the Academy of Canadian Cinema and Television (for best motion picture and achievement in sound editing), and the Foreign Critics' Gene Moskowitz Prize for best film screened at the Budapest festival in February 2000. Szabó is perhaps most renowned for his cinematic meditations on Central Europe and its Habsburg history, with *Mephisto* (1981) and *Colonel Redl* (1985), both of which investigate the relationship between morality and power in the specific context of Central European culture, history, and society. He co-wrote the screenplay of *Sunshine* with American screenwriter Israel Horowitz. *Sunshine* tells the story of a Jewish-Hungarian family, the Sonnenscheins, in several generations and recounts how they are compelled to assimilate, to change their religion, and to change their surname from the German Sonnenschein (Sunshine) to the Hungarian Sors (Fate) in order to rise in Hungarian society. According to Szabó, the story of the Sonnenscheins "is not simply a question of ethnicity or race. From mobility among the various strata of society in recent Hungarian life to the waves of economic and political emigration in Europe today, people must face the challenge of surrendering the self or deliberately demonstrating their identity" (Press Conference, 31st Hungarian Film Week, Budapest, February 1999).

What makes *Sunshine* a powerful epochal experience is the intimacy of the stories and the vitality of the personalities explored. Szabó and his international cast transport us back through the events that shaped the past century as members of this Jewish family experiences both success and catastrophes. Yet this moving historical account never loses sight of the personal details that shape the legacy of an intergenerational family, transforming the tragedy of twentieth-century Jewry into a work of redemptive power. Visually beautiful, historic Budapest locations appear throughout the film, in sequences shot in the state opera house, grand museums built in the nineteenth century, the synagogue in Dohány Street, the parliament, the grand *Nyugati* railway station, etc.

As exemplified in the films briefly and broadly discussed here, over the past decade after the demise of the communist era, Central and East European film makers have demonstrated in documentary and fiction film making an engagement with social, historical, and personal terrain denied, avoided, or suppressed over the course of two previous generations. Among Central and East European cinemas, in Hungary the discourses of younger film makers such as Attila Jánisch, János Szász, Péter Forgács, Ibolya Fekete, and Péter Tímár are of note while in Austria the experimental group "Six-Pack," working in both fiction and non-fiction, go far to translate the vicissitudes of this post-communist, pre-millennial moment. Their evaluation of Hungary's and Austria's post-war past, and their respective relationships to the former Soviet Union or the former Yugoslavia; reconsideration of each nation's responsibilities for and experience of the Holocaust; and their reassessments of their distinct national destinies increasingly intermingled "European" cinemas and raise further questions with regard to style, film language, and audience. The privatization of film studios, the altered climate of production, and the consequences of new media technologies are inscribing new horizons for the third millennium and beyond. For just as the nations of Central Europe must face the challenges of globalization and confront the re-making of identity within and beyond their borders, so, too must those of us who work within the parameters of the arts and culture interrogate the reconfigured meanings of national cinema and the politics of co-production. These and many other post-communist films from the region gesture symbolically against recruiting the idea of Central Europe into a politics of exclusion.

WORKS CITED

Albert, Barbara, dir. *Nordrand*. Color, 103 min. Prod. Erich Lackner. Wien: Zero Film, Berlin: Fama Film, Bern: Lotus Film, 1999.
"Anti-Immigrant Rightists Gain in Austrian Province." *New York Times* (20 September 1999): A8.
Boujut, Michel. *Le Cinéma retrouvé*. Paris: Adam Biro-France-Culture, 1994.
Deltcheva, Roumiana. "Comparative Central European Culture: Displacements and Peripheralities." *Comparative Central European Culture*. Ed. Steven Tötösy de Zepetnek. West Lafayette: Purdue UP, 2002. 149–68.
Geyrhalter, Nikolaus, dir. *Pripyat*. Black and white, 100 min. Wien: Nikolaus Geyrhalter Filmproduktion, 1999.
Portuges, Catherine. "Memory, Nostalgia, and Mourning in Post-Socialist Hungarian Cinema." *Cinemas in Transition: Post-Communist Cinema in East Central Europe*. Ed. Catherine Portuges and Daniel Goulding. London: Flick Books, forthcoming.
Portuges, Catherine. "Recent Balkan Cinema." *American Historical Review* 104.2 (1999): 693–94.
Portuges, Catherine. "Jewish Identity in Post-Communist Hungarian Cinema." *Assaph-Studies in the Cinema and Visual Arts* 1.1 (1998): 83–101.
Portuges, Catherine. "Border Crossings: *Bolshe Vita*. A Review Essay." *American Historical Review* 102.3 (1997): 939–40.
Portuges, Catherine. "Hungarians in Hollywood." *Post-Communist Cinema*. Thematic Issue of *Film Criticism* 21.2 (1996–97): 50–59.
Portuges, Catherine. "Between Worlds: Re-Placing Hungarian Cinema." *Before the Wall Came Down: Soviet and East European Film Makers Working in the West*. Ed. Graham Petrie and Ruth Dwyer. New York: UP of America, 1990. 63–70.
"Press Note: *Pripyat*." *AustriaKultur Newsletter* 11.2 (2000): no pag.
"Real to Reel: Niki Geyrhalter." *Austrian Film International News* 2 (1999): 9–11.

Suleiman, Susan Rubin. "Central Europe, Jewish Family History, and *Sunshine.*" *Comparative Central European Culture.* Ed. Steven Tötösy de Zepetnek. West Lafayette: Purdue UP, 2002. 169-88.

Szabó, István, dir. *Sunshine.* Color, 180 min. Prod. Robert Lantos and András Hámori. Toronto: Alliance Atlantic Pictures, 1999.

Tötösy de Zepetnek, Steven. "Comparative Cultural Studies and the Study of Central European Culture." *Comparative Central European Culture.* Ed. Steven Tötösy de Zepetnek. West Lafayette: Purdue UP, 2002. 1-32.

Comparative Central European Culture: Displacements and Peripheralities

Roumiana Deltcheva

A decade after the collapse of the Soviet empire, the cultural discourse of Central and East Europe continues to be permeated by one dominant metaphor of intent, namely the road to Europe. In spite of the differentiation of manifestations the symbol has undergone in the past ten years, the semantic scope encompasses a common perception of peripherality, marginality, isolation, outsidedness. Geographically within Europe, yet culturally excluded from it, the countries of Central and East Europe are still in a process of defining their identity based on a double binary opposition: by consciously differentiating themselves from the former center of Soviet political power, and equally strongly attempting to integrate themselves within the Western center of cultural legitimization. The West continues to be perceived as a homogeneous unity with impermeable, or at best semi-permeable, borders. The paradigm is further complicated by the intrusiveness of powerful American cultural domination which has de facto subsumed the earlier mythology of Western Europeanness. Here, I discuss some changes that the metaphor of the road with its underlying premises of exile and return has undergone in Central and East European film.

In the period prior to the 1989 changes the dominant discourse of the region was already, both politically and culturally, subordinated to a metaphor of movement. At that time, however, the movement was effected along the axiologically determined vertical axis. The ultimate representation of the concept found its most clear expression in the five-year plan as the basic ideological-temporal unit governing all aspects of socialist society—economy, politics, sports, culture, etc. On paper the five-year plans were always over-accomplished, thus narrowing the distance and time to the utopian ideal. The vertical orientation of the movement led to the perfection of a specific epic discourse, devoid of grounding in reality, in which the present was displaced not by a frozen past but, rather, by a hypothetical future (see Deltcheva 1997). Yet, in the 1980s, within the cultural and ideological space of the region, the possibility of horizontal movement—by definition subdued and allegorically disguised—received a direct, if predominantly formal, sanctioning directly by the communist center of ideology in Mikhail Gorbachev's formulation of a "common European home" (*obshchii evropeiskii dom*). Thus, *perestroika* should be understood an important factor that already in the 1980s presets the conditions in the various reorientations of the subsequent decade, following the demise of the Soviet empire. In the post-1989 period, the vertical, ideologically charged axis is entirely obliterated by a horizontal axis, primarily determined by spatial markers, border crossings, and the paradoxical erection of a new "Iron Curtain," far more impermeable than the old one, namely the Schengen Agreement (see Daskalovski). In other words, the ahistorical symbolism of "high"-"above"-"better" has been simplified into a concrete spatio-temporal metaphor of travel, the geographically determined "road to Europe." Traditionally, external traveling is implicitly connected with inner growth. Be it the picaresque novel and the Bildungsroman, the "road movie," or the "return of the prodigal son" motif in painting, the road always symbolizes life: it is on the road that the protagonists learn about themselves and come to terms with the surrounding world in the process (see also Portuges). Consequently, the topic is adjacent to the theme of exile and its implications on identity formation, especially in the framework of post-colonial studies.

In this context, I approach the Central and East European situation in the post–Cold War period from the angle of (post)colonial studies and systems theory as developed by Steven Tötösy (see 1995–2002). Tötösy postulates that owing to its geographical location and historical developments, Central and East Europe can be viewed as a periphery of two sides. On the one hand, the West as a traditional cultural center has unavoidably a exerted strong influence on the East. On the other hand, there is a second center of power which acts from the East, i.e., the former Soviet Union through the mechanism of a "filtered" colonialism, that is, the cultural leverage of the former USSR is not primary but of the second order, "through ideological, political, social, cultural, and other means" (Tötösy 1998, 131). The paradigm is further complicated by the fact that the cultural influence of the West is not a post–Cold War development only but has been on going for centuries with particular impetus since the nineteenth century. Moreover, the conscious attempt on the part of Central and East Europe to emulate the West is not viewed as colonialism but as a process of integration, "the way to Europe." Tötösy calls this peculiar geo-political and cultural disposition of Central and East Europe "in-between peripherality," a specific and mediating *altérité*. It can be argued, then, that in-between peripherality is a theoretically viable framework that can be used to integrate Central and East Europe into the domain of Western critical thought and comparative cultural studies (for the concept of "comparative cultural studies," see Tötösy 2002. Furthermore, the very permeability of Tötösy's concept—grounded in a cross-cultural, multidisciplinary, and systemic and empirical methodology—allows for its expansion and/or readjustment as the region progresses in its painful transitional period. In its situation of in-between peripherality Central and East Europe oscillates between two centers of power and the centripetal forces they emanate. Thus, the road metaphor I propose acquires two distinct manifestations with respect to each center: An overtly geographical spatial parameter to the West and an internal, ideologically marked attitude toward Russia and this is particularly the case with regard to Bulgaria, for obvious historical reasons.

It is not my intention here to homogenize the concept or disregard specific peculiarities of the collective national psychologies of the respective countries belonging to Central and East Europe. At the same time, I believe that there is some justification in maintaining that there are some aspects that construct a common Central and Central European identity. I propose that this is, in the Western cultural milieu, manifested via the mediation of the road. The dialogue with Russia, albeit present, is more subdued and less visible. It can be expected to develop as the next stage in identity construction, once more time has elapsed and allowed for a less emotionally charged reevaluation of the years of political, economic, and cultural colonialism. That is why, the focus of this discussion is primarily oriented towards the East-West horizontal axis and the implications of geographical nomadism on identity construction. In that sense, the function of geographical setting transcends the decorative and should be viewed as a crucial parameter in identity construction. Moreover, after years of not only economic, but even more so spatial stagnation, the transgression of borders can be postulated as one of the fundamental elements of the emerging post-communist identity of Central and East Europe. Already in the late 1980s and especially in the first years after the fall of totalitarianism, the dominant gesture that accompanied the dramatic socio-political changes in the region was that of an exodus of vast proportion. Everyone was on the road—Poles, Czechs, Serbs, Croats, Bulgarians, Romanians, Hungarians, Albanians—all in pursuit of prosperity, "normality," and the American dream. For example, according to unofficial information in the Bulgarian press, about one million young, highly educated Bulgarians left the country after 1989. For comparison, the entire population of Bulgaria was around nine million after the last census.

These tendencies were reflected both in the political discourse and the cultural production of the region. The trend was exacerbated even further after the fall of the Berlin Wall—the last symbol of forced immobility. Suddenly, Central and East Europe was on a mission to join Europe, as soon and as quickly as possible. Politically, this was accompanied by a frenzied strife towards joining international and European structures, such as the Council of Europe, the European Union, NATO. Economically, national currencies gave way to the Deutschmark and the American dollar, while Central and East Europeans *en masse* became used cars salespeople suddenly boosting another Central European locus, Austria and in this case its auto retail industry. The implications for culture were even more drastic: with the disappearance of the Iron Curtain and state funding for the arts, after years of semi-clandestine existence American popular culture surfaced with a vengeance. The urban landscape of the Slavic countries using Cyrillic script, for instance, provided the opportunity for free English instruction for all. The Bulgarian newspaper *Kultura*, for instance, had an on going debate in 1998 regarding the advantages and viability of switching to the Latin script given the advent of technological revolution and the sweeping effects of the Internet in all domains of life.

Paradoxically, these processes were accompanied a counter directed tendency expressed in "the resurgence of nationalism and conflicting self-determination claims" (Miller and Bayard vii). The events in the former Soviet republics, Yugoslavia, and Czechoslovakia infused the cartographer profession with a fresh breath of life and the reshuffling of the *status quo* is far from over. From this vantage point, the slogans of internationalism, tolerance, and cooperation that defined the now defunct Council for Mutual Economic Assistance (COMECON) have become the big joke in the modern history of the East Central European countries. In the course of the 1990s, the default state of homogenized political, social, and economic indeterminacy of Central and East Europe, often verging on chaos, underwent subtle changes. In fact, the adoption of designations such as "Central Europe," Central and East Europe," or "East Central Europe" as an alternative appellation to the earlier dominant "Eastern Europe" or "Eastern Bloc" is indicative of the newly acquired fluidity of the region. The change in nomenclature suggests a paradigmatic shift in the intra-regional configurations where the earlier homogeneity established by a common denominator in the political system is being substituted by clear economic, as well as cultural, differentiation. Thus, to some degree, East and Central are no longer automatically interchangeable, despite such homogenizing tendencies from the perspective of North American scholarship. As a result in part to historical development, in part to West European double-standard politics, "Central" (Poland, The Czech Republic, Slovakia, Slovenia, Hungary) has gradually attained positive valorization, thus drawing closer to the Western center of ideological power, while "East" and "Eastern" (Bulgaria, Romania, Serbia, Croatia, Ukraine, Albania) continues to be entrenched in an unambiguously marginal position (see also Deltcheva 1999).

In their introduction to a *Canadian Slavonic Papers* special issue devoted the problems of nationalism and self-determination in the multicultural societies of East Central Europe, the guest editors—Stefania Szelek Miller and Caroline Bayard—implicitly reinforce such an axiological assessment by comparing the nationalistic tendencies in former Yugoslavia and Czechoslovakia, respectively: "The gross abuses of human rights in the disintegration of the former Yugoslavia demonstrate the problems of secession in multi-ethnic states as well as the unpreparedness of the international community in its response. The process of separation in Czechoslovakia and the subsequent agreements between the Czech Republic and Slovakia, on the other hand, indicate that conflicting claims can be resolved in a peaceful manner" (vii). The binarism adopted by the Miller and Bayard and illustrating a broader intellectual tendency, while indicative of some trends insofar as the development of the various countries in the region are concerned, also suggests a divergence in experience that eventually could lead to further nationalistic confrontation. This situation is reflected in the already tangible syndrome of Central and East European countries—in their fast-track attempt to wipe out the past—to construct new mythologies of uniqueness and exclusivity.

Instead of automatically discarding shared past experience, I employ, as previously mentioned, the theoretical notions embedded in comparative cultural studies, an approach intended to pluralize and paralellize the study of culture without hierarchization (Tötösy 2002). Thus, in addition to the advantages of theory and method Tötösy's framework offers, it entails also an ideological dimension I agree with. In my analysis here, I focus on cinematic texts produced by directors of the said region in the last two decades while the most recent films I refer to were shown at the Montréal World Film Festival, 27 August to 6 September 1999.

Despite the drastic fall in the cinematic production of the region after the dismantling of the complex machinery of socialist state funding for the arts (see Portuges), the films that have appeared during these years clearly reflect the turbulence of the times. Moreover, there is an uncanny similarity in perception across Central and East European countries thus referring us to the notion of variable similarities in the cultures of the region (see also Tötösy 2002). As I state in the beginning, the metaphor of the road appears to be one such ubiquitous constant. Its realization, however, has undergone an interesting transformation. In the years prior to and immediately after the demise of communism, the image of the road is unambiguously unidirectional: away from the oppressive atmosphere of Central and East Europe. In the 1980s, this oppression results from a combination of communist dogmatism and economic shortage. In the early 1990s, it is primarily an escape from the chaos of the primary accumulation of capital, paradoxically in search of the greater opportunities offered by models available in Western democracies. Importantly, practically all films of the 1980s and early 1990s dealing contemporary subject matters incorporate the motif of traveling and its implications. The 1984 Croatian farce *In the Jaws of Life* (*U raljama zivota*), directed by Rajko Grlic, follows the life of a middle-aged TV executive (Gorica Popovic) making a soap opera about an unhappy confused young woman (Vitomira Loncar) searching for Mr. Right. The film intercuts the two stories which in the end converge through their common happy ending. Throughout the narrative, Western values, such as extreme consumerism, the fetishization of the eternally young, artificial female body, jogging *ad absurdum* as a marker of belonging to the yuppie stratum, are subtly implemented in the Balkanic reality, in Croatian, stressing the comical element. Notably, the film's happy ending is unambiguously marked by the road metaphor, both symbolically and literally. The soap protagonist is able to go on her first date with Mr. Right only after she joins an English language institute in the final episode of the television series—English with all its connotations becomes her path to spiritual and physical comfort. After their first class, the two characters decide to go for coffee speaking in a ridiculously stilted broken English. Similarly, the series' producer finds happiness with her long-time secret love when he invites her to join him on his trip to America, where he intends to start a new, "normal" life.

Maciej Dejczer's 1989 film *300 Miles to Heaven* (*300 mil do nieba*) explores two brothers' quest to reach Denmark from a much more serious angle. Set in an ominously ugly Polish socialist reality, the film highlights the risks that such an undertaking carried under the old system. Eventually, the two adolescents are able to reach their goal, "the prosperous, though cold, 'capitalist' landscapes" of the West (Haltof 18). The final sequence depicts them in a telephone conversation with their parents back in Poland, in which their father seals the uni-directionality of their journey with the words: "Don't ever return here." Jan Sverak's award-winning *Kolya* (1996) further promotes the idea of travel. Made after 1989, yet following events of the last months of communism in Czechoslovakia, the film subtly introduces a bi-directionality in the travel metaphor that will eventually become a defining component in the film production of the late 1990s. The Western presence is implicitly strong: in the course of the film narrative, we learn that the protagonist's brother has long established himself as an emigrant outside Czechoslovakia. The protagonist, Louka (Ždenek Sverak), himself becomes the vehicle for yet another travel narrative. Out of economic considerations, he reluctantly agrees to marry the Russian citizen Nadezhda (Irena Livanova) who needs Czech papers in order to facilitate her trip to Germany. The film also depicts Soviet military presence in then Czechoslovakia. The initial ideological hostility toward the powerful occupators manifested by the protagonist and particularly his mother (Stella Zazvorkova), subtly reinforced by the refusal on the part of all to speak Russian, clashes with Louka's inherent humanism when he is faced with the task of looking after Nadezhda's son, Kolya (Andrej Chalimon), after his grandmother unexpectedly dies. The film's humanist message is contained in the idea that beyond politics, ideology, and oppression, we are all human. In the end, Louka begins to communicate with Kolya in Russian while the little boy pronounces his first words in Czech; as an ironic counterpoint, in the background the Western broadcasts of *Deutsche Welle* and Radio Free Europe intermingle with the political demagogy of the official totalitarian regime. Throughout the film, Kolya voices the constant tension between center and periphery by the simple binary "ours" (Russian) *versus* "yours" (Czech). The ironic twist contained in the fact that Nadezhda needs the help of the periphery (Czech papers) to achieve her own escape from the Russian center further relativizes the relationship between center and periphery. Moreover, the film does not treat the West as the unambiguous paradise. It is not accidental that Louka remains the quintessential Czech: he has been banned from the philharmonic as a result of his brother's defection but he does not covet to leave himself; while he does not speak Russian, neither does he speak any other Western language. During his fictitious marriage ceremony, Nadezhda's mother (Lilian Mankina), a cynical Russian who has no faith in anything beyond material prosperity, makes a remark that highlights the historical roots of the perennial marginality of the region: "First you don't like the Germans. Then you don't like the Russians."

Similar tensions are treated with less lyricism in the 1996 Ukrainian black comedy *A Friend of the Deceased* by director Viatcheslav Kryshtofovich. The post-totalitarian chaotic space of Kiev is dominated by markers of West European and, even more so, American presence. Racketeering, blackmail, and currency fraud define the atmosphere. Parodying the genre of the gangster film, the film tells the story of a desperate Ukrainian who has lost the battle with early capitalist lawlessness. As a last measure to ensure the survival of his family, he hires an assassin to kill him but eventually changes his mind. However, it is too late to stop the uncontrollable impetus of change. The murder takes place anyway, but with a twist. In the end, the assassin takes the place of the deceased in the hearts of his wife and child. Despite the comedy throughout the film, darker overtones highlighting the current lack of structure in Central and East Europe pose more questions than provide answers. The mirage of the West, refracted through the image of the beautiful Viennese streets is also a motif in Lazar Ristovski's 1996 comedy *The White Suit* (*Belo odelo*). Produced in a very turbulent period of Yugoslav history and as a politically correct effort intended to defend the reputation of the Yugoslav army, the plotline is purposefully fairy-tale like and idealized. The details, however, reflect the tangible reality of the socio-cultural changes in Yugoslavian society and the implicit lack of faith in the future. The dominant atmosphere throughout the film is one of drunken stupor, blaring music combining Western rock and Balkan *chalga,* and a string of surrealist events, reminiscent of the world in the works of Dusan Makavejev and Emir Kusturica. Not by accident, the action takes place on a train going to Belgrade, filled with colorful characters and their stories. A group of prostitutes accompanied by their pimp is en route to Vienna. On one level, this detail adds to the verisimilitude of the narrative; yet, there is a curious twist that needs to be addressed. The star prostitute of the group is Russian. She tries to manipulate her pimp and border guard in an attempt to escape to Austria on her own. In the end, however, the guard shoots her. The sequence is short and somewhat disconnected from the rest of the plot as it takes place outside the train.

Similar to *Kolya,* the representation of the Russian in a clearly disadvantageous position suggests the establishment of a new motif in post-totalitarian Central and East European art: the manifestation of direct revenge against the former omnipotent ruler. The Russian motif is raised to a symbolic level at the end of the film. The final sequence and the film credits roll against the background of a song in praise of the army by the famous Russian bard Vladimir Vysotsky. The choice of that particular score can be interpreted as an ironic commentary about the detrimental consequences that the communist past has inflicted on the present lack of values in a morally corrupt society built on myths of nationalistic grandeur devoid of content. However, it is also an acknowledgement that this past can neither be denied nor easily resolved. In this sense, the Yugoslav film presents an interesting new development in Central and East European cinema of the late 1990s as it foregrounds the issue of continuity between past, present, and future, suggesting that dealing and coming to terms with the past is also part of the horizontal axis of movement.

Central and East European films of the 1990s not only introduce the new theme of "revenge" against the former colonial power but also reconceptualize the earlier uni-directionality of the road metaphor. Unlike the earlier films of the 1980s and the first years after the demise of the Soviet empire, the later films foreground a new component. The path to Europe now begins to encompass the long return home after experiencing the West. The new situation complicates and exacerbates even more the notion of "in-betweenness" in that the characters have truly lost a sense of identity, not having achieved acceptance abroad, yet unable to readapt to the new conditions of a constantly changing (hyper)reality, a state the Bulgarian émigrée Julia Kristeva has defined as being "étrangers à nous-mêmes." The long return home as a component of the voyage is already suggested in Krzysztof Kieslowksi's 1993 *White*. The film is the second part of the director's color trilogy *Bleu, Blanc, Rouge*. Exploiting the symbolism of the colors of the French flag—*liberté, égalité, fraternité*—*White* focuses on the East-West dialogue by carnivalizing the notion of equality in the post-modern world of inverted values. The film tells the story of an ill-fated Pole whose beautiful French wife divorces him because he is no longer able to perform sexually. The major section of the film takes place in the new Poland which the protagonist eventually reaches, hidden in a suitcase. In Poland, he is able to adapt to the new circumstances, become a *nouveau riche,* and finally plan his revenge on his wife. One of the strategies he adopts is faking his own death, a symbolic gesture that suggests the idea that the new Central and East European situation has become incomprehensible if we apply to it old values and structures.

The same metaphor is foregrounded in Krsto Papic's 1998 *When the Dead Start Singing (Kad mrtvi zapjevaju)*. Two Croats decide to return home after years of economic emigration in Germany. One of them, Cinco (Ivo Gregurevic), literally returns in a coffin, having faked his death for the German authorities with the intent of enjoying his benefits in his homeland. Moreover, on the road the Cinco encounters another former compatriot, a Bosnian, pulling the same scam. In spite of a series of unexpected adventures on German soil, the two friends manage not only to evade the orderly German system unharmed, but they represent a symbolic victory of Balkanic dodginess and *joie de vivre* over the apathy, complacency, and hidden evil of a well-oiled Western society. It is back in their villages, absurdly separated by an "international" border with Yugoslavia, that the real troubles begin. Very much in the absurdist tradition of Emir Kusturica, the director shows the tragic consequences of a failed experiment—the Yugoslav federation. At the same time, the film is intercut with romanticized flashbacks in which all Yugoslavs were able to coexist and instead of hating each other were united in undermining the inadequate totalitarian ideology. The film's dénouement features a blood bath between Serb *chetniks* and Croats which is triggered not by an attack by either side but by a damaged muffler. This time, the ever entrepreneurial Cinco cannot survive—his corpse falls lifeless in the prepared grave. While Papic's film directly criticizes ethnic intolerance that defines Balkan history of the 1990s, indirectly it also raises the issue of the extent to which in-between peripherality—in other words, the secondary and hence inferior assessment of the region by the West—becomes a factor for the explosion of nationalism.

Ivan Nichev's 1999 *After the End of the World* (*Sled kraia na sveta*) also explores the question of ethnic tolerance on the Balkans. His film follows the return to a post-communist Bulgaria of Albert Cohen (Stefan Danailov), a renowned Jewish scholar of Byzantine. Having officially left Bulgaria in the 1960s, Cohen relives his childhood memories in Plovdiv when Bulgarians, Armenians, Turks, Jews, Greeks, and Roma all lived peacefully side by side. The idyllic existence abruptly comes to an end with the advent of communism. The Gypsies are driven away to the north of Bulgaria, the Turks leave on their own accord after the local party leaders desecrate their cemetery, and the Jews are allowed to emigrate to Israel. The film also focuses on the hardships endured by a wealthy Armenian family. Instead of being allowed to go to Paris, the mother and the daughter end up dispatched to a remote village while the father spends some years in a communist labor camp. Too many lives were sacrificed in the name of the utopian ideal, the film seems to suggest. Yet, it goes beyond its status of being a mere document of communist repression and a nostalgic reverie for the idyllic pre-communist past of childhood memories. In fact, the importance of Nichev's film is in the parallel plot which follows Cohen's contemporary experiences in democratic Bulgaria: corruption, blackmail, racketeering, threats, poverty, and chaos surround him at every step. When he refuses to bend to the desires of the new mobsters, he is threatened and badly beaten. And the film ends on an utterly pessimistic note: the Plovdiv home of the old photographer is burned down by the mob, thus obliterating a century of memories and history. While in spite of their efforts and mindless cruelty, the communists were ultimately unable to destroy the human bond between the people, the new forces—grounded not in ideological but in economic considerations—operating in the country with a nominally democratic system are causing destruction of grand proportions.

A further development of this newer trend of looking at Central and East European identity from within is reflected in the films that emerge from films in the Czech Republic, Poland, and Hungary. In general, the concept of traveling is much more subdued, it has been internalized, and there is a subtle orientation toward its inner rather than outer manifestations. Traditionally defined as lyrical, in the post-communist period Czech cinema seems to be perpetuating the trend. The focus is distinctly on the existential dimension, that is, how to reconcile the spiritual needs in an overtly materialistic and cynical society. Such is the underlying subject matter of Saša Gedeon's 1999 *Return of the Idiot* (*Návrat idiota*). The film's inspiration is taken directly from Dostoevsky (acknowledged in the film's opening credits). Once again, the motif of the journey is clearly defined—in part motivated by Dostoevsky's novel, in part as a symbol of the fluidity of the times. Gedeon's gesture of interpreting the new present through the mediation of the Russian cultural past is a subtle indicator that, indeed, the countries from Central and East Europe are able to a greater degree to reconceptualize both past and present. The fact that a contemporary Czech film is directly inspired by a Russian writer also points to variation within the larger notion of Central and East European identity. It suggests a degree of emancipation of Czech cultural discourse, namely its ease, without intimidation or fear, to look at cultural traditions represented by the former Russian center of power. This tendency becomes even clearer when posited against the recent cinematic production in Ukraine, for instance. As Bohdan Nebesio's survey article "Rebuilding a National Cinema: Ukraine in the 1990s" suggests, Ukrainian film makers are striving along the lines of constructing a national Ukrainian cinematic tradition that is clearly distinct from the Russian tradition. In this sense—and naturally as a result of different starting conditions—Ukrainian cinema is still consciously addressing the issue of national identity construction through extreme differentiation.

In his article on Polish cinema after 1989, Marek Haltof suggests that "film ideology is of minor significance and will remain so until a new antagonist is found" (15). While contemporary Polish film continues to be concerned less with ideology and more with universal issues, there is some indication that such a new antagonist has been found: namely, the lack of meaning in an empty existence predicated by violence, sex, and extreme commercialism. This idea is promoted in Urszula Urbaniak's feature *début, The Junction (Torowisko, 1999)*.

The film tells the story of a trapped young woman, Maria (Karolina Dryzner), who works as a signalperson at a remote railway junction and lives with her pragmatic mother and drug dealing brother. Through a series of details and events, the film demonstrates how entrenched the Western/American sensibility has become even in the furthest corner of Poland. *Hustler* and *Playboy* magazines, casinos, brothels, cocaine, and the pervasive presence of cans of pop are intentionally foregrounded by the camera throughout the film. On TV, the shows are Polish clones of American games and talk shows. There is never meaningful communication, only incessant consumerism. And while the protagonist manages to leave the oppressive and stagnant atmosphere in the end, there is little hope that she will be able to find a better alternative the next junction she stops at.

In the course of the narrative, Maria's brother (Marcin Dorocinski) gets deeper and deeper into drug dealing. At the same time, he is presented as a truly sympathetic and sensitive character. The only time he feels comfortable is when listening to blaring heavy metal music or when interacting with Andrzej, a mentally handicapped boy. Maria's brother expresses the subtle criticism of the new Polish generation with regard to the one-sided treatment of the socio-political changes by the older, more emotionally engaged generation. Looking at an old tree at the bus stop, the young man remembers that the tree was probably planted by his father as an ideological toward against the old regime and then cynically wonders how it has remained untouched. In general, the film subtly juxtaposes the difference in attitudes to past and present expressed by the younger and older generations.

This conclusion is reinforced when recent films from Central and East Europe are compared with the production of older directors, especially *émigrés* living outside the region. One such parallel can be drawn between the omnibus film *Prague Stories* (*Praha ocima,* 1999) and Vojtech Jasny's *Which Side Eden* (*Návrat ztraceného ráje,* 1998). In the first film, four directors, three from the Czech Republic and one from France, present contemporary Czech life from four different perspectives, all emphasizing the state of spiritual uncertainty of their protagonists. Without infusing the film with an overt ideological dimension, politics dissects the protagonists' personal lives and the relationships they enter into. This is particularly clear in the first segment, Vladimír Michálek's "The Cards Are Dealt" ("Karty jsou rozdany"). The segment follows the numbing routine of an award-winning journalist (Jan Machacek). In spite of his professional achievements, he feels trapped, unsatisfied, and bored by the endless nagging of his ever-pregnant wife, the miniature apartment he shares with her, and his two young children, and above all, the editorial meetings which prove to be as restrictive as those in communist times. The only respite from his despair prove to be drugs, easily available everywhere in Prague's seedy pubs. Martin Sullk's contribution, "Pictures from a Visit" ("Obrázky ž vyletu") subtly evokes the separation of Czechoslovakia into the Czech and Slovak republics. The female protagonist's mother comes to visit her from a remote Slovakian town and is initially surprised at her daughter's libertarian life style. In the end, she ends up not only accepting the young woman's openness but also ends up enjoying her momentary freedom from a defunct marriage. Upon her arrival, she reproaches her daughter for not speaking Slovakian but beyond that remark, the episode does not touch upon the political dimension again. Paradoxically, the segment that actualizes the before-now dichotomy the most is the one made by the French director Artemio Benki. His piece, "The Dive" ("Riziko") ends the omnibus film and focuses on a French couple who has come to Prague on a working trip. Richard (Arnaud Giovanietti) searches for the Prague he used to know years earlier but is unable to find even the slightest vestiges of it. His relationship with Marie (Laurence Coté) is equally unstable and becomes doomed when she meets the Czech Pável (David Cerny). Marie, who does not carry preconceived ideas, is able to enjoy herself much more. To this detached yet introspective look at contemporary Czech society the Czech-American *Jasny* offers an emotional, nostalgia-charged interpretation of his personal experience as an emigrant who never forgot his homeland, largely predicated on idealized assumptions. The film opens with a sequence of images emphasizing the director's adoration of New York City as one side of paradise.

Later on, the protagonist and director's alter-ego (Vladimir Pucholt) returns to Moravia and meets his compatriots after an absence of thirty years. Through a series of flashbacks, we learn about his family's plight with Nazis and Communists and his subsequent relocation to the United States. There, he attains success as a well-respected professor (from a short sequence, we also learn that his beloved is also in the academic milieu in Germany). The film abounds in symbolism, nostalgia for the past, and stereotypes that at times promote intolerance (e.g., the episode of the boy being abducted by Gypsies). In my interpretation however, the writer/director's excessive search for a unique Czech identity suppresses the more universal, humanist level achieved by the new Czech film makers.

The objective of Central and East Europe's access to the West and the physical presence of so many legal and illegal Central and East Europeans has resulted in the interest and parallel appearance of some Western films that deal with the emergence of the region's "Other" in Western society. Such an instance is Jean-Marc Barr's 1999 *Lovers*. Depicting a love story between a Yugoslav illegal alien (Dragan Nicolic) in Paris and a French girl, Jane (Elodie Bouchez), the director violates the viewers' expectations from the very beginning by making Dragan a sensitive, erudite painter, more interested in Dante Gabriel Rossetti than in making a quick buck. Further toying with preconceived ideas, Dragan explains that he has no interest for materialist prosperity: as a child of communism he has been spoilt by the system (in the process driving his French girlfriend on the verge of a break-down with his lengthy long-distance calls and excessive heating of the apartment). Unlike the frenetic hallucinatory atmosphere of Kusturica or Makavejev, Barr opts for a more subdued representation of Yugoslavian immigrants in France. Their parties are exclusive and intense precisely because they are avoided by the French and they drink mostly out of hopelessness and the need to forget their situation. The police are polite but ubiquitous. One of the most ironic remarks in the film is made by Dragan who tells his girlfriend that only on French soil his friend Zlatan (Sergei Trifunovic), known for his public singing of anti-Tito songs, became afraid, restrained, and observant of law and order. Barr's film also shows Jane's gradual marginalization from her own milieu intercut by direct instances of French racist attitudes towards the Yugoslavian. In an ideologically charged gesture, throughout the film Dragan refuses to identify himself: when Jane asks him "What are you? Serb? Croat?" all he responds is "Yugo." Barr's *Lovers* is perhaps one of the most effective films of recent treating the complex European East-West dialogue from the point of view of the West. That the director is also aware of new trends such as the "path to Europe" metaphor is reflected in the fact that the end there is no bloody shoot-out or an alternative melodramatic *grand finale* for the protagonist. He simply returns home after having been ordered to leave France by the authorities.

Another film dealing with Central and East Europe's obsession to belong is the black comedy *Beresina ou les derniers jours de la Suisse* (1999) by Swiss director Daniel Schmid, and, notably, an Austrian and Swiss co-production. Clearly intended as a bitter satire against the myths of the Swiss democracy, the film exposes the corruption and double standards governing Swiss politics and society. What is significant is the fact that the protagonist, who eventually brings about the downfall of Switzerland, is a naive Russian call girl who truly believes in the great Swiss myths. Throughout the film, the idea is visualized farcically by the representation of the heroine dressed in traditional Alpine outfits. The film has a happy ending as Irina is crowned the queen of a presumably purified Switzerland. And yet, despite all her efforts, dreams, and expectations she does not become a Swiss citizen, only a queen: the coveted Swiss passport evades her.

Ironically, even the fairy tale plot refuses to allow such fantasy as Swiss citizenship for a foreigner. Barr's and Schmid's films promote the awareness of Western film makers of the consequences of the new, postcommunist world order. What is even more encouraging is their effort to go beyond traditional stereotypes in the attempt to understand dynamic tendencies in and of Central and East Europe. In this, the directors are not only reflecting a highly volatile state of affairs which is directly or indirectly predicated on the road metaphor, but they are also truly contribute to the on going complex and often conflict-ridden dialogue on Euro-identity.

At the dawn of a new millennium and ever-greater globalization, fluidity, and differentiation within the geographical space formerly known as the "Eastern block" continue to be defining parameters. Within the East-Central axis, the Balkans remain a region of political conflict and ethnic confrontation. Movement continues to be a central gesture manifested not only as coveted immigration but also as forced migration (an issue that yet remains to be addressed). At the same time, there is also a new development expressed in the journey back home, on the one hand, and in the renewed interest of Central and East Europeans to inscribe and re-inscribe themselves in the paradigm of globalized economy and border dissolution. The younger generation of film makers, both from Central and East Europe and from the West, have already begun depicting the process. At this point, the final destination appears to be a long way off. Yet, with its quest for the right way and for self-determination, Central and East Europe promises to raise numerous propositions that will continue to make the inquiry into identity construction an inexhaustible field in comparative cultural studies.

WORKS CITED

Daskalovski, Zhidas. "Ten Years Later: Schengen's Iron Curtain." *Central Europe Review* 1.25 (1999): <http://www.ce-review.org/25/daskalovski25.html>.

Deltcheva, Roumiana. "Western Mediations in Reevaluating the Communist Past: A Comparative Analysis of Gothár's *Time Stands Still* and Andonov's *Yesterday.*" *CLCWeb: Comparative Literature and Culture: A WWW Journal* 1.4 (1999): <http://clcwebjournal.lib.purdue.edu/clcweb99-4/deltcheva99-2.html>.

Deltcheva, Roumiana. "East Central Europe as a Politically Correct Scapegoat: The Case of Bulgaria." *CLCWeb: Comparative Literature and Culture: A WWW Journal* 1.2 (1999): <http://clcwebjournal.lib.purdue.edu/clcweb99-2/deltcheva99.html>.

Deltcheva, Roumiana. "Totalitarian Journalism from a Systemic and Dialogic Perspective: The Case of Bulgaria." *The Systemic and Empirical Approach to Literature and Culture as Theory and Application.* Ed. Steven Tötösy de Zepetnek and Irene Sywenky. Edmonton: Research Institute for Comparative Literature, U of Alberta and Siegen: Institute for Empirical Literature and Media Research, 1997. 237–54.

Haltof, Marek. "A Fistful of Dollars: Polish Cinema after the 1989 Freedom Shock." *Film Quarterly* 48.3 (1995): 15–25.

Miller, Stefania Szelek, and Caroline Bayard. "Introduction: Nationalism and Self-Determination in Multicultural Societies: Eastern Europe." *Canadian Slavonic Papers/Revue Canadienne des Slavistes* 37.3–4 (1995): vii–viii.

Nebesio, Bohdan. "Rebuilding a National Cinema: Ukraine in the 1990s." *Cinemas in Transition: Post-Communist Cinema in East Central Europe.* Ed. Catherine Portuges and Daniel Goulding. Forthcoming.

Portuges, Catherine. "Comparative Central European Culture: Austrian and Hungarian Cinema Today." *Comparative Central European Culture.* Ed. Steven Tötösy de Zepetnek. West Lafayette: Purdue UP, 2002. 133–48.

Tötösy de Zepetnek, Steven. "Comparative Cultural Studies and the Study of Central European Culture." *Comparative Central European Culture.* Ed. Steven Tötösy de Zepetnek. West Lafayette: Purdue UP, 2002. 1–32.

Tötösy de Zepetnek, Steven. "Configurations of Postcoloniality and National Identity: Inbetween Peripherality and Narratives of Change." *The Comparatist: Journal of the Southern Comparative Literature Association* 23 (1999): 89–110.

Tötösy de Zepetnek, Steven. "Cultures, Peripheralities, and Comparative Literature." *Comparative Literature: Theory, Method, Application.* By Steven Tötösy de Zepetnek. Amsterdam-Atlanta, GA: Rodopi, 1998. 121–72.

Tötösy de Zepetnek, Steven. "Post-Colonialities: The 'Other,' the System, and a Personal Perspective, or, This (Too) Is Comparative Literature." *Postcolonial Literatures: Theory and Practice/Les Littératures post-coloniales. Théories et réalisations.* Ed. Steven Tötösy de Zepetnek and Sneja Gunew. Thematic Issue of *Canadian Review of Comparative Literature/Revue Canadienne de Littérature Comparée* 22.3-4 (1995): 399–407.

Central Europe, Jewish Family History, and *Sunshine*

Susan Rubin Suleiman

An English-language film with an almost exclusively Anglo-American cast, produced in Canada, filmed in Hungary, with a screenplay cowritten by an American playwright and a Hungarian director who is best known in North America for an Oscar-winning film in German (*Mephisto*, 1981), István Szabó's *Sunshine* is nothing if not transnational.

Released in Canada in 1999 and in Europe and the United States in Spring 2000, *Sunshine* was produced by Canadian-Hungarian producer Robert Lantos. The screenplay is by Szabó and Israel Horowitz, based on an original story by Szabó; the film's stars are Ralph Fiennes, Rosemary Harris, Jennifer Ehle, and William Hurt. *Sunshine* sums up the history of Jews in the Austro-Hungarian empire and Hungary by telling the story of a single family over four generations. Emmanuel Sonnenschein (the surname means "Sunshine" in English), while still a boy, leaves the village where his father, the local tavern keeper, has been killed by an explosion in his distillery, and makes his way to Budapest, the capital. We are in the mid-nineteenth century, just before the period of Hungary's greatest economic and cultural flowering under the dual

Austro-Hungarian monarchy (1867–1918). By the time the story begins in earnest—when Ralph Fiennes makes his appearance as Emmanuel's young adult son—the Sonnenscheins have become rich through Emmanuel's distillery, which fabricates the tonic he calls a "taste of sunshine" (A *napfény íze,* the film's title in Hungarian).

While the narrative mode of the film is that of the historical epic, Szabó introduces, from the start, a mediating presence: the story is told with voice-over narration by the last male descendant of Emmanuel Sonnenschein, his great-grandson Ivan. Ivan's voice (in English, Ralph Fiennes's voice, for he plays all three roles of son, grandson, and great-grandson) opens and closes the film, and intervenes at various moments throughout—not so often as to disrupt the realist narration, but often enough to indicate that the story is recounted by a specific individual who is also a participant in it, not by an omniscient camera-narrator. This point is worth emphasizing, for it has not been sufficiently taken into account in the critical responses to the film. After the prologue, the story divides neatly into three historical periods; extending the meteorological metaphor suggested by the film's title, we can call them the "sunlit age," roughly 1890–1914; the "stormy age," roughly 1914–1944; and the "overcast age," 1945 to our day. By the time Emmanuel's two sons, Ignatz and Gustave, reach young manhood, in the 1890s, Hungarian prosperity and cultural achievement have attained remarkable heights; and Jews—along with other ethnic minority groups such as the substantial German-speaking population of the country—play a prominent role in it.

Historians have often described the "assimilationist contract" that linked the liberal nobility to Jewish industry and finance in the period of the Dual Monarchy. The liberals, inspired by the ideals of the Enlightenment as well as by Magyar patriotism, sought to modernize a backward, quasi-feudal country and to create a unified nation despite the number of minority ethnic groups scattered over its large territory. The "assimilationist contract" gave Jews, especially those living in Budapest, an opportunity to participate fully in the liberals' modernization project and in the creation of a modern Hungarian identity and culture. In return, "Hungarian Jews were expected to demonstrate total loyalty to the Hungarian state, to accept the political hegemony of the nobility, and to strive for complete assimilation within the Hungarian community" (Kovács 50; for recent work on the history of Jews in Hungary, see Braham; Fejtö; Ozsváth *Orpheus;* Patai; on *Sunshine* see also Portuges).

Ignatz Sonnenschein becomes a lawyer and is quickly promoted to the high position of a central court judge; but since, as his Christian patron tells him, "a central court judge cannot have a name like Sonnenschein," he changes his name to Sors ("fate" in Hungarian). His brother Gustave, a physician, does likewise, and so does his adopted sister, Valerie, who soon becomes his wife. Drafted into the officer corps as a military judge during the First World War, Ignatz remains a lifelong loyalist to the emperor, Franz Joseph. Gustave follows a more radical route, joining the socialist party and later the short-lived communist government of Béla Kun (1919). After the fall of the Kun regime, he is forced to leave Hungary.

"Magyarizing" one's name in the period before the First World War (starting with the mid- to late-1800s did not have the same anxious connotation (hiding one's Jewishness for fear of persecution) that it would acquire during the 1930s and it was practiced not only by Jews but by other ethnic minorities in Hungary who wanted to affirm their loyalty. For Jews, who had acquired their Germanic names in the eighteenth century by royal decree under the Habsburg emperor Joseph II, magyarizing their name was a sign of patriotism as well as of belief in the promises of assimilation (for a source of magyarized Jewish surnames, see Szentiványi). It did not necessarily imply a renunciation of Jewish self-identification or of Jewish practice, although assimilated Jews in Budapest generally practiced a reform brand of Judaism in opposition to the Orthodox practice of most Jews in the provinces. Thus, by changing their name when they do, Ignác, Gusztáv and Valéria (their first names in Hungarian) are not giving up their Jewishness, but rather affirming their Hungarianness. The vexing question asked by this film is whether—and how—one can be both Jewish and Hungarian after the Holocaust. For as it turned out, the "assimilationist contract" was much more fragile than it seemed to the Jews of Ignatz and Gustave Sonnenschein/Sors's generation. The contract did not foresee—and could not, ultimately, withstand—the economic crisis and the aggravated nationalism that followed the dismemberment of the Habsburg Empire after World War I, when Hungary lost two-thirds of its territory. Nor did it foresee the revolutionary upheavals in Russia and Hungary (where the short-lived Kun regime, dominated by assimilated Jews, was brutally put down by the authoritarian regime of Miklós Horthy), or the rise of Nazism and radical anti-Semitism in Germany.

Many Jews, seeing the handwriting on the wall, emigrated from Hungary in the early years of the Horthy regime and in the 1930s. Those who stayed faced increasing hostility and persecution by their own government, culminating in the Jewish laws of 1938 and 1939, which virtually excluded Jews from Hungarian economic, cultural, and political life. Ignatz Sors does not live to see that day, for he dies shortly after the First World War; but his two sons, István and Adam, experience virulent anti-Semitism while they are still teenagers. Adam, who takes up fencing after being attacked by his own schoolmates, becomes a national and Olympic champion, and an ardent patriot. By that time, however, Jewishness and Hungarian patriotism coexist only in a highly problematic fashion. When Adam is told that in order to be allowed to join the officers' fencing club (which has the best fencers) he must convert to Catholicism, he does so—accompanied by his brother and by the women they will marry. In 1941, the Hungarian government—an ally of Germany—conscripted most Jewish men into forced labor service where they were subjected to treatment that ranged from harsh to homicidal. Adam is tortured to death in a forced labor camp by Hungarian gendarmes when he insists on wearing a white armband (signaling that he is a convert) and on identifying himself as "Ádám Sors, an officer in the Hungarian army and Olympic gold-medal winner." Adam's teenage son, Ivan (our narrator) watches helplessly as his father is stripped naked, beaten, strung up on a tree and doused with cold water, slowly turning into an ice statue—refusing unto death to call himself a Jew.

In March 1944, the Germans invaded Hungary and began the systematic deportation of Jews from the provinces, an operation that was administered and carried out by Hungarian officials and police under the supervision of Adolf Eichmann. Two thirds of Hungary's Jews, close to half-a-million people, perished through deportation and other forms of murder. The deportations never reached Budapest, which accounts for the relatively large number of Jews (when compared to Poland, for example) who remained in Hungary after the war. However, in the last winter of the war, Budapest Jews were hounded by Hungarian Nazis, the Arrow Cross, led by Ferenc Szálasi, who had replaced Horthy as head of the government in October 1944. Adam Sors's family is murdered by the Arrow Cross; the only survivor, besides Ivan, is his grandmother Valerie, who returns to an empty apartment in 1945. Ivan's story brings us up to the present. Like many young Jews after the war, Iván becomes an ardent communist. He works for the dreaded secret police, the ÁVÓ—until his boss and friend Andor Knorr (William Hurt), a survivor of Auschwitz, is arrested on trumped-up charges of "Zionist conspiracy" and tortured to death by the communist regime. We are in 1952, just as the anti-Jewish Slansky trial is starting in Czechoslovakia and the "doctor's plot" is about to be launched in the Soviet Union. Iván quits the police, eventually becomes a leader of the failed 1956 revolution, and spends several years in prison. In the 1960s, after Valerie's death, he finds a letter addressed by his great-grandfather Manó (Emmanuel) to his son Ignác, advising him to stay true to himself and his origins. Taking this letter to heart, Ivan changes his name back to Sonnenschein—and for the first time in his life, he announces in a final voice-over, he "breathes freely" in the streets of Budapest.

In *Sunshine*, Szabó aims to tell a story about individuals that a spectator can identify with and care about, and at the same time to give an accurate representation of a complex and extended collective history. Szabó has stated in interviews that he is fascinated by "how people's private lives have been influenced by history and politics" (qtd. in Gener). Indeed, one can see *Sunshine* as the culmination or combination of several of his earlier films in German and Hungarian, which focused on individual lives in smaller segments of the long historical period treated in this film. István Deák's review of the film, devoted exclusively to its historical aspects not to its formal qualities, vouches for its overall historical accuracy, give or take a few details. Inevitably, however, Szabó must rely on a certain schematicism and simplification, if for no other reason than the huge temporal sweep of the narrative. Characters tend to function as types, rather than as fully developed "round" figures; plot and narration are linear, avoiding flashbacks, dream sequences, and other fragmenting modernist techniques that one finds in Szabó's earlier films, especially those of the 1960s and 1970s (for overviews of Szabó's work up to the early 1990s, see De Marchi; Hirsch; Paul). Correlatively, the narrative in *Sunshine* relies on repetition and parallelism as its most important tropes. These tropes occur not only on the level of plot and characters, but in the *mise en scène* as a whole, including decor, lighting, and music. The family's apartment and the building in which it is located are one major repeated element, used to great effect: the physical deterioration of these spaces tracks and "doubles" both the family's and Hungary's decline. Similarly, colors are used to mark the film's movement from sunshine to darkness and back to at least a partial sunshine.

The musical score (by Maurice Jarre) is also highly patterned, with the leitmotif borrowed from Schubert's Fantasia in F Minor for two pianos accompanying the family's evolution. Played by Valerie and Ignatz as young lovers, the Schubert piece becomes the Sonnenschein theme music, sometimes fully orchestrated, at other times reduced to a single piano. In the sequence of Adam's murder, there is no music at all; in the concluding sequence, when the Sonnenschein name is revived, the Schubert melody swells again to full orchestration, perhaps indicating a return in musical memory to the family's history during the monarchy. Szabó makes use of other musical motifs as well; the Hungarian folk song "Spring Wind" ("Tavaszi szél"), which is played at Valerie and Ignatz's wedding and recurs often, underlines the family's love of Hungary and its deep sense of "Hungarianness," according to Szabó's commentary in an interview (see Mülner; all translations from the Hungarian are mine).

On the level of plot and characters, repetition and parallelism are used to ensure narrative cohesion as well as to underline the film's major themes—this is in keeping with the epic-realist genre, which relies on a high degree of redundancy (for redundancy in realist narrative, see Suleiman 1983). Repetition in the film, including Fiennes's three-generational acting, works well to communicate a meaning cinematically that is not stated verbally. Early in the film, for example, we see Ignatz dressed in military uniform, approaching a palace which the voiceover tells us is that of the emperor Franz Joseph: it is the First World War, and Ignatz, a military judge, is going to have a private audience with the emperor. The meeting lasts only a minute and is perfunctory, but Ignatz is deeply moved: afterward, approaching the staircase, he touches his shoulder where the emperor briefly placed his hand, like a teenager who has been touched by a rock idol (Deák finds this detail one of the rare false historical notes in the film: the emperor would never have touched a commoner in such a familiar way). One of the hostile critics of the film in Budapest, Péter György, remarked that the scene with the emperor was put into the film to please American audiences, who "like palaces." The easy jibe reveals the critic's ill will, for the palace scene is in fact crucial to the film's theme of assimilation/accommodation, and is repeated with variations in both Adam's and Ivan's stories. Adam, after his Olympic victory, enters a similar grand building, also dressed in uniform, and receives a military decoration; afterward, he descends the staircase, ramrod stiff, moved beyond words. Ironically, it is this same military stiffness and loyalty to the "homeland" that will get him killed later: he is singled out by the camp guard while wearing his army coat. The scene of Adam's decoration thus both "repeats" his father's meeting with the emperor and foreshadows his own death; more importantly, it exacerbates the theme of assimilation.

What in Ignatz is an understandable loyalty to a system that has encouraged his advancement (at least, in his own eyes) becomes a tragic blindness in his son, who remains loyal even to a system that seeks his destruction. There is yet a third decoration scene, which pushes the accommodation theme even further: Ivan, on Stalin's birthday, is decorated along with other police officers in a public ceremony in the state opera house (another grand building), and is the one chosen to give the formal speech of thanks. Standing on the stage in his uniform before a large crowd, Ivan shouts his words in a monotone: "Comrade Stalin has shown us the way!" His eyes stare ahead, oddly recalling the boy's stare at his father being tortured. Afterward, he is shown descending a grand staircase—but there is no pride in his face, only his usual pained look. This sequence "repeats" the two earlier ones, but turns the wheel once more: whereas his father and grandfather were men of will and power, Ivan is an automaton. His face constantly frozen into an anxious mask, he is the embodiment of trauma.

George Schöpflin has remarked in his review of the film that Szabó's heroes are singularly devoid of irony (otherwise a standard characteristic of Central European culture). This strikes him as a fault, aesthetically and historically; for the typical defense of the Jewish "insider/outsider" against the daily small (or large) humiliations he had to endure even in the best of times was, precisely, irony. The irony of the Jewish insider/outsider acted, according to Schöpflin, as a corrective to the "kitsch and sentimentalism" that always threatened the "intense emotions generated by nationalism." This ironic distance from their own assimilation is precisely what the Sonnenschein men lack. Indeed, one is hard put to find a Szabó hero, in his oeuvre as a whole, who displays the kind of "corrective" irony Schöpflin describes, at once self-deprecating and subversive of the system to which the insider/outsider belongs (and does not belong). However, all of the Sonnenschein men engage in socially transgressive sexual behavior. Ignatz marries his first cousin and adopted sister Valerie, against his father's wishes; Adam, the proper patriot, engages in an adulterous love affair with his brother's wife. True, it is she who pursues him and he hates himself for yielding to her; but it is significant that their first sexual encounter takes place immediately after he descends the grand staircase with his decoration, as if to "correct" his rigid conformism and propriety. Similarly, it is while descending the staircase after his "praise of Stalin" speech that Ivan has his first encounter with Carol, the married blond policewoman who teases him about his anxious look ("the sad man," she calls him); in the next scene she shows up in his office, where they make breathless love on his desk. Transgressive sexuality presents itself as the subversive counterpart to "good boy" integration into the system, a possibility of individual self-affirmation outside institutional or political norms. The Sonnenschein women display an independent-mindedness characteristic of many women in the bourgeois elite in Central Europe; in this equation, women function as outsiders to authority, possible vehicles of freedom—but they are also, by the same token, outside the political realm and outside history. In an interview, Szabó states: "Women stand with two feet on the ground. . . . They are much closer to nature, to every part of nature, including blood, than men . . . For that very reason, they are less likely to fall prey to the attractions of ideologies and of history, they are more able to safeguard their identity than men" (qtd. in Mülner). A compliment, but also a sexist stereotype.

Furthermore, the women in *Sunshine* are not only outside politics—a positive trait in this context—but appear to be outside ordinary ethical standards as well. Adultery is not only a societal transgression; it is also a personal betrayal, and the women in *Sunshine* become increasingly crass. As in other repetitive patterns in the film, the progression is downward as the generations advance. Valerie, who leaves Ignatz for another man after the First World War, declaring him too much of a conformist to the empire, returns to him when he becomes an outcast during the Kun regime; Adam's sister-in-law, by contrast, never regrets betraying her husband with his own brother. As for Carol, she betrays not only her husband but her lover Ivan: despite their passionate lovemaking, she drops him immediately when he falls from official grace; and when they meet by chance on the subway years later, she escapes, refusing to have any contact with him. On the other hand, and perhaps in keeping with his theory about women's firmer grasp of reality, Szabó makes the old Valerie (Rosemary Harris) into the moral center of the film. Enduring through all four generations, Valerie expresses the ethical norms of the film when she tells Ivan that politics and history are not the important things in life; what really matters is the appreciation of life's beauty, despite the destructiveness of history. If there is a "message" in the film, this affirmation of individualist values—and of art, for Valerie is for a time a professional photographer—may well sum it up (for recent work on Central European women's literature and women in literature, see Imre; Tötösy 177–214).

Just as repetitive patterning and linear narration are hallmarks of historical realism and the epic mode, so self-reflection and the disruption of linear narration are hallmarks of modernism. While *Sunshine* clearly belongs to the former, it contains modernist elements that recall Szabó's early Hungarian films, which, as critics have noted, were much influenced by the French new wave, especially Truffaut. The voice-over narration with Ivan as narrator recalls the voice-over narration in *Father* (1966), where the story is also refracted through the main character rather than through an omniscient camera. Similarly, inserted newsreels function as intertextual allusions to the earlier films, which used similar or identical footage. A dead horse on the street in Budapest in 1945 and blown-up bridges on the Danube are among the opening shots of *Father,* and also appear in *Sunshine;* footage of foreign soldiers on horseback in Budapest, "restoring order" in 1919 after the fall of the Kun regime, recalls similar horsemen who appear in *Firemen's Street 25* (1973). These early films thus become retrospectively glossed in the new film. Indeed, it is possible to see *Sunshine* as a rereading—and rewriting—of *Father,* or more exactly of what Joshua Hirsch has called the "repressed" Jewish story in *Father.* The protagonist of that film is identified as Catholic, but a number of implicit indications, akin to Freudian slips, suggest that he comes from a Jewish (or formerly Jewish) family.

Hirsch's paper, "István Szabó: Problems in the Narration of Holocaust Memory," appeared before *Sunshine,* but his analysis appears confirmed by Szabó's latest film. What is repressed in *Father,* manifesting itself only as symptoms, becomes explicitly stated and narrativized in *Sunshine.* Hirsch mentions as one "symptom" the fact that the protagonist's father was rounded up by the Arrow Cross in 1944—this is recounted to the boy by his mother, but she leaves unstated why the Arrow Cross (whose main activity in 1944 was rounding up Jews) pursued him. Another "symptom," not mentioned by Hirsch, occurs later, when the young boy asks his mother: "Did you ever think of leaving Hungary?" and she replies that his father did not want to leave, since he was "very Magyar." Again, no explanation is offered, but if one reads this exchange in light of Adam's story in *Sunshine,* its repressed meaning becomes clear and this repression may correspond to Szabó's own attitude toward his family's Jewish background. In the long interview he gave to Italian critic, Bruno de Marchi in 1976, Szabó mentions the autobiographical elements in *Father* without ever mentioning the protagonist's—or his own—ethnic or religious background (see De Marchi). This was no doubt in keeping with the taboo on discussing Jewishness during the communist regime in Hungary. In recent interviews, as well as in the 1994 essay by David Paul, Szabó's family's Jewish background is explicitly mentioned.

Szabó often includes *mises en abyme* (sometimes in the form of theatrical performances, as in *Mephisto* or *Hanussen*) in his films, and they are always highly significant. In *Father,* for example, it is only in a *mise en abyme* that the Jewish yellow star appears: a crowd of extras wearing the yellow star are marched over a bridge in a reenactment of what actually happened in 1944, while a dictatorial director yells instructions at them through a loudspeaker. This oblique visual reference is all that we see of the Holocaust in Hungary in *Father;* the one character who is actually identified as a Jew, the protagonist's girlfriend, talks at some length about her family's persecution during the war and about her own problems of identity as a Jew and a Hungarian, but the camera shows only her face, not the past she evokes. In *Sunshine,* by contrast, the Holocaust representation is direct: Szabó not only shows the sadistic murder of Adam in the labor camp, but also inserts a piece of archival footage showing a line of Jews wearing the yellow star, being herded on a street in Budapest in 1944. The *mise en abyme* in *Sunshine* is concerned, rather, with historical representation in general, and with political manipulation and lying by means of film. An unnamed director (played by the Hungarian actor Péter Halász), interrogated by Ivan after the war, made propaganda films showing Soviet atrocities on the Russian front. We actually see an excerpt from one of his films, viewed by Ivan; but when pressed by Ivan, the director admits that the film was staged and filmed in a small town near Budapest. In other words, the presumed documentary was a fake—and the director tells this to Ivan as a plea in his favor, to show that he did not really travel to the Russian front during the war. "You shit!" is Ivan's comment. The director reappears later, filming Ivan when he receives his decoration—and later still, filming the 1956 crowds. It is because of his film that Ivan ends up in jail.

What is the difference between documentary, fake documentary, and historical realist fiction? What constitutes authenticity in film, and how can we tell when a film lies? What is the responsibility of a director to his audience, to his sponsors, to himself? How can one survive, make films, and succeed in not being "a shit"? These are among the questions raised, implicitly and cinematically, by the self-reflexive sequences in *Sunshine*. Why is the ending of *Sunshine,* Ivan's giving up his magyarized name, so shocking (one commentator called it "astounding," see Földes) to Hungarian viewers? That question leads us into the very center of Jewish identity and its dilemmas in contemporary Hungary and probably in all of Central Europe (with the difference that most Jews have disappeared from Poland and other Central European countries, whereas the Jewish population of Hungary is still significantly large; the usual number given is around 100,000). Szabó himself has offered interpretations of his ending in interviews. For him, the film's real theme is that of personal identity: by taking back his Jewish-sounding name, Ivan breaks the pattern of accommodation to authority, with its attendant alienation of self, that was begun by his grandfather. Szabó clarifies in an interview that "the obligation to accommodate, the terrible desire to fit in, transmitted from father to son, is what the story's last hero, Ivan, breaks with" (qtd. in Mülner). And in the same interview, he explains: "The protagonist finally understands who he is, and assumes that identity. That is much more important than the change of name. Ivan realizes that in order to be part of society, he does not have to renounce his self." In an interview with a Canadian journalist, he generalizes this theme to include not only Jews, and not only Hungary: "The film is about an identity crisis. . . . This is not only a Jewish problem. Millions of people suffer from the same question. Who am I? Should one, for the promise of a better life, cut off one's roots? I used the Jewish family simply as an example, because I know that world. I think that similar worries exist among the Turks in Germany and one sees this problem in England, Ireland, and Kosovo" (Adelman).

As Szabó well knows, Jews in Hungary are not really comparable to Turkish *Gastarbeiter* (guest workers) in Germany, nor to Asian and African immigrants in England. The specificity of Hungarian Jews until the Holocaust (and since then, but much more problematically, that is the point) is that they *felt* Hungarian: they were not exiles, Hungary was their home. Furthermore, as we have seen, they played an important historical role in the modernization of Hungary and in the creation of modern Hungarian identity. Jewish intellectuals—writers, journalists, publishers—played major roles in Hungarian cultural life as they did all over Central and East Europe, and the liberal professions were at times more than 50 percent Jewish. The Jewish laws of the late 1930s were designed precisely to do away with this Jewish "domination." They suddenly informed the Jews, even upper-class, assimilated, or converted Jews like Adam Sors, that they were not true Magyars; that in true Magyar eyes, they were pariahs. For over forty years after the Second World War, Jews who had survived and had decided to remain in Hungary persuaded themselves that anti-Semitism was a thing of the past: Jewishness was irrelevant in communist Hungary. Many Jews born after the war did not even realize until much later that their family was Jewish: "How I learned that I was a Jew" became practically a canonical subgenre of autobiography starting in the mid-1980s (see Erös et al.). Until the last years of the commmunist period, the word "Jew" could hardly be printed in the newspaper, nor were overtly anti-Semitic writings publishable. It is true that the official anti-Zionist discourse of the Soviet block, starting in 1949 and revived periodically afterward, was often a convenient cover for anti-Semitism, in Hungary as elsewhere. Still, Hungarian nationalism and the anti-Semitism that has traditionally accompanied it were not overtly endorsed by the communist regime.

After 1989 and the lifting of official censorship of the press and of book publishing, traditional anti-Semitic discourse once again became possible and actual (naturally, the same was true of other discourses, including Zionist and anti-anti-Semitic ones). The MDF, the center-right party that came to power in the 1990 elections, tolerated an extreme xenophobic and nationalist wing which eventually split off and formed its own party, the "Magyar Truth and Justice Party" (MIEP) led by the writer István Csurka. Csurka edits *Magyar Fórum,* the party's weekly newspaper, which is unabashedly and explicitly anti-Semitic. Evinced in the 1994 elections, the MIEP bounced back in 1998 and is currently quite close to the governing party, the once liberal but now conservative "Young Democrats" (FIDESZ) led by Viktor Orbán. In 1999, the Hungarian public heard, for the first time in more than half a century, a member of the government refer to the "Jewish question" in Hungary. This provoked a certain indignation, whereupon a government spokesman published an open letter in the newspaper *Magyar Hírlap* (16 August 1999) in an attempt to explain the minister's meaning as not anti-Semitic (see also Miklós Szabó). The current Hungarian government—in 2000–2001—has been the only one, so far, to welcome an official visit by the Austrian chancellor whose government has been boycotted by the European Union for accepting an alliance with Jörg Haider's extreme right-wing party (see Haraszti "Haider's"). Despite these troubling manifestations, however, it would be a mistake to compare today's Hungary to the 1930s, let alone the 1940s. For one thing—leaving aside the obviously different world situation—the majority of Hungarians does not appear to be in favor of anti-Semitism; for another, the Jews of Hungary have reacted vigorously, on the whole, to the reemergence of anti-Semitism from under the rug. Many assimilated Jewish intellectuals who had never spoken, or even, one surmises, thought much about their Jewish ancestry have in recent years begun writing or speaking about it. As one such intellectual told me when I was living in Budapest in 1993, "I have no contact with Jewishness, but now that there are anti-Semites I affirm that I'm a Jew" (see Suleiman 1996, 124–26). Since then, I have heard the same from others as well.

Aside from the assimilated Jews, there is a thriving Jewish community (or more exactly, a plurality of communities) in today's Hungary, almost all in Budapest: synagogues, Jewish schools, Jewish cultural journals—notably, *Szombat* (*Sabbath*), a monthly edited by Gábor T. Szántó, and *Múlt és Jövő* (*Past and Present*), a quarterly edited by János Kőbányai, who has also started a publishing house devoted to literature by Jewish writers—all indicate a significant Jewish presence. One does not have the feeling in Hungary, as one does in some neighboring countries, that only a few old people are left who know anything about Judaism and Jewish practice. Szabó's film is not about these relatively un-problematically self-identified Hungarian Jews; nor, one might say, is it chiefly addressed to them. Rather, the addressees are assimilated Jews who, like Szabó himself, have only recently begun avowing (publicly or privately) their Jewish ancestry. By a fascinating but not altogether surprising twist, the critics who have most passionately attacked *Sunshine* in Hungary belong precisely to this group.

"I left the movie sad and puzzled," wrote the well-known journalist Anna Földes in the liberal (formerly socialist) daily, *Népszabadság*. Szabó's "answer" to the search for identity is, according to Földes, the "worst possible" one, for it supports those (i.e., the anti-Semites) who "contest our inherited Hungarianness" (see Földes). If Ivan Sors can find his true identity only by becoming Sonnenschein, why should not all the *Kovács* and *Kis* (common Hungarian names) whose families changed their name generations ago be advised by the anti-Semites to take back their *Kohn* name? In fact, the extreme right-wing press has taken recently to "outing" assimilated Jews by digging up their family's original Germanic name; the anxiety expressed by the journalist alludes to this nasty habit. Similar anxiety is found in what has so far been the most detailed and sweeping critique of the film, published in the most respected cultural weekly in Hungary. The author, Péter György, a well-known intellectual, criticizes Szabó for bowing to global market pressures in producing a film chiefly for an "American" audience (see György). For the sake of this audience, Szabó has simplified Hungarian reality and presented a negative view of Hungary: he does not show any "decent," ordinary non-Jewish Hungarians, nor any extraordinary ones who sheltered Jews during the war. This is the image "the world will have of our Hungarian history, and this one-sidedness pains me," writes György. But his biggest worry, a veritable *cri de coeur,* is that "Israelite" and "non-Israelite" Hungarians will be driven apart by the "example" proposed in the film's ending. Szabó is wrong to insist on Jewish "difference" with Ivan's change of name, György maintains. Take the great modernist poet Miklós Radnóti: "He was born Glatter, he became a Catholic, and he is a Hungarian poet as Radnóti (for recent work on Radnóti, see Ozsváth "Radnóti, Celan") Would Szabó himself not be outraged if some "nobody" suddenly started referring to the poet as Glatter?

Fascinating question: could a Miklós Glatter be a great Hungarian poet? What György does not say, because it is known to all who read him, is that Miklós Radnóti was murdered in 1944 by Hungarian soldiers, while on a forced march with a group of other Jewish prisoners. For all his love of Hungary and the Hungarian language—he refused all his adult life to call himself a Jew or a Jewish poet, and converted to Catholicism in the early 1940s—Radnóti suffered the same fate as thousands of other Hungarian Jews. The problem that *Sunshine* struggles with is precisely the problem so sharply posed by the life and work of Radnóti, and of the other murdered Hungarian Jews who thought of themselves as Hungarians like any other.

Tamás Ungvári, one of the many well-known intellectuals who responded to György's article, puts it well: Szabó's film opens up sensitive wounds. It is about people who "chose a fate [a play on words on the name 'Sors,' meaning fate, also in György's title], but whom that fate did not choose. Another fate chose them, one they did not choose" (see Ungvári). Ungvári is pessimistic. The world over, he writes, combined identities have become the rule: African-American, Catalan-Spanish, Breton-French, Scottish-English; the only combination that its own society tolerates with difficulty, Ungvári adds, is that of Jewish Hungarian (for the voluminous critical debate about the film in Hungarian, see also the January 2000 issue of the journal *Múlt és Jövő,* with a special section devoted to *Sunshine*). Although its anxious critics read Szabó's ending as equally pessimistic, the film in fact seems to offer a more optimistic possibility. To be "outed" as a Jew is humiliating, but to come out of the closet—to take back one's Jewish name willingly—is liberating. Ivan breathes freely in Budapest at last as Sonnenschein; he does not leave Hungary, but makes his life there. The film's final panorama of Budapest, beneath a muted sky, suggests that the beauty of the city so closely identified with the Sonnenscheins' history may console Ivan for the losses and humiliations his family has suffered. To the North American viewer, even a Jewish-American born in Hungary, this ending seems quite plausible: one can be Hungarian even with a Jewish name; pluralistic democracy can work in Hungary. In sum, a multiculturalist dream which I, for one (being of a postmodern persuasion) am drawn to applaud. Yet, for reasons quite different from those of the Hungarian critics, I am a bit troubled: the dream is tenuous, even as a dream. The change of name is secondary, Szabó has stated; what matters is the recovery of roots and of a suppressed identity. But at the end of this film, Ivan has nothing but the name to tie him to Jewishness or to his family's past. He is the baptized son of two Catholic converts and he has thrown out all traces that might constitute a cultural archive. Photographs, letters, all the papers carefully saved by the faithful (Catholic) family servant during the war, even the famous black notebook that was at the origin of the family fortune—Ivan discards them all. The notebook falls to the ground, unseen and unrecognized by him, then joins the rest of the archive in the garbage truck. Nor does Ivan have progeny, as far as we can see: he is the last of the Sonnenscheins, alone in the city crowds. Yet, the ending of the film is clearly meant to be upbeat: the pan over Budapest, the swelling music, Ivan's final voice-over announcing that he feels free, all indicate a hopeful mood. A triumph of individualism and an affirmation of the individual artist, as some commentators have suggested? Miklós Haraszti suggests, as I have, that Valerie is the true mouthpiece of the film's values—not as a woman, but as an artist and an individualist (see Haraszti "Hívasson"). Perhaps. But I cannot help thinking of the final image of Szabó's last film before *Sunshine*, *Sweet Emma, Dear Böbe* (1992), which is bitterly ironic. What if, instead of reading the final images of *Sunshine* as a promise, we were to read it as ironic: not Szabó's dream, but a delusion of his traumatized hero? This interpretation may be reinforced by Ivan's statement, at the end, that he wants to follow in his grandmother's footsteps and photograph the world around him. In fact, he has shown not the slightest inclination for artistic expression up to this point, when he is more than thirty years old.

Finally, like the Danube that flows through Budapest, beautiful but full of Jewish ghosts, *Sunshine* is a deeply moving, troubled, and troubling film.

NOTE

This paper is adapted from a longer version, Susan Rubin Suleiman, "Jewish Assimilation in Hungary, the Holocaust, and Epic Film: Reflections on István Szabó's *Sunshine*," published in the *Yale Journal of Criticism* 14.1 (2001): 233–52. The author thanks Éva Forgács, Christoph Hüvös, János Köbányai, Eric Rentschler, Brooks Robards, George Schöpflin, and Michael Suleiman for their helpful comments. Special thanks to Steven Tötösy for his editorial help and his advice in producing this version of my work.

WORKS CITED

Adelman, Sid. "*Sunshine*'s Story Based on Director's Life . . . Sort of." *The Toronto Star* (3 December 1999).
Braham, Randolph. *The Politics of Genocide: The Holocaust in Hungary.* 2nd ed. New York: Columbia UP, 1994.
De Marchi, Bruno. *István Szabó.* Firenze: La Nuova Italia, 1977.
Deák, István. "Strangers at Home." *The New York Review of Books* (20 July 2000): 31.
Erös, Ferenc, András Kovács, and Katalin Lévai. "Hogyan jöttem rá hogy zsidó vagyok" ("How I Came to Realize I am Jewish"). *Medvetánc* 2.3 (1985): 129–44.
Fejtö, François. *Hongrois et Juifs.* Paris: Balland, 1997.
Földes, Anna. "Sors út" ("The Road of Fate"). *Népszabadság* (19 February 2000).
Gener, Randy. "Fiennes, Ehle, Harris Play across Generations in *Sunshine* Film." *Theatre.com News* (8 June 2000): <www.theatre.com/news/public/newsbrief.asp?newsid=7710>.

György, Péter "Sorsválasztók" ("Those Who Chose Their Fate"). *Élet és Irodalom* (11 February 2000).
Haraszti, Miklós. "Haider's Shadow Falls to the East." *New York Times* (2 May 2000).
Haraszti, Miklós. "Hívasson esztétát!" ("Call Upon an Art Critic!"). *Élet és Irodalom* (25 February 2000).
Hirsch, Joshua. "István Szabó: Problems in the Narration of Holocaust Memory." *Journal of Film and Video* 51.1 (1999): 3–21.
Imre, Anikó. "Comparative Central European Culture: Gender in Literature and Film." *Comparative Central European Culture*. Ed. Steven Tötösy de Zepetnek. West Lafayette: Purdue UP, 2002. 73-94.
Kovács, András. "Jews and Politics in Hungary." *Values, Interests and Identity: Jews and Politics in a Changing World*. Thematic Issue *Studies in Contemporary Jewry: An Annual* 11 (1995): 50–63.
Mülner, Dóra. "Itt vigyázni kell" ("Here We Must be Careful"; Interview with István Szabó). *Népszabadság* (8 February 2000).
Ozsváth, Zsuzsanna. "Radnóti, Celan, and Aesthetic Shifts in Central European Holocaust Poetry." *Comparative Central European Culture*. Ed. Steven Tötösy de Zepetnek. West Lafayette: Purdue UP, 2002. 53-72.
Ozsváth, Zsuzsanna. *In the Footsteps of Orpheus: The Life and Times of Miklós Radnóti*. Bloomington: Indiana UP, 2000.
Patai, Rafael. *The Jews of Hungary: History, Culture, Psychology*. Detroit: Wayne State UP, 1996.
Paul, David. "Szabó." *Five Filmmakers*. Ed. Daniel Goulding. Bloomington: Indiana UP, 1994. 156–208.
Portuges, Catherine. "Comparative Central European Culture: Austrian and Hungarian Cinema Today." *Comparative Central European Culture*. Ed. Steven Tötösy de Zepetnek. West Lafayette: Purdue UP, 2002. 133–48.
Schöpflin, George. Review of *Sunshine*. *Centre for the Study of Democracy Online* (26 January 2000): <http://www.ucl.ac.uk/cds/gsbr1.htm>.
Scott, A.O. "Serving the Empire, One After Another After . . . ." Review of *Sunshine*. *The New York Times* (9 June 2000): E12.
Szabó, István, dir. *Sunshine*. Color, 180 min. Prod. Robert Lantos and András Hámori. Toronto: Alliance Atlantic Pictures, 1999.
Szabó, Miklós. "A fogadott prókátor üzeni: a zsidók ne merjenek félni" ("A Message from the Official Spokesman: The Jews are not Allowed to Be Afraid"). *Magyar Hírlap* (1 September 1999).
Suleiman, Susan Rubin. *Budapest Diary: In Search of the Motherbook*. Lincoln: U of Nebraska P, 1996.
Suleiman, Susan Rubin. *Authoritarian Fictions: The Ideological Novel as a Literary Genre*. New York: Columbia UP, 1983.

Szentiványi, Zoltán. *Századunk névváltoztatásai. Helyhatósági és miniszteri engedéllyel megváltoztatott nevek gyűjteménye 1800–1893 (The Century's Changes of Surnames: A List of Surnames Changed by Ministerial and Municipal Permits 1800–1893)*. Budapest, 1895.

Tötösy de Zepetnek, Steven. "Women's Literature and Men Writing about Women." *Comparative Literature: Theory, Method, Application*. By Steven Tötösy de Zepetnek. Amsterdam-Atlanta, GA: Rodopi, 1998. 173–214.

Ungvári, Tamás. "Választott sors?" ("A Fate Chosen?"). *Élet és Irodalom* (10 March 2000).

Selected Bibliography for the Study of Central European Culture

Steven Tötösy de Zepetnek

This is a selected bibliography for the study of Central European culture of work ranging from studies in culture, literature, sociology, history, economics, architecture, political science, the arts, comparative cultural studies, etc. Central European culture is designated as a real and imagined space from Austria and the former East Germany to Romania and Bulgaria and Serbia to Galicia in the Ukraine, etc., including the Habsburg lands and their spheres of influence at various times of history. While the bibliography is with focus on the period of and after the 1989–1990 collapse of the Soviet empire and communism, essential studies about previous periods of the region are included. Although cumulative as well as selected bibliographies of work in all languages of the region including work published in the major languages of the West would be best, recognizing the universality of English as today's language of research and communication, the studies selected for this bibliography are mostly English-language publications although selected seminal studies in German, French, and Italian are included.

After the Fall. Thematic Issue *Media Studies Journal* 13.3 (1999): 1–204.
Ágh, Attila, ed. *The Emergence of East Central European Parliaments: The First Steps.* Budapest: Hungarian Centre for Democracy Studies, 1994.
Altermatt, Urs. *Nation, Ethnizität und Staat in Mitteleuropa.* Wien: Böhlau, 1996.
Anderson, Benedict. *Imagined Communities: Reflection on the Origin and Spread of Nationalism.* London: Verso, 1991.
Antohi, Sorin, and Vladimir Tismaneanu, eds. *Between Past and Future: The Revolutions of 1989 and Their Aftermath.* Budapest: Central European UP, 2000.
Arens, Katherine. "Politics, History, and Public Intellectuals in Central Europe after 1989." *Comparative Central European Culture.* Ed. Steven Tötösy de Zepetnek. West Lafayette: Purdue UP, 2002. 115–32.
Arens, Katherine. "Central Europe and the Nationalist Paradigm." *Working Papers in Austrian Studies* 96.1 (1996): <http://www.cas.umn.edu/wp961.htm>.
Arens, Katherine. *Austria and Other Margins: Reading Culture.* Columbia: Camden House, 1996.
Ash, Timothy Garton. *History of the Present: Essays, Sketches, and Dispatches from Europe in the 1990s.* New York: Random House, 2000.
Ash, Timothy Garton. "The Puzzle of Central Europe." *The New York Review* (18 March 1999): 18–23.
Ash, Timothy Garton. *The Magic Lantern: The Revolution of '89 Witnessed in Warsaw, Budapest, Berlin and Prague.* New York: Vintage, 1993.
Ash, Timothy Garton. *The Uses of Adversity: Essays on the Fate of Central Europe.* Cambridge: Granta, 1991.
Banac, Ivo, ed. *Eastern Europe in Revolution.* Ithaca: Cornell UP, 1992.
Barcsay, Thomas. "Entrepreneurial Traditions in East-Central Europe." *Essays in Economic and Business History* 10 (1992): 66–81.
Baske, Siegfried. "Charakteristika der Entwicklung und der gegenwärtigen Gestalt des Bildungswesens in Mitteleuropa im inter- und intrasystemaren Vergleich." *Zeitschrift für Ostforschung* 39.2 (1990): 226–37.
Beauprêtre, Gerard, ed. *L'Europe centrale. Realité, mythe, enjeu, XVIIe–XXe siècles.* Warsaw: U of Warsaw P, 1991.
Beller, Steven. "Reinventing Central Europe." *Working Papers in Austrian Studies* 92.5 (1992): <http://www.socsci.umn.edu/cas/925.htm>.
Berend, Iván T. *Decades of Crisis: Central and Eastern Europe before World War II.* Berkeley: U. of California P, 1998.
Berend, Iván T. *Central & Eastern Europe 1944–1993: Detour from the Periphery to the Periphery.* Cambridge: Cambridge UP, 1996.

Berend, Iván T. "German Economic Penetration in East Central Europe in Historical Perspective." *Can Europe Work? Germany and the Reconstruction of Postcommunist Societies*. Ed. Stephen E. Hanson and Willfried Spohn. Seattle: U of Washington P, 1995. 129–50.
Berend, Iván T., and György Ránki. *The European Periphery and Industrialization, 1780–1914*. Cambridge: Cambridge UP, 1982.
Berry, Ellen E., ed. *Postcommunism and the Body Politic*. Thematic Issue *Genders* 22 (1995): 1–431.
Bertens, Hans, and Douwe Fokkema, eds. "The Reception and Processing of Postmodernism: Central and Eastern Europe." *International Postmodernism: Theory and Literary Practice*. Amsterdam: John Benjamins, 1997. 413–59.
Beyme, Klaus von. *Transition to Democracy in Eastern Europe*. London: Macmillan, 1996.
Bibó, István. *Histoire des petites nations d'Europe centrale*. Paris: Albin Michel, 1993.
Bibó, István. *Democracy, Revolution, Self-Determination: Selected Writings*. Boulder: East European Monographs, 1991.
Biskupski, M. B. "Re-Creating Central Europe: The United States 'Inquiry' into the Future of Poland in 1918." *International History Review* 12.2 (1990): 249–79.
Björling, Fiona, ed. *Through a Glass Darkly: Cultural Representation in the Dialogue Between Central, Eastern, and Western Europe*. Lund: Slavica Lundensia, 1999.
Bojtár, Endre. *East European Avant-garde Literature*. Budapest: Akadémiai, 1992.
Bojtár, Endre. "Die Postmoderne und die Literaturen Mittel- und Osteuropas." *Neohelicon: Acta comparationis litterarum universarum* 16.1 (1989): 113–28.
Borghello, Giampaolo. "Svevo e la letteratura mitteleuropea: Appunti e riflessioni." *Neohelicon: Acta comparationis litterarum universarum* 23.2 (1996): 21–35.
Borsody, Stephen. *The New Central Europe: Triumphs and Tragedies*. Boulder: East European Monographs, 1993.
Boyer, John W. "Some Reflections on the Problem of Austria, Germany, and Mitteleuropa." *Central European History* 22 (1989): 301–15.
Braham, Randolph L. *Studies on the Holocaust: Selected Writings*. Boulder: East European Monographs, 2000.
Brînzeu, Pia. *Corridors of Mirrors: The Spirit of Europe in Contemporary British and Romanian Fiction*. Lanham: UP of America, 2000.
Bristol, Evelyn, ed. *East European Literature*. Berkeley: U of California Berkeley Slavics Specialities, 1982.

Bucur, Maria, and Nancy M. Wingfield, eds. *Staging the Past: The Politics of Commemoration in Habsburg Central Europe, 1848 to the Present.* West Lafayette: Purdue UP, 2001.
Bugge, Peter. "The Use of the Middle: Mitteleuropa vs. Stredni Evropa." *European Review of History* 6.1 (1999): 15–35.
Burian, Jarka. "Aspects of Central European Design." *The Drama Review* 28:2 (1984): 47–65.
Cacciari, Massimo. *Posthumous People: Vienna at the Turning Point.* Trans. Rodger Friedman. Stanford: Stanford UP, 1996.
Camerino, Giuseppe Antonio. "Lo specifico mitteleuropeo e i maggiori giuliani del primo novecento." *Neohelicon: Acta comparationis litterarum universarum* 23.2 (1996): 9–19.
Carneci, Magda. "Europe, Europe: Le Siècle de l'avant-garde en Europe Centrale et Orientale." *Euresis* 1–2 (1994): 275–77.
Casmir, Fred L., ed. *Communication in Eastern Europe: The Role of History, Culture, and Media in Contemporary Conflicts.* Mahwah: Lawrence Erlbaum, 1995.
Charguina, Ludmilla. "The Typology of Symbolism in Central and Eastern Europe." *Actes du VIIIe Congrès de l'Association Internationale de Littérature Comparée/Proceedings of the 8th Congress of the International Comparative Literature Association.* Ed. Béla Köpeczi and György M. Vajda.. Stuttgart: Bieber, 1980. Vol. 1, 545–50.
Collins, R. G., and Kenneth McRobbie, eds. *The Eastern European Imagination in Literature.* Thematic Issue of *Mosaic: A Journal for the Comparative Study of Literature and Ideas* 6.4 (1974): 1–238.
Comtet, Roger. "Langue et nation en Europe Centrale et Orientale du XVIIe siècle à nos jours." *Revue des Etudes Slaves* 69.3 (1997): 401–15.
Corcoran, Farrel, and Paschal Preston, eds. *Democracy and Communication in the New Europe: Change and Continuity in East and West.* Cresskill: Hampton P, 1995.
Cornis-Pope, Marcel. "Cultural Dialogics before and after 1989." *The Unfinished Battles: Romanian Postmodernism before and after 1989.* By Marcel Cornis-Pope. Iaşi: Polirom, 1996. 7–29.
Cornwall, Mark. *The Undermining of Austria-Hungary: The Battle for Hearts and Minds.* New York: Palgrave, 2000.
Crampton, R. J. *Eastern Europe in the Twentieth Century.* London: Routledge, 1997.
Czerwinski, E. J. "The Oldest Dying Profession: Poetry in Eastern Europe." *World Literature Today* 59.2 (1985): 203–07.
Dalbert, Claudia, and Hedvig Katona Sallay. "The 'belief in a just world' Construct in Hungary." *Journal of Cross-Cultural Psychology* 27 (1996): 293–314.

Dassanowsky, Robert von. "Lernet-Holenia and the Return of Central Europe." *Pro Europa: A Lodge of Literati* (2001): <http://www.proeuropa.gr/athenaeum/dassanowcv.html>.
Deletant, Dennis, and Harry Hanak, eds. *Historians as Nation-Builders: Central and South-East Europe.* New York: Macmillan, 1988.
Delsol, Chantal, and Michel Maslovski. *Histoire des idées politiques de l'Europe centrale.* Paris: PU de France, 1998.
Deltcheva, Roumiana. "Comparative Central European Culture: Displacements and Peripheralities." *Comparative Central European Culture.* Ed. Steven Tötösy de Zepetnek. West Lafayette: Purdue UP, 2002. 149–68.
Deltcheva, Roumiana. "East Central Europe as a Postcoloniality: The Prose of Viktor Paskov." *Colonizer and Colonized.* Ed. Theo D'Haen and Patricia Krüs. Amsterdam-Atlanta, GA: Rodopi, 2000. 589–97.
Deltcheva, Roumiana. "East Central Europe as a Politically Correct Scapegoat: The Case of Bulgaria." *CLCWeb: Comparative Literature and Culture: A WWWeb Journal* 1.2 (1999): <http://clcwebjournal.lib.purdue.edu/clcweb99-2/deltcheva99.html>.
Deltcheva, Roumiana. "The Difficult Topos In-Between: The East Central European Cultural Context as a Post-Coloniality." *Post Colonialism in Central Europe* Thematic Issue of *Sarmatian Review: A Forum for Central European Cultures* 23.3 (1998): <http://www.ruf.rice.edu/~sarmatia/998/deltcheva.html>.
Don, Yehuda, and Viktor Karády, eds. *A Social and Economic History of Central European Jewry.* New Brunswick: Transaction, 1990.
Dor, Milo. *Mitteleuropa, mythe ou réalité.* Paris: Fayard, 1999.
Drakulić, Slavenka. "Who Is Afraid of Europe?" *Eurozine* (9 November 2000): <http://www.eurozine.com/online/index.html>.
Drakulić, Slavenka. *Café Europa: Life after Communism.* New York: Norton, 1997.
Drakulić, Slavenka. *How We Survived Communism and Even Laughed.* New York: Harper, 1991.
Dupcsik, Csaba. "Postcolonial Studies and the Inventing of Eastern Europe." *East Central Europe* 26.1 (1999): 1–14.
Duṭu, Alexandru. *Political Models and National Identities in "Orthodox Europe."* Bucureşti: Babel, 1998.
Eagle, Herbert. "Czechoslavak, Polish, and Hungarian Cinema under Communism." *Cross Currents: A Yearbook of Central European Culture* 11 (1992): 175–92.
Eidsvik, Charles. "Mock Realism: The Comedy of Futility in Eastern Europe." *Comedy/Cinema/Theory.* Ed. Andrew S. Horton. Berkeley: U of California P, 1991. 91–109.

Enyedi, György. "Urbanisation in East Central Europe: Social Processes and Societal Responses in the State Socialist Systems." *Urban Studies* 29.6 (1992): 869–80.

Esbenshade, Richard S. "Remembering to Forget: Memory, History, National Identity in Postwar East-Central Europe." *Representations* 49 (1995): 72–96.

Fábry, Andrea. "A Comparative View of Modernism in Central European Literature." *Comparative Central European Culture*. Ed. Steven Tötösy de Zepetnek. West Lafayette: Purdue UP, 2002. 33–50.

Fanger, Donald. "Central European Writers as a Social Force." *Partisan Review* 59.4 (1992): 639–65.

Fehér, Ferenc. "On Making Central Europe." *Eastern European Politics and Societies* 3.3 (1989): 412–47.

Ferry, William E., and Roger Kanet, eds. *Post-Communist States in the World Community*. New York: St. Martin's P, 1998.

Fitzmaurice, John. "A Tale of Four Elections: Central Europe September 1997–September 1998." *Czech Sociological Review* 8.1 (2000): 93–101.

Fitzmaurice, John. *Politics and Government in the Visegrad Countries: Poland, Hungary, the Czech Republic and Slovakia*. New York: Palgrave, 1998.

Fleischer, Manfred P., ed. *The Harvest of Humanism in Central Europe*. St. Louis: Concordia P, 1992.

Fox, Patricia D. "What's Past Is Prologue: Imagining the Socialist Nation in Cuba and in Hungary." *CLCWeb: Comparative Literature and Culture: A WWWeb Journal* 1.1 (1999): <http:// clcwebjournal.lib.purdue.edu/ clcweb99-1/fox99.html>.

Fraser, Angus. *The Gypsies*. Oxford: Blackwell, 1992.

Fried, István. "The Literary-Historical Process in East Central Europe." *Acta Litteraria Academiae Scientiarum Hungaricae* 31.1–2 (1989): 149–59.

Fried, István. "East-Central Europe: Controversies over a Notion." *Danubian Historical Studies* 2.1 (1988): 7–17.

Fried, István. "On the Formation of East Central European Novel." *Acta Litteraria Academiae Scientiarum Hungaricae* 27.1–2 (1985): 173–88.

Fried, István. "Les Possibilités de la comparaison dans l'analyse des littératures de l'Europe centrale et orientale." *Acta Litteraria Academiae Scientiarum Hungaricae* 24.3–4 (1982): 383–94.

Funk, Nanette, and Magda Mueller, eds. *Gender Politics and Post-Communism*. New York: Routledge, 1993.

Gal, Susan, and Gail Kligman, eds. *Reproducing Gender: Politics, Publics, and Everyday Life after Socialism*. Princeton: Princeton UP, 2000.

Gitelman, Zvi, Lubomyr Hajda, John-Paul Himka, and Roman Solchanyk, eds. *Cultures and Nations of Central and Eastern Europe*. Cambridge: Harvard UP, 2000.

Glatz, Ferenc. *Minorities in East-Central Europe: Historical Analysis and a Policy Proposal.* Budapest: Europa Institut, 1993.
Goldfarb, David A. "Cinema in Transition: Recent Films from East and Central Europe" *Slavic and East European Performance* 13:2 (1993): 51–54.
Goldfarb, Jeffrey. *After the Fall: The Pursuit of Democracy in Central Europe.* New York: HarperCollins, 1992.
Good, David F., and Tongshu Ma. "The Economic Growth of Central and Eastern Europe in Comparative Perspective, 1870–1989." *European Review of Economic History* 3.2 (1999): 103–37.
Gotovska-Popova, Todoritchka. "Nationalism in Post-Communist Eastern Europe." *East European Quarterly* 27.2 (1992): 171–86.
Goulding, Daniel J. "East Central European Cinema: Two Defining Moments." *The Oxford Guide to Film Studies.* Ed. John Hill and Pamela Gibson. New York: Oxford UP, 1998. 471–77.
Graubard, Stephen R., ed. *Eastern Europe . . . Central Europe . . . Europe.* Boulder: Westview P, 1991.
Gross, Jan T. "Social Consequences of War: Preliminaries to the Study of Imposition of Communist Regimes in East Central Europe." *Eastern European Politics and Societies* 3.2 (1989): 198–214.
Hacohen, Malachi Haim. "Dilemmas of Cosmopolitanism: Karl Popper, Jewish Identity, and 'Central European Culture'." *Journal of Modern History* 71.1 (1999): 105–49.
Halecki, Oscar. *Borderlands of Western Civilization: A History of East Central Europe.* New York: Ronald P, 1952.
Harrison, Thomas. *1910: The Emancipation of Dissonance.* Berkeley: U of California P, 1996.
Havranek, Jan. "Central Europe, East-Central Europe and the Historians 1940–1948." *Verbürgerlichung in Mitteleuropa.* Budapest: Akadémiai, 1991. 299–309.
Hawkesworth, Celia, ed. *Literature and Politics in Eastern Europe.* New York: St. Martin's P, 1992.
Hegyi, Lóránd. "Central Europe as a Hypothesis and a Way of Life." *The Heartland Project: Exploring the Heartlands of Central Europe and the American Midwest: Aspects/Positions Thematic Issue 50 Years of Art in Central Europe 1949–1999* (Essays): <http://www.aspectspositions.org/essays/hegyi1.html>.
Heimerl, Daniela. "L'Unification de l'Allemagne. Vue de l'Europe du Centre-Est: Reminesces, espoirs." *Revue d'Allemagne et des Pays de Langue Allemande* 31.1 (1999): 123–37.
Held, Joseph, ed. *The Columbia History of Eastern Europe in the Twentieth Century.* New York: Columbia UP, 1992.
Higley, John, and György Lengyel. *Elites after State Socialism: Theories and Analysis.* Lanham: Rowman and Littlefield, 2000.

Holmes, Leslie. *The End of Communist Power.* New York: Oxford UP, 1993.
Homosexuality in Eastern Europe. Thematic Issue Central Europe Review1.7 (1999): <http://www.cereview.org/_archives99.html#issue _seven>.
Huntington, Samuel P. *The Third Wave: Democratization in the Late Twentieth Century.* Norman: U of Oklahoma P, 1991.
Hupchik, Dennis P. *Culture and History in Eastern Europe.* New York: St. Martin's P, 1994.
Imre, Anikó. "Comparative Central European Culture: Gender in Literature and Film." *Comparative Central European Culture.* Ed. Steven Tötösy de Zepetnek. West Lafayette: Purdue UP, 2002. 71–90.
Ingrao, Charles. "Ten Untaught Lessons about Central Europe: An Historical Perspective." Habsburg Web Site Occasional Papers 1 (1996): <http://www2.hnet.msu.edu/~habsweb/occasionalpapers/untaughtlessons.html>.
Janaszek-Ivaniĉková, Halina. "Postmodern Literature and the Cultural Identity of Central and Eastern Europe." *Postcolonial Literatures: Theory and Practice/Les Littératures post-coloniales. Théories et réalisations.* Ed. Steven Tötösy de Zepetnek and Sneja Gunew. Thematic Issue *Canadian Review of Comparative Literature/Revue Canadienne de Littérature Comparée* 22.3–4 (1995): 805–11.
Janos, Andrew C. *East Central Europe in the Modern World: The Politics of the Borderlands from Pre- to Postcommunism.* Stanford: Stanford UP, 2000.
Janowski, Maciej. "Pitfalls and Opportunities: The Concept of East-Central Europe as a Tool of Historical Analysis." *European Review of History* 6.1 (1999): 91–100.
Jászi, Oscar. *The Dissolution of the Habsburg Monarchy.* Chicago: U of Chicago P, 1929.
Johnson, Lonnie R. *Central Europe: Enemies, Neighbors, Friends.* New York: Oxford UP, 1996.
Johnston, William M. *The Austrian Mind: An Intellectual and Social History 1848–1938.* Berkeley: U of California P, 1976.
Judt, Tony. "The Rediscovery of Central Europe." *Daedalus: Journal of the American Academy of Arts and Sciences* 119.1 (1990): 23–54.
Kaufmann, Thomas DaCosta. *Court, Cloister & City: The Art and Culture of Central Europe 1450–1800.* Chicago: U of Chicago P, 1995.
Keane, John, ed. *The Power of the Powerless: Citizens against the State in Central-Eastern Europe.* Armonk: M.E. Sharpe, 1990.
Kennedy, Michael D. "An Introduction to East European Ideology and Identity in Transformation." *Envisioning Eastern Europe: Postcommunist Cultural Studies.* Ed. Michael D. Kennedy. Ann Arbor: U of Michigan P, 1994. 1–45.

Kennedy, Michael D., ed. *Envisioning Eastern Europe: Postcommunist Cultural Studies*. Ann Arbor: U of Michigan P, 1994.
King, Jeremy. "The Nationalization of East Central Europe: Ethnicism, Ethnicity, and Beyond." *Staging the Past: The Politics of Commemoration in Habsburg Central Europe, 1848 to the Present*. Ed. Maria Bucur and Nancy M. Wingfield. West Lafayette: Purdue UP, 2001. 112–52.
Király, Béla K., and Dimitrije Djordjević, eds. *East Central European Society and the Balkan Wars*. Boulder: Eastern European Monographs, 1987.
Kis, Csaba G. "Contradictions of the National Image in East Central European Anthems." *Acta Litteraria Academiae Scientiarum Hungaricae* 29.3–4 (1987): 381–401.
Klobucka, Anna. "Theorizing European Periphery." *symplokē: a journal for the intermingling of literary, cultural and theoretical scholarship* 5.1–2 (1997): 119–35.
Konrad, Helmut. "Urbane Identität in Zentraleuropa. Überlegungen zu einer vergleichenden Studie." *Österreichische Osthefte* 37.1 (1995): 13–23.
Konrád, George, and Iván Szelényi. *The Intellectuals on the Road to Class Power*. Trans. Andrew Arato and Richard E. Allen. Brighton: Harvester, 1979.
Konrád, György. *The Melancholy of Rebirth: Essays from Post-Communist Central Europe, 1989–1994*. Trans. Michael Henry Heim. New York: Harcourt Brace, 1995.
Konrád, György, Václav Havel, Danilo Kis, and Claudio Magris. *Central Europe*. London: The Austrian Cultural Institute, 1998.
Konstantinović, Zoran. "Variationen der Mitteleuropaidee 1848 und danach." *1848 Revolution in Europa. Verlauf, politische Programme, Folgen und Wirkungen*. Ed. Heiner Timmermann. Berlin: Drucker and Humblot, 1999. 367–79.
Konstantinović, Zoran. "Das Mitteleropa-Verständnis in der Literatur der Gegenwart." *Mitteleuropa. Idee, Wissenschaft und Kultur im 19. und 20. Jahrhundert. Beiträge aus österreichischer und ungarischer Sicht*. Ed. Richard G. Plaschka, Horst Haselsteiner, and Anna M. Drabek. Wien: Verlag der Österreichischen Akademie der Wissenschaften, 1997. 73–89.
Konstantinović, Zoran. "Das Projekt 'Mitteleuropa' in der neuen Architektur Europas." *Die neue Architektur Europas*. Ed. Helmut Reinalter. Wien: Thaur, 1997. 53–65.
Konstantinović, Zoran. "Les Slaves du Sud et la Mitteleuropa." *Revue germanique internationale* 1 (1994): 45–60.
Konstantinović, Zoran. "Verspielte Chancen mitteleuropäischer Literaturausblicke. Über die Zukunft regionaler Literaturen." *Identität und Nachbarschaft. Die Vielfalt der Alpen-Adria Länder*. Ed. Manfred Prisching. Wien: Böhlau, 1994. 219–52.

Konstantinović, Zoran. "Figurationen mitteleuropäischer Geistigkeit: Versuch einer literarhistorischen Periodisierung." *Die deutsche Literaturgeschichte Ostmittel- und Südosteuropas von der Mitte des 19. Jahrhunderts bis heute. Forschungsschwerpunkte und Defizite.* Ed. Anton Schwob. München: Südostdeutsches Kulturwerk, 1992. 9–18.

Konstantinović, Zoran. "Die Literatur in Mitteleuropa der zwanziger Jahre. *La Mitteleuropa negli anni venti. Culture et società.* Ed. Quirion Principe. Gorizia: Istituto per gli incontri culturali mitteleuropei, 1992. 83–97.

Konstantinović, Zoran. "Universitas complex: Überlegungen zu einer Literaturgeschichte Mitteleuropas." *"Kakanien" Aufsätze zur österreichischen und ungarischen Literatur, Kunst und Kultur um die Jahrhundertwende.* Ed. Eugen Thurnher, Walter Weiss, János Szabó, and Attila Tamás. Budapest: Akadémiai, 1991. 9–30.

Konstantinović, Zoran. "Gibt es eine mitteleuropäische Literatur?" *Europa und Mitteleuropa. Eine Umschreibung Österreichs.* Ed. Andreas Pribersky. Wien: Böhlau, 1991. 201–12.

Konstantinović, Zoran. "Mitteleuropäische Literatur und kulturelle Identität." *Mitteleuropäische Perspektiven.* Ed. Arno Truger and Thomas H. Macho. Wien: Böhlau, 1990. 17–31.

Konstantinović, Zoran, and Fridrun Rinner, eds. *Eine Literaturgeschichte Mitteleuropas.* Innsbruck: Studien Verlag, 2001.

Kontler, László. *Pride and Prejudice: National Stereotypes in 19th and 20th Century Europe East to West.* Budapest: Central European UP, 1995.

Kopczynski, Maciej. "The Second Generation of Democratic Elites in Eastern and Central Europe." *Polish Sociological Review* 1.129 (2000): 129–35.

Kostecki, Wojciech, Katarzyna Zukrowska, and Bogdan J. Goralczyk, eds. *Transformations of Post-Communist States.* New York: St. Martin's P, 2000.

Kundera, Milan. "The Tragedy of Central Europe." *The New York Review of Books* 31.7 (26 April 1984): 33–38.

Kurczaba, Alex. "East Central Europe and Multiculturalism in the American Academy." *Post Colonialism in Central Europe* Thematic Issue of *Sarmatian Review: A Forum for Central European Cultures* 23.3 (1998): <http://www.ruf.rice.edu/~sarmatia/998/kurczaba.html>.

Kürti, László, and Juliet Langman, eds. *Beyond Borders: Remaking Cultural Identities in the New East and Central Europe.* Boulder: Westview P, 1997.

Laskowski, Timothy. "Naming Reality in Native American and Eastern European Literatures." *Melus: The Journal of the Society for the Study of the Multi-Ethnic Literature of the United States* 19.3 (1994): 47–59.

Lawday, David. "Central Europe: The Return of the Habsburgs." *The Economist* (18 November 1995): 5–24.
Leitner, Erich, ed. *Educational Research and Higher Education Reform in Eastern and Central Europe*. Bern: Peter Lang, 1998.
Lengyel, György. "The Post-Communist Economic Elite." *A Society Transformed*. Ed. Rudolf Andorka, Tamás Kolosi, Richard Rose, and György Vukovich. Budapest: Central UP, 1999. 85–96.
Lewis, Virginia L. "The Other Face of Modernization: The Collapse of Rural Society in East Central European Realism and Naturalism." *Neohelicon: Acta comparationis litterarum universarum* 22.2 (1995): 221–45.
Liebich, André, and André Reszler, eds. *L'Europe centrale et ses minorités. Vers une solution européenne*. Paris: PU de France, 1993.
Lojkó, Miklós. "C. A. Macartney and Central Europe." *European Review of History* 6.1 (1999): 37–57.
Lojkó, Miklós. "The Failed Handshake on the Danube: The Story of Anglo-American Plans for the Liberation of Central Europe at the End of the Second World War." *Hungarian Studies* 13.1 (1998–99): 119–27.
Lomax, Bill. "Eastern Europe: Restoration and Crisis: The Metamorphosis of Power in Eastern Europe." *Critique* 25 (1993): 47–84.
Lutzkanova-Vassileva, Albena. "Testimonial Poetry in East European Post-Totalitarian Literature." *CLCWeb: Comparative Literature and Culture: A WWWeb Journal* 3.1 (2001): <http://clcwebjournal.lib.purdue.edu/clcweb01-1/lutzkanova-vassileva01.html>.
Magocsi, Paul Robert. *Of the Making of Nationalities There Is no End*. Boulder: East European Monographs, 2000.
Marácz, László, ed. *Expanding European Unity: Central and Eastern Europe*. Thematic Issue *Yearbook of European Studies/Annuaire d'Etudes européennes* 11 (1999): 1–171.
Matejka, Ladislav. "Milan Kundera's Central Europe." *Cross Currents: A Yearbook of Central European Culture* 9 (1990): 127–34.
Mayhew, Alan. *Recreating Europe: The European Union's Policy towards Central and Eastern Europe*. New York: Cambridge UP, 1998.
McNair, Brian. "Lovebirds? The Media, the State, and Politics in Central and Eastern Europe." *The Public* 2.1 (1995): 75–91.
Mendoza, Celia. "Die Entwicklung des ost- und westeuropäischen gesellschaftlichen Bewusstseins im Vergleich." *Jahrbücher für Geschichte Osteuropas* 47.2 (1999): 244–53.
Michel, Bernard. "Pour une image vraie de l'Europe Centrale." *Historiens et Geographes* 80.329 (1990): 69–73.
Michta, Andrew A., ed. *America's New Alliances: Poland, Hungary, and the Czech Republic in NATO*. Seattle: U of Washington P, 2000.

Molnár, Miklós, and André Reszler, eds. *La Génie de l'Autriche-Hongrie. Etat, société, culture*. Paris: PU de France, 1989.
Moore, David Chioni. "Is the Post- in Postcolonial the Post- in Post-Soviet? Toward a Global Postcolonial Critique." *PMLA: Publications of the Modern Language Association of America* 116.1 (2001): 111–28.
Moravánszky, Ákos. *Competing Visions: Aesthetic Invention and Social Imagination in Central European Architecture, 1867–1918*. Cambridge: MIT P, 1998.
Morton, Frederic. *Thunder at Twilight: Vienna 1913/1914*. New York: Macmillan, 1989.
Morrison, John, ed. *Ethnic and National Issues in Russian and East European History*. New York: St. Martin's P, 2000.
Motyl, Alexander J. "Reform, Transition, or Revolution? The Limits to Change in the Postcommunist States." *Contention: Debates in Society, Culture, and Science* 4.1 (1994): 141–60.
Nemeti, Ludmila Sargina. "Le Modernisme et l'idée de la fin de siècle dans les littératures d'Europe centrale et orientale." *Neohelicon: Acta comparationis litterarum universarum* 5.1 (1988): 113–23.
Nemoianu, Virgil. "Learning over Class: The Case of the Central European Ethos." *Cultural Participation: Trends since the Middle Ages*. Ed. Ann Rigney and Douwe Fokkema. Amsterdam and Philadelphia: John Benjamins, 1993. 79–107.
Niedermüller, Péter. "The Image of Eastern Europe and European Identity: An Anthropological Approach." *Watching Europe: A Media and Cultural Studies Reader*. Ed. Ute Bechdolf, Pia Kalliopi Hatzistrati, Torsten Storm Johannsen, Michi Knecht, Hardy Kromer, Tanja Marquardt, Bas Raijmakers, Maarten Reesink, and Ralph Winkle. Amsterdam: Amsterdam Cultural Studies Foundation, 1993. 68–78.
Okey, Robin. *The Habsburg Monarchy: From Enlightenment to Eclipse*. New York: Palgrave, 2001.
Okey, Robin. "Central Europe/Eastern Europe: Behind the Definitions." *Past & Present* 137 (1992): 102–33.
Okey, Robin. *Eastern Europe 1740–1985*. Minneapolis: U of Minnesota P, 1986.
Ozsváth, Zsuzsanna. "Radnóti, Celan, and Aesthetic Shifts in Central European Holocaust Poetry." *Comparative Central European Culture*. Ed. Steven Tötösy de Zepetnek. West Lafayette: Purdue UP, 2002. 51–70.
Paul, David W., ed. *Politics, Art and Commitment in the East European Cinema*. New York: St. Martin's, 1983.
Perczel, Csilla Ottlik. *A History of Architecture in the Carpathian Basin (1000 A.D.–1920)*. Boulder: East European Monographs, 2000.

Péter, László. "Central Europe and Its Reading into the Past." *European Review of History* 6.1 (1999): 101–11.
Petro, Peter. "Austroslovakism in Anton Hykisch's Novel about Maria Theresa." *Comparative Central European Culture*. Ed. Steven Tötösy de Zepetnek. West Lafayette: Purdue UP, 2002. 91–102.
Pichova, Hana. "Milan Kundera and the Identity of Central Europe." *Comparative Central European Culture*. Ed. Steven Tötösy de Zepetnek. West Lafayette: Purdue UP, 2002. 103–14.
Pilon, Juliana Geran. *The Bloody Flag: Post-Communist Nationalism in Eastern Europe*. New Brunswick: Transaction Publishers, 1992.
Pók, Attila. "Atonement and Sacrifice: Scapegoats in Modern Eastern and Central Europe." *East European Quarterly* 32.4 (1999): 531–48.
Portuges, Catherine. "Comparative Central European Culture: Austrian and Hungarian Cinema Today." *Comparative Central European Culture*. Ed. Steven Tötösy de Zepetnek. West Lafayette: Purdue UP, 2002. 133–48.
Portuges, Catherine. "Border Crossings: Recent Trends in East and Central European Cinema." *Slavic Review* 51.3 (1992): 531–35.
Portuges, Catherine, and Daniel P. Goulding, eds. *Cinemas in Transition: Post-Communist Cinema in East Central Europe*. London: Flicks Books, forthcoming.
Pospíšil, Ivo, and Miloš Zelenka, eds. *Centrisme interlittéraire des littératures de l'Europe Centrale*. Brno: Masaryk U, 1999.
Prazmowska, Anita J. *Eastern Europe and the Origins of the Second World War*. New York: St. Martin's P, 2000.
Puskás, Julianna, ed. *Overseas Migration from East-Central and Southeastern Europe, 1880–1940*. Budapest: Akadémiai, 1990.
Quart, Barbara. "A Few Short Takes on Eastern European Film." *Cinéaste* 19.4 (1993): 63–64.
Rai, Shirin, Hilary Pilkington, and Annie Phizacklea, eds. *Women in the Face of Change: The Soviet Union, Eastern Europe, and China*. New York: Routledge, 1992.
Ramet, Sabrina P., ed. *The Radical Right in Central and Eastern Europe since 1989*. University Park: Pennsylvania State UP, 1999.
Renne, Tanya. *Ana's Land: Sisterhood in Eastern Europe*. Boulder: Westview P, 1996.
Reszler, André. "Latent Pluralism in Central Europe." *Plural Societies* 18.2–3 (1989): 30–44.
Rinner, Fridrun. "Die Literatur Mitteleuropas als Bestimmung von Raum und Zeit." *Space and Boundaries of Literature*. Ed. Roger Bauer. München: Iudicium, 1990. 83–87.
Rosenberg, Tina. *The Haunted Land: Facing Europe's Ghosts after Communism*. New York: Vintage, 1996.

Rothschild, Joseph. *Return to Diversity: A Political History of East Central Europe since World War II.* Oxford: Oxford UP, 1993.
Rozman, Gilbert, et al., eds. *Dismantling Communism.* Baltimore: Johns Hopkins UP, 1992.
Rupnik, Jacques. "Central Europe or Mitteleuropa?" *Daedalus: Journal of the American Academy of Arts and Sciences* 119 (1990): 249-78.
Rupnik, Jacques. *The Other Europe.* New York: Schocken Books, 1989.
Russocki, Stanislaw. "Pour une histoire de la culture politique et juridique de Centre-Est de l'Europe." *Acta Poloniae Historica* 62 (1990): 191-203.
Ryszka, Franciszek. "'Mitteleuropa': Does It Still Exist, Or Is It a Mere Geopolitical Abstraction?" *World Futures* 29.3 (1990): 219-26.
Sadowski-Smith, Claudia. "Post-Cold War Narratives of Nostalgia." *The Comparatist: Journal of the Southern Comparative Literature Association* 23 (1999): 117-27.
Salamander, Rachel, ed. *The Jewish World of Yesterday, 1860-1938.* New York: Rizzoli, 1992.
Savage, Mike. "Making Capitalism without Capitalists: Class Formation and Elite Formation in Post-Communist Central Europe." *Sociological Review* 48.3 (2000): 491-92.
Saydak, Paul A. "Nato Enlargement and Stabilizing Central and Eastern Europe: The First Wave and Beyond." *Polish Review* 43.3 (1998): 337-54.
Schöpflin. George. *Politics in Eastern Europe.* Oxford: Blackwell, 1993.
Schöpflin, George. "Post-Communism: Constructing New Democracies in Central Europe." *International Affairs* 67.2 (1991): 235-50.
Schöpflin, George, and Nancy Wood, eds. *In Search of Central Europe.* Cambridge: Polity P, 1989.
Schorske, Carl E. *Fin-de-siècle Vienna: Politics and Culture.* New York: Vintage, 1980.
Schramm, Gottfried. "Ein Rundgespräch über 'Ostmitteleuropa': Vom sinvollen Umgang mit einem Konzept für unsere Zukunft." *Jahrbücher für Geschichte Osteuropas* 48.1 (2000): 119-22.
Schramm, Tomasz. "La Formation des frontières en Europe Centrale après la première guerre mondiale." *Relations Internationales* 64 (1990): 359-70.
Schwartz, Herman. *The Struggle for Constitutional Justice in Post-Communist Europe.* Chicago: U of Chicago P, 2000.
Sharman, J. C., and Roger E. Kanet. "The Challenge of Democratic Consolidation in Post-Communist Europe." *International Politics* 35.3 (1998): 333-51.
Shumaker, David. "The Origins and Development of Central European Cooperation: 1989-1992." *East European Quarterly* 27.3 (1993): 351-73.

Škvorecký, Josef. "Eastern European Literature in Transition." *The Review of Contemporary Fiction* 17 (1997): 98–107.
Spohn, Willfried. "United Germany as the Renewed Center in Europe: Continuity and Change in the German Question." *Can Europe Work? Germany and the Reconstruction of Postcommunist Societies*. Ed. Stephen E. Hanson and Willfried Spohn. Seattle: U of Washington P, 1995. 79–128.
Stenberg, Peter. *Journey to Oblivion: The End of the East European Yiddish and German Worlds in the Mirror of Literature*. Toronto: U of Toronto P, 1991.
Stern, J.P. *The Heart of Europe: Essays on Literature and Ideology*. Oxford: Blackwell, 1992.
Stirk, Peter, ed. *Mitteleuropa: History and Prospects*. Edinburgh: Edinburgh UP, 1994.
Stokes, Gale. *The Walls Came Tumbling Down: The Collapse of Communism in Eastern Europe*. Oxford: Oxford UP, 1993.
Suleiman, Susan Rubin. "Central Europe, Jewish Family History, and *Sunshine*." *Comparative Central European Culture*. Ed. Steven Tötösy de Zepetnek. West Lafayette: Purdue UP, 2002. 169–88.
Sussex, Roland. *Culture and Nationalism in Nineteenth-Century Eastern Europe*. Columbus: Slavica, 1985.
Svob-Djokić, Nada, ed. *The Cultural Identity of Central Europe*. Zagreb: Institute for International Relations Europe House, 1997.
Szakolczai, Arpad. "In a Permanent State of Transition: Theorising the East-European Condition." *Limen: Journal for Theory and Practice of Liminal Phenomena* 1.1 (2001):<http://www.mi2.hr/limen/limen1-2001/arpad_szakolczai.html>.
Taras, Ray, ed. *National Identities and Ethnic Minorities in Eastern Europe*. New York: St. Martin's P, 1998.
Teichova, Alice, ed. *Central Europe in the Twentieth Century: An Economic History Perspective*. Brookfield: Ashgate, 1997.
Teleky, Richard. "Towards a Course on Central European Literature in Translation." *Comparative Literature: History and Contemporaneity/Littérature Comparée: Histoire et contemporanéité*. Ed. Milan V. Dimić and Steven Tötösy de Zepetnek. Thematic Cluster *Canadian Review of Comparative Literature/Revue Canadienne de Littérature Comparée* 23.1 (1996): 113–23.
Ten Years after 1989: Postcommunist Reflections. Thematic Cluster *Dissent* (Fall 1999): 5–19.
Tismaneanu, Vladimir. *Fantasies of Salvation: Democracy, Nationalism and Myth in Post-Communist Europe*. Princeton: Princeton UP, 1998.
Tismaneanu, Vladimir. *Reinventing Politics: Eastern Europe from Stalin to Havel*. New York: The Free Press, 1992.

Tomaszewski, Jerzy. *The Socialist Regimes of East Central Europe: Their Establishment and Consolidation 1944–67.* New York: Routledge, 1989.
Tóth, István György. *Literacy and Written Culture in Early Modern Central Europe.* Budapest: Central European UP, 2000.
Tötösy de Zepetnek, Steven. "Comparative Cultural Studies and the Study of Central European Culture." *Comparative Central European Culture.* Ed. Steven Tötösy de Zepetnek. West Lafayette: Purdue UP, 2002. 1–32.
Tötösy de Zepetnek, Steven. "Configurations of Postcoloniality and National Identity: Inbetween Peripherality and Narratives of Change." *The Comparatist: Journal of the Southern Comparative Literature Association* 23 (1999): 89–110.
Tötösy de Zepetnek, Steven. "Ethnizität und Zentrum/Peripherie. Deutschland, (östliches) Mitteleuropa und das kanadische Modell." *Kultur, Identität, Europa. Über die Schwierigkeiten und Möglichkeiten einer Konstruktion.* Ed. Reinhold Viehoff and Rien T. Segers. Frankfurt: Suhrkamp, 1999. 425–41.
Tötösy de Zepetnek, Steven. "Women's Literature and Men Writing about Women." *Comparative Literature: Theory, Method, Application.* By Steven Tötösy de Zepetnek. Amsterdam-Atlanta, GA: Rodopi, 1998. 173–214.
Tschernokoshewa, Elka. "Born in Eastern Europe: Reality and Imagination." *Watching Europe: A Media and Cultural Studies Reader.* Ed. Ute Bechdolf, Pia Kalliopi Hatzistrati, Torsten Storm Johannsen, Michi Knecht, Hardy Kromer, Tanja Marquardt, Bas Raijmakers, Maarten Reesink, and Ralph Winkle. Amsterdam: Amsterdam Cultural Studies Foundation, 1993. 60–78.
Turner, Barry, ed. *Central Europe Profiled: Essential Facts on Society, Business and Politics in Central Europe.* New York: St. Martin's P, 2000.
Turnock, David. *Eastern Europe: An Historical Geography, 1815–1945.* London: Routledge, 1989.
Valiani, Leo. *The End of Austria-Hungary.* Trans. Eric Mosbacher. New York: Knopf, 1973.
Verdery, Katherine. *What Was Socialism and What Comes Next?* Princeton: Princeton UP, 1996.
Wagner, Francis S., ed. *Toward a New Central Europe.* Astor Park: Danubian P, 1970. Rpt. Hamilton: Hunyadi P, 1991.
Wallace, Claire. "The Eastern Frontier of Western Europe: Mobility in the Buffer Zone." *New Community* 22.2 (1996): 259–86.
Wallerstein, Immanuel. "The Relevance of the Concept of Semiperiphery to Southern Europe." *Semiperipheral Development: The Politics of Southern Europe in the Twentieth Century.* Ed. Giovanni Arrighi. Beverly Hills: Sage, 1985. 31–39.

Wandycz, Piotr S. *The Price of Freedom: A History of East Central Europe from the Middle Ages to the Present.* New York: Routledge, 1992.

Weinberg, Leonard. "Communism and the Intellectuals: The Beginning and the End of the Cold War." *Halcyon: A Journal of the Humanities* 13 (1991): 181–91.

White, Steven, Judy Batt, and Paul G. Louis, eds. *Developments in Central and Eastern European Politics 2.* Durham: Duke UP, 1998.

Whitefield, Stephen, ed. *The New Institutional Architecture of Eastern Europe.* London: Macmillan, 1993.

Willett, John. "Is There a Central European Culture?" *Cross Currents: A Yearbook of Central European Culture* 10 (1991): 1–16.

Wiszniowska, Marta. "To Die of Politics: An Exclusively East-Central European Malady?" *East Central European Traumas and a Millennial Condition.* Ed. Zbigniew Bialas and Wieslaw Krajka. Boulder: East European Monographs, 1999. 107–24.

Wolff, Larry. *Inventing Eastern Europe: The Map of Civilization on the Mind of the Enlightenment.* Stanford: Stanford UP, 1994.

Contributors

Katherine Arens's interests are in Austrian and German literature and culture, nineteenth century to the present, the history of psychology and psychoanalysis, history of nineteenth-century linguistics, and contemporary French theory. She is author of *Structures of Knowing: Psychologies of the Nineteenth Century* (1989), *Austria and Other Margins* (1996), *Empire in Decline: Fritz Mauthner's Critique of Wilhelminian Germany* (2000), and numerous articles on literature and intellectual history. Her recent work focuses on defining Germanophone literature from the eighteenth through the twentieth centuries in other than the nationalist paradigm. Address: Department of Germanic Studies, The University of Texas at Austin, Austin, Texas 78712 USA. E-mail: <k.arens@mail.utexas.edu>.

Roumiana Deltcheva's interests are in comparative literature, Central and East European literature and culture, film-literature relations, media studies, and identity politics and post-colonial studies. She has published articles in the *Canadian Review of Comparative Literature/Revue Canadienne de Littérature Comparée* (1994, 1995), *Studies in the*

Humanities (1996), *The Russian Review* (1997), *Europe-Asia Studies* (1996), *The Sarmatian Review* (1998), *CLCWeb: Comparative Literature and Culture: A WWWeb Journal* (1999), and others, and co-edited *Literature and Film: Models of Adaptation,* a thematic issue of the *Canadian Review of Comparative Literature / Revue Canadienne de Littérature Comparée* (1996). Deltcheva works in new media technology in Montréal. Address: 209-3445 chemin de la Côte-de-Neiges, Montréal, Québec, Canada H3H 1T5. E-mail: <rdeltche@yahoo.com>.

Andrea Fábry's interests are cultural studies, modernism and silent film, Central and East European film, socialist culture, and feminism. She has published in *CLCWeb: Comparative Literature and Culture* (1999): <http://clcwebjournal.lib.purdue.edu/clcweb994/fabry99.html> and she has presented papers on feminist approaches in film theory at several gender and media studies conferences. Fábry is organizer of an East European film series and of a pedagogical workshop at the Humanities Institute at SUNY Stony Brook. She is now completing her Ph.D. dissertation on Central European modernism. Address: Department of Comparative Literature, State University of New York Stony Brook, Stony Brook, New York 11794 1901. E-mail: <andrea_fabry@hotmail.com>.

Anikó Imre's interests are in film studies, feminist criticism, cultural studies, and the cultures and literatures of Central and East Europe. She has published "White Man, White Mask: Mephisto Meets Venus" in *Screen* 40.4 (1999) and a review article of Richard Teleky's *Hungarian Rhapsodies* (1997) and Rudolf Andorka et al.'s *A Society Transformed: Hungary in Time-Space Perspective* (1999) in the *Slavic and East European Journal* (2000). At Washington, she is now completing her Ph.D. dissertation about theory transfer and the application of feminist and postcolonial theories in the study of Central European literatures and cultures. Address: Department of English, University of Washington, Seattle, Washington 98195-5840 USA. E-mail: <aimre@u.washington.edu>.

Zsuzsanna Ozsváth's interests include the translation of poetry from the German and Hungarian into English, the history of ideas, and Holocaust literature. She has published in journals such as *German Studies Review* (1978), *Research Studies* (1983), *Judaism* (1985), *Partisan Review* (1989), *The Hungarian Quarterly* (1998), and in anthologies such as *The Holocaust in Hungary: Fifty Years Later* (ed. Randolph L. Braham and Attila Pók, 1997) and *The Life and Poetry of Miklós Radnóti: Essays* (ed. George Gömöri, 1999). Her volumes of poetry translations (with Frederick Turner) include, *Foamy Sky: The Major Poems of Miklós Radnóti* (1992) and *The Iron-Blue Vault: Selected Poems* (1999). Her most recent book is *In the Footsteps of Orpheus: The Life and Times of Miklós Radnóti* (2000). Address: School of Arts and Humanities, The University of Texas at Dallas, Richardson, Texas 75083 USA. E-mail: <zozsvath@utdallas.edu>

Peter Petro's interests are in Czech, Polish, Russian, and Slovak literatures and cultures. He is author of *Modern Satire: Four Studies about Modern Czech, English, Russian, and American Texts* (1982), *History of Slovak Literature* (1995), a translation of Milan Simecka's novel as *The Year of the Frog* (1993). He also published an edited volume, *Critical Essays on Milan Kundera* (1999) and a translation of Alexej Fulmek's novel as *Dispatches from the Home Front* (2000), as well as, in learned journals, many articles on various topics in literature. Address: Department of Germanic and Slavic Studies, The University of British Columbia, Vancouver, British Columbia, Canada V6T 1Z1. E-mail: <petro@interchange.ubc.ca>.

Hana Pichova's interests are in Czech and Russian literatures and cultures and she has published her work in learned journals such as the *Slavic and East European Journal* (1992), *Comparative Literature Studies* (1997), *Russian Literature* (1998), *European Studies Journal* (1998), and *Brown Slavic Contributions* (1999). She is also author of *The Art of Memory in Exile: Vladimir Nabokov and Milan Kundera* (2001). She is now working on another book, *Visions of Post-World War II Prague: A Literary and Cultural Study.* Address: Department of Slavic Languages and Literatures, The University of Texas at Austin, Austin, Texas 78713 USA. E-mail: <pichova@mail.utexas.edu>.

Catherine Portuges's interests are in French and Central and East European cinema and video, international film makers, and the intersections of cinema, culture, and gender, representations of minorities, globalization, and migration, and the restructuring of Central European national cinemas. Portuges is author of *Screen Memories: The Hungarian Cinema of Márta Mészáros* (1993) and she co-edited *Gendered Subjects: The Dynamics of Feminist Pedagogy* (1985) and *Cinema in Transition: Post-Communist Cinema in East-Central Europe* (2001). A frequent contributor of essays on film in the *American Historical Review, Film Criticism,* and *Slavic Review,* she has also published in *Yale French Studies, Genders, Discourse,* and other journals and collected volumes. Address: Department of Comparative Literature, University of Massachusetts at Amherst, Amherst, MA 01003 USA. E-mail: <portuges@complit. umass.edu>.

Susan Rubin Suleiman's interests are in modern French literature and comparative literature and culture. To date, she is author or editor of half a dozen books and more than seventy articles on modern literature and culture, and has also published poetry and a memoir. Her critical books include *Risking Who One Is: Encounters with Contemporary Art and Literature* (1994), *Subversive Intent: Gender, Politics, and the Avant-Garde* (1990), *Authoritarian Fictions: The Ideological Novel as a Literary Genre* (1983, 1993), and the edited volumes *The Female Body in Western Culture* (1986), and *Exile and Creativity* (1998). Her memoir, *Budapest Diary: In Search of the Motherbook,* appeared in 1996. Most recently she has co-edited an anthology of *Contemporary Jewish Writing in Hungary,* forthcoming from the University of Nebraska Press. Address: Department of Comparative Literature, 517 Boylston Hall, Harvard University, Cambridge, MA 02138 USA. E-mail: <suleiman@fas.harvard.edu>.

Steven Tötösy's interests are in the humanities and the social sciences; in theory, contemporary fiction, minority writing, communication studies, editing, new media scholarship, etc. He is author of four and editor of eighteen books and over one hundred articles, book chapters, bibliographies, and encyclopedia entries published on both sides of the Atlantic and elsewhere. His most recent single-authored book is *Comparative Literature: Theory, Method, Application* (1998). He edited 1989–1997 the *Canadian Review of Comparative Literature* and he is founding and current editor of *CLCWeb: Comparative Literature and Culture: A WWWeb Journal,* published by Purdue University Press at <http://clcwebjournal.lib.purdue.edu/>. Address: 8 Sunset Road, Winchester, MA 01890 USA. E-mail: <totosy@lib.purdue.edu>.

Index

Aesthetic convention, 7
Albania, 154
Albert, Barbara, 135
altérité, 151
American cultural domination, 149
American cultural studies, 4
American dream, 152
American film audience, 183
American popular culture, 153
Anderson, Benedict, 8, 115
Antifeminist movement, 84
Anti-nationalist rhetoric, 120
Anti-Semitism, x, 14, 181
Antschel, Paul. *See* Celan, Paul
Appelfeld, Aharon, 54
Arens, Katherine, xii, xv, 115
Arrow Cross, 144, 173
Assimilation, 19
Auerbach, Erich, 38
Austria, vii, ix, 12, 17, 22, 94, 97, 117, 128, 135
Austrian empire, 8
Austrian film, xiii, 135, 139, 166
Austro-Hungarian empire, xiii, 14, 18, 20, 92, 94, 131, 143, 169
Austro-Hungarian monarchy, 170
Austroslovakism, xi, 94, 100

Bacsó, Péter, 34

Bajza, Jozef Ignac, 99
Balkans, 115
Baltic countries, 8, 118
Banat, 126
Barr, Jean-Marc, 165
Bayard, Caroline, 154
Bel, Matej, 98
Belgium, 7
Belgrade, 123
Benki, Artemio, 164
Berlin Wall, xii, 25, 131, 133, 152
Berman, Marshall, 33
Bhabha, Homi, 10
Biedermeier, 77
Bohemia, 94
Bosnia, 85
Bratislava, 21, 92, 97
British cultural studies, 4
Brouwer, Adrian, 122
Brussig, Thomas, 23
Bucharest, 66, 67
Budapest, 12, 27, 139, 169, 175, 185
Bukovina, 53, 67
Bulgakov, Mikhail, 94
Bulgaria, vii, 8, 24, 151, 154, 160–161

Cărtărescu, Mircea, 26
Canada, ix, 7, 14, 91, 107, 169
Celan, Paul, x, 51

Chalfen, Israel, 53
Chetniks, 160
Chvatík, Květoslav, 107
Cold War, xii, 151
Colonialism, 4, 151
Comecon, 153
Communist nomenclatura, 9
Comparative cultural studies, vii, viii, ix, x, 1-3, 6, 11, 27, 49, 135, 151, 154, 167
Comparative literature, vii, 1, 2, 19
Connor, Ralph, 14
Constructivism, 6. See Radical constructivism
Contextual approach, viii, xiv, xv, 6, 93. See Systemic and empirical approach
Cornis-Pope, Marcel, 10
Croatia, 128, 154
Csurka, István, 182
Cultural discourse, 149
Cultural legitimization, 149
Cultural studies, 1, 2
Cultural subjugation, 72
Czech film, 161, 162
Czech literature, 107-109
Czech Republic, 104, 154, 161, 163
Czechoslovakia, xii, 17-18, 21, 91-93, 97, 103-105, 153-154, 156, 163, 173

De Marchi, Bruno, 179
Deák, István, 173
Dejczer, Maciej, 156
Deltcheva, Roumiana, xiii, 149, 150
Democracy, xi
Denes, Magda, 18, 20
Diaspora, 123
Dobozy, Tamas, 15
Donnhjofer, Diego, 135
Dor, Milo, xii, 115
Dornheim, Robert, 135
Dunn, Christopher Chase, 10
DuPlessis, Rachel Blau, 71

Eastern German, 27
Eichmann, Adolf, 173
Eidsvik, Charles, 33
Eisenstein, Zillah, 83
Eksteins, Modris, 15
Emigration, 13
Eroticism, 24, 82
Esterházy, Péter, 23, 26, 81
Ethnic minorities, 171
Eurocentrism, 3, 72-73, 79
European Parliament, 116

Even-Zohar, Itamar, 6, 11
Exile, 13, 57, 103, 105, 109-110, 137-138, 149-150, 181

Fábry, Andrea, x, 33
Faludy, György, 13
Fándly, Juraj, 99
Fekete, Ibolya, 141, 145
Feminism, 74, 78
Feminist critics, 71
Fischer, Tibor, 15
Foerster, Heinz von, 6
Földes, Anna, 183
Forgács, Péter, 145
Forman, Miloš, 34
France, 163, 165
Furst, Alan, 15
Furst, Desider, 18, 22
Furst, Lilian R., 18, 22

Gedeon, Saša, 161
Gender, 71, 72, 73, 76, 135
German literature, 54
Germany, 7, 11, 17, 72, 107, 117, 128, 144, 156, 164, 172
Germany, East, vii, 8, 25, 116
Geyrhalter, Nikolaus, 135, 141
Glasersfeld, Ernst von, 6
Glatter, Miklós. See Radnóti, Miklós
Globalization, 5
Goethe, Johann Wolfgang von, 65
Gorbachev, Mikhail, 83, 150
Gothár, Péter, 34
Goulash communism, 75
Grlic, Rajko, 155
György, Péter, 175, 183
Gypsies (Roma), 15, 18, 79, 160, 164

Hašek, Jaroslav, x, 34, 43
Habsburg, vii, 8, 26, 133
Habsburg empire, xi, 35, 93
Habsburg, Otto von, xii, 115
Haider, Jörg, 139
Haltof, Marek, 162
Handke, Peter, xii, 115
Haraszti, Miklós, 185
Havel, Vaclav, 83, 104, 112
Hell, Maximilian, 99
Heterosexuality, 80
Hoffmann, Eva, 15
Holland, 7
Holocaust, x, xv, 14, 16, 19, 21, 68, 143, 179
Holocaust literature, 16
Horowitz, Israel, 144, 169
Horthy, Miklós, 172

Hrabal, Bohumil, 34
Humanities, 2, 4, 5, 6
Hungarian film, xiii, 75, 143, 178
Hungarian literature, 21, 27, 75, 78, 83
Hungary, 7, 8, 10, 12, 14, 16–17, 19–22, 24–26, 52, 55, 57, 59, 73, 75, 77, 78, 81, 83, 92, 94, 100, 135, 143, 144, 154, 161, 169, 171–172, 179–184
Hus, Jan, 117
Hybridity, 13
Hykisch, Anton, xi, 91

Identity, xi–xii, xiv–xv, 53, 55, 74, 101, 103–104, 108, 110–111, 120, 125, 130–131, 134, 146, 149, 150, 152, 159, 161, 166–167, 170, 179–181, 183
Ignatieff, Michael, 15
Imagined community, vii, xiv, 16, 115, 136
Imre, Anikó, xi, 71
In-between peripherality, x, xiii, 1, 10–11, 13, 151
Intellectuals, 105, 107, 129, 131–132, 181–182, 184
Interdisciplinarity, 3
International visual culture, 133
Internet, 153
Intertextuality, 75, 178
Interwar period, 17
Intra-disciplinarity, 5
Iron Curtain, 76, 153
Ishiguro, Kazuo, 15
Israel, 7
Istria, 128
Italy, 7

Janaszek-Ivaničková, Halina, 9
Jánisch, Attila, 145
Jasny, Vojtech, 163
Jené, Edgar, 55
Jewrie, 14, 18–19, 23
Joyce, James, x, 43
Jungmann, Milan, 105

Kafka, Franz, x, 34, 41
Kalman Naves, Elaine, 18
Kalman, Judith, 18
Kertész, Imre, 16
Khudojnazarov, Bakhtiar, 135
Kieslowksi, Krzysztof, 159
Kiossev, Alexandar, 72
Klíma, Ivan, 110
Klobucka, Anna, 10
Kollár, Adam Frantisek, 97

Kollár, Ignac, 97
Kollár, Jan, 98
Koltai, Jenő, 17
Koltai, Róbert, 34
Komlós, Aladár, 55
Konrád, György, 79
Kosik, Karel, 35
Král, Petr, 107
Kreisky, Bruno, 140
Kryshtofovich, Viatcheslav, 34, 157
Kukorelly, Endre, 25, 83
Kun, Béla, 171
Kundera, Milan, xi, 12, 13, 36, 101, 103
Kusturica, Emir, 34, 158

Lantos, Robert, 169
Lewis, Matthew, 14
Ljubljana, 12
Localization, 5
Longinović, Tomislav, 10
Love lyric, 71
Luhmann, Niklas, 6
Lukács, György, 36, 42, 48, 75

Magris, Claudio, 131
Magyarization, 20, 171, 180
Makavejev, Dusan, 158
Malak, Amin, 10
Marginalization, 6
Maria Theresa, 92, 97
Masculinity, 79
Mass media, 129
Master theory, 2
Matějka, Ladislav, 103, 108
Memoir, x, 1, 20, 23, 25, 26, 27
Menzel, Jiří, 34
Metaphorical interpretation, 7
Meta-theory, 5
Methodology, 1, 3–6, 11
Minh-ha, Trinh, 11
Minorities, 20
Modernism, x
Modernist literature, 34
Modernity, 34
Monovalency, 7
Moravia, 164
Moskowitz, Gene, 144
Multiculturalism, 185
Multi-disciplinarity, viii, 5

Nádas, Péter, 26
Narratives of change, 24, 27
Nationalism, xi, 20, 22, 54, 71–75, 80, 83, 100, 115, 126–127, 131, 134, 153–154, 160, 172, 176, 181
Nationalist narrative, 132

NATO, 129, 153
Naves, Elaine Kalman, 19
Nebesio, Bohdan, 162
Neofascism, 129
Nichev, Ivan, 160–161
Nkrumah, Kwame, 83
Nomadism, 152
Nostalgia, xi, 17, 21, 23, 98, 133, 164
numerus clausus, 52

Orbán, Viktor, 182
Ottoman conquest, 97
Ozsváth, Zsuzsanna, x, xv, 51

Paneuropa, 117
Pannonia, 98
Papic, Krsto, 159
Papoušek, Jaroslav, 34
Paradigm shift, 5
Paré, François, 10
Patriotism, 21, 170–172
Paul, David, 179
Paviani, Nicola, 16
Pedagogy, 2, 4
Petrík, Vladimir, 92
Petro, Peter, xi, xv, 91
Pichova, Hana, xi, xv, 103
Pluri-disciplinarity, 5
Poetry, x, xv, 51, 54, 56, 59, 62, 66–68, 71, 73–74, 78, 80
Pogany, Eugene L., 16
Poland, 8, 10, 14, 21–22, 24, 154, 159, 161, 173
Polish film, 162
Polysystem, 11
Polyvalence convention, 7
Pornography, xi, 81–82, 85, 106
Portugal, 8, 10
Portuges, Catherine, xii, 133
Postcolonial nativism, 75
Postcolonial studies, xi, 8, 72
Postcoloniality, x, 1, 8, 11, 13, 24
Postmodern film, 134
Postmodern literature, 75
Postmodernism, 76–77
Postmodernity, xi, 10
Post-socialist film, 33
Prague, 27, 139, 163, 164
Proust, Marcel, 40
Public intellectuals, xii, xv, 115
Purdue University Press, ix

Radical constructivism, 2, 6
Radnóti, Miklós, x, 51, 184
Radokovic, Zarko, 121
Resnais, Alain, 142

Riegler, Alex, 6
Ristovski, Lazar, 158
Romania, vii, 8, 12, 25, 53, 154
Romanian literature, 27

Sachs, Nelly, 57
Salamon, Julie, 18
Salecl, Renata, 84
Salih, Taleb, 78
Sandoval, Chela, 85
Sarajewo, 128
Schengen Agreement, 150
Schiele, Egon, 82
Schmid, Daniel, 166
Schmidt, Siegfried J., 6
Schöpflin, George, 176
Self-referentiality, 3, 8, 11
Serbia, vii, 122, 125, 128, 154
Sexist stereotype, 177
Sexual narrative, 25
Sexuality, 71–72, 74, 76
Sharpe, Jenny, 78
Shields, Jody, 15
Shoah, 23, 51. *See* Holocaust
Silesia, 96
Škvorecký, Josef, 13, 15, 107
Slovak literature, 98, 107
Slovakia, 73, 91–94, 97–98, 117, 154
Slovenia, 121, 154
Social sciences, 2, 4
Soviet colonialism, xi, xiv, 10, 24
Soviet empire, xii, xiv, 149, 159
Soviet invasion, 105, 106
Soviet Republic, 52
Soviet Union, 72, 151
Spielberg, Steven, 18
Stein, André, 16
Subversion, 75
Suleiman, Susan Rubin, xiii, xv, 18, 21–22, 84, 169
Sullk, Martin, 163
Sverak, Jan, 34, 156
Swiss film, 166
Switzerland, 166
System(s) of culture, 7
Systemic and empirical approach, viii, 1, 5–7, 13
Szabó, István, xiii, 19, 143, 169, 170
Szász, János, 145
Szelek Miller, Stefania, 154

Taxonomy, xiv
Team work, 1
Textual analysis, 2
Tímár, Péter, 34, 145
Tiso, Jozef, 93

Topol, Jachim, 109
Tötösy, Steven, ix, x, xiv, 48, 72, 83, 135, 151, 154
Transnationality, 136
Trianon Peace Treaty, 52
Tschofen, Monique, 78
Tweedle, Jill, 15

Ukraine, vii, 8, 14, 141, 154
Ukrainian film, 162
Ungvári, Tamás, 184
United States, 7, 14
Urban space, 135
Urbaniak, Urszula, 162
Urbanity, 25
Ustascha, 127

Vaculík, Ludvik, 110

Vienna, 12, 15, 22, 67, 97, 128, 130, 138
Viewegh, Michal, 109
Vlasopolos, Anca, 17

Wallerstein, Immanuel, 6, 10
Walsh, Jill Paton, 15
Warsaw, 12
Weöres, Sándor, 77
Wertmüller, Lina, 16
West, Rebecca, 115
Western film, 165–166
Willet, John, 17

Yugoslav film, 158
Yugoslavia, 8, 124, 153, 154

Zelitch, Simone, 15

About the Editor

Steven Tötösy de Zepetnek, previously at the University of Alberta, Canada, 1984–2000, resides in Winchester at Boston. He is author, editor, or co-editor of two dozen books and author of over one hundred articles, book chapters, bibliographies, and encyclopedia entries in culture and literary theory, Canadian, European, and US contemporary fiction, minority writing, communication studies, editing, new media and knowledge management, history, etc. Tötösy is founding and current editor of *CLCWeb: Comparative Literature and Culture: A WWWeb Journal,* a peer-reviewed quarterly published by Purdue University Press online at <http://clcwebjournal.lib.purdue.edu/> and series editor of Books in Comparative Cultural Studies, also published by Purdue University Press. Tötösy's Curriculum Vitae and list of publications are available online at <http://clcwebjournal.lib.purdue.edu/totosycv.html>.

www.ingramcontent.com/pod-product-compliance
Lightning Source LLC
Chambersburg PA
CBHW071711160426
43195CB00012B/1651